100

CANADIAN
HEROINES

100 Canadian Heroines
Famous and Forgotten Faces

By Merna Forster

THE DUNDURN GROUP
TORONTO

Copy-Editor: Heather Sanderson
Design: Andrew Roberts
Printer: Transcontinental

Library and Archives Canada Cataloguing in Publication

Forster, Merna, date.
   100 Canadian heroines : famous and forgotten faces / Merna Forster.

Includes bibliographical references and index.
ISBN 1-55002-514-7

   1. Heroines--Canada--Biography.   2. Women--Canada--Biography.   3. Canada--Biography.   I. Title.   II. Title: One hundred Canadian heroines.

FC26.W6F67 2004   920.72'0971   C2004-904461-3

1   2   3   4   5   08   07   06   05   04

We acknowledge the support of the **Canada Council for the Arts** and the **Ontario Arts Council** for our publishing program. We also acknowledge the financial support of the **Government of Canada** through the **Book Publishing Industry Development Program** and **The Association for the Export of Canadian Books**, and the **Government of Ontario** through the **Ontario Book Publishers Tax Credit** program, and the **Ontario Media Development Corporation's Ontario Book Initiative**.

Care has been taken to trace the ownership of copyright material used in this book. The author and the publisher welcome any information enabling them to rectify any references or credits in subsequent editions.

J. Kirk Howard, President

Printed and bound in Canada
Printed on recycled paper

www.dundurn.com

Dundurn Press
8 Market Street
Suite 200
Toronto, Ontario, Canada
M5E 1M6

Gazelle Book Services Limited
White Cross Mills
Hightown, Lancaster, England
LA1 4X5

Dundurn Press
2250 Military Road
Tonawanda, NY
U.S.A. 14150

FOR JOYCELYN DUFRESNE AND GRACE LATIMER

Table of Contents

J

K

L

M

Huron County Library

--- Currently checked out ---

Title: Maclean's : Clinton Branch [magazine]
Date due: 13 December 2011 23:59

Library name: Clinton Branch Library
User ID: 06492001674632

Title: 100 Canadian heroines : famous and forgotten faces
Date due: 16 December 2011 23:59

Sunday hours resume on Sept. 11 (towns)

"They planted the trees so we could enjoy the shade."

— Dora Nipp, from an old Chinese saying

Foreword
by Rt. Hon. Kim Campbell

In virtually all societies, leadership is gendered masculine. This is not because women do not lead, but because the positions that define leadership have been dominated by men. When women occupy these positions, they are not seen to "belong" there in the same way that men are seen naturally to do. Rather than revise their predispositions about women and leadership, people are more likely to find ways around the contradiction, for instance by seeing the woman leader as an anomaly. Her story may simply be forgotten, for, if women are not to be leaders, why do we need to keep their stories alive to inspire girls? Worse, the stories of courageous women get rewritten. That is why it is so important that Merna Forster gives us back the true story of Laura Secord, whose extraordinary feat of courage and endurance has been diminished to a tale of a "stroll with a cow." I was glad to see the story of Marie Guyart included in this book. I have had the good fortune to visit the museum of the Ursulines in Quebec City, and to see first hand what kinds of hardy, brave women founded our country. The term "weaker sex" should make one's blood boil after reading this book!

Merna Forster's celebration of one hundred Canadian women of extraordinary accomplishment has a very serious purpose. Of course the stories of these women entertain and inspire us, but more importantly, they contribute to changing the understanding that determines how societies define the roles of women. Throughout my life, I have found myself in positions where I was the first female — starting with my election in the spring of 1963 as student council president of my high school. In the course of my political career I had many perplexing experiences that I suspected were related to my sex, but which I didn't know how to analyze. Since 1993, when an election thrust me into "political retirement," I have had the opportunity to read a great deal of research on gender and how it plays out in the way we see leaders in Western societies. For several years I taught a course called "Gender and Power" at the John F. Kennedy School of Government at Harvard, and I travel around the world speaking on this subject. What I have learned is this: human beings are "pattern makers" who transform what they observe and learn into hypotheses that enable them to function in a complex world. Among the most powerful hypotheses that children create are those related to the social construction of sex, or what we call "gender roles."

My generation of "baby boomer" women was told that all we needed in order to succeed was to be good at what we did. However, many women became frustrated at finding that this was not enough. Social science research confirms what they suspect — that there are deep, underlying preconceptions about femininity that dramatically affect the way women are perceived and that can override empirical observation. Harvard economist Claudia Goldin discovered that when symphony orchestras audition musicians behind a screen, they hire 25 percent more women — the screen filtering out the negative preconceptions about women musicians. In *Why So Slow? The Advancement of Women*, psychologist Virginia Valian tells how hypotheses about height lead men and women to judge men to be as much as 3 1/2 inches taller than women of equal height. In *Closing the Gender Gap*, Marie Wilson, one of the founders of the White House Project (whose purpose is to elect a woman as U.S. president), tells of research that revealed that the ratio of men to women on the influential Sunday morning news programs in the United States is 9 to 1, rising to 13 to 1 after 9/11. Not only do the networks not feature women who hold key committee chairmanships in Congress, but they also call as commentators men who are former holders of such positions rather than the women who currently hold the positions.

These and other similar situations reflect the difficulty faced by women in overcoming deeply rooted notions of where leadership lies. That is why this book is so important. The only way to open up the full scope of opportunities for women is to "reprogram" the way people see gender roles. This is not a simple task. Research shows that by the time children arrive at school, they already have clear ideas about gender. But if we tell the stories of women who defy the stereotypes, we contribute to changing the social landscape from which children derive their views of how the world works.

For Canadians, whose worldview cannot escape the powerful influence of our neighbour to the south, telling these Canadian stories counteracts another form of invisibility. From 1996 to 2000, I served as Canada's Consul General in Los Angeles. The key issues I dealt with included Canada's position in the global film industry and our cultural policies relating to Canadian content. Canada has one of the most open media markets in the world, but living next door to the world's largest economy guarantees that many Canadians see more Americans than Canadians in their media and entertainment.

Having lived in the United States for most of the past eight years, I can confirm that Canada and Canadians are largely invisible in American media. As Merna Forster shows in this book, Canadian women have made their mark at home and abroad, and our country has attracted women who wanted an opportunity to flourish.

Of course, there are many more courageous and brilliant Canadian women than can fit into this book, and I await with anticipation the sequel to this volume, but these stories are a great contribution to our understanding of women and a corrective to the standard histories. Celebrating these one hundred Canadian heroines reminds us that Canadian women do amazing things, and it will be a loss to our whole country if we forget them.

Introduction

Laura Secord is number one. Surveys show she's the most popular heroine from Canadian history, though pollsters suggest this has more to do with the tasty line of chocolate treats that bear her name than knowledge of Laura's heroism in warning British troops of a planned American attack.[1] Madeleine de Verchères was once a key historical heroine in French Canada, but her popularity declined somewhat with the passage of time.[2]

Who is your favourite Canadian heroine? How can you possibly pick without knowing the stories of notable women in the history of Canada? Perhaps pilot Helen Harrison who ferried Spitfires and other military planes during World War II, mountaineer Phyllis Monday, the first woman to climb the highest peak in the Canadian Rockies, or maybe Gudridur the Viking, the adventurous Icelandic explorer who visited North America five hundred years before Columbus. What about singing sensation La Bolduc or painter Helen McNicoll? Maybe the best-selling author Mazo de la Roche or explorer Agnes Deans Cameron?

If you've never heard of these people it's not surprising. Women are practically invisible on the pages of Canadian history textbooks, too often overshadowed by the feats of famous men. The faces of politicians such as Sir John A. Macdonald and Sir Wilfrid Laurier stare at us from crumpled bills in our wallets, but there is never a female face to greet us — aside from the Queen of England. At least more and more Canadian women are showing up on commemorative stamps, reminding us of some of the notable women who have helped develop Canada.

Are there really few heroines in Canadian history that we would be interested in knowing about and remembering? Perhaps the word *heroine* conjures up visions of women in Greek mythology, or the legendary Joan of Arc. But are there heroines in Canadian history?

Dictionaries define a heroine as a woman noted for courage and daring action, or a woman noted for special achievement in a particular field. Every country has its heroines, and Canada is no exception. Our history is coloured with amazing women who have done fascinating things.

Many Canadian heroines should be recognized for their brave deeds or heroic actions. Countless other heroines made notable achievements in many fields. Heroines in sport, science and medicine, business, arts and entertainment, exploration, literature, politics, social reform, and many other fields. Some faced incredible obstacles to fight for their beliefs and to improve the quality of life for others. They battled prejudice, discrimination, repression, and worse to follow their dreams and excel in their chosen paths.

There are women mountaineers and Olympic medallists, famous dancers and daring adventurers. Pilots, painters, and poets. Farmers, fugitives fleeing slavery, fighters for the freedom to vote and to be called a person. Aboriginal storytellers. Nurses, nuns, and novelists. Gold seekers on the Chilkoot Trail. Miners, mothers, and lovers, stars on stage and the silver screen. Inventors and Inuit artists.

Each of these heroines in Canadian history, being neither a mythological character nor a super-heroine from a comic book, is a human being: an imperfect person with strengths and weaknesses. A woman who reflects social behaviours and attitudes of her time — some of which are objectionable by modern standards. Were her achievements any less? Can we still celebrate the achievements of the heroines while acknowledging their flaws?

This book is a collection of stories celebrating the accomplishments of a small selection of women who made significant contributions to society. I chose people from throughout Canadian history, a variety of fields, and most regions of the country — trying to include heroines of many races and backgrounds. Most of the women were born in Canada and lived their entire lives in this country. Others immigrated to Canada or spent just a short time here, but left an important legacy. Some of the heroines were Canadians who achieved great things in other countries. We claim all these women as heroines for Canada.

Some of them are famous. For example, actress Mary Pickford and artist Emily Carr. You may recognize the names of others profiled in this book, but may not be familiar with their stories. Did you know that the first Canadian best-seller was the autobiography of a dog, penned by author Margaret

Saunders? Or that politician Agnes MacPhail, the first woman elected to the federal parliament, was so stressed by her early days on the Hill that she lost twelve pounds and, despite an impressive career in politics, she died in fear of poverty with the unfulfilled dream of getting a seat in the Senate?

Unfortunately, many of the stories of Canadian heroines have been forgotten. They are buried in books that are out of print or gathering dust in libraries. Hidden away in old letters and photo albums, records brittle with age. Some are lost in unwritten legends or tales of centuries past, but many are waiting for us to discover — or rediscover. In recent years some remarkable stories have been rescued from obscurity by passionate researchers who came across mentions of unfamiliar names and faces. Stories of great Canadian women that should be part of our history.

"When I was growing up, I heard, and I actually believed that there had never been any great women artists. This was the wisdom of the day," said the gifted Canadian artist Dorothy McCarthy in 1999.[3] How terribly sad.

I hope that this book will help acquaint you with a few of the count-less heroines in Canadian history — women that can inspire us to achieve our own dreams. Visionaries. Rebels. Strong women who can encourage us as we learn of the pain of their struggles and hardships, their determination, and the glory of their remarkable achievements. Many of the women featured here are role models who have made a significant impact in Canada or beyond its borders, distinguishing themselves by heroic deeds or excellence in their fields.

There are so many amazing women in the history of Canada. Faces that should not be forgotten — but recognized and celebrated as Canadian heroines.

Specialist of the Heart

Maude Abbott
1868–1940

It was a tough time for a Canadian woman to become a doctor, but Maude turned every opportunity she got into a major accomplishment.

Maude Abbott.

Maude Abbott gained fame abroad as a distinguished medical researcher and teacher, yet never gained the academic promotions she deserved at McGill University — where she spent most of her career. Refused admittance to the program of medicine at McGill University in 1890 because she was a woman, Maude was forced to continue her studies at the University of Bishop's College. In 1883 Augusta Stowe had become the first woman to graduate with a medical degree from a Canadian institution, but there was still considerable opposition to the idea of respectable young women becoming medical doctors. Throughout her impressive career Maude Abbott struggled to overcome the barriers that were presented to early Canadian women eager for success in the profession of medicine.

Maude was fortunate to have received encouragement for her education from the loving maternal grandmother who raised her and her sister, Alice. Born in the village of St. André d'Argenteuil, Quebec in 1868,[4] Maude was the daughter of Frances Abbott and a French-Canadian Protestant clergyman named Jérémie Babin. Her father had been acquitted of a charge of murdering his invalid sister, but the community was apparently unconvinced of his innocence. When Frances died of tuberculosis he moved to the United States and left the baby girls with their grandmother, Mrs. William Abbott. She changed their surname to Abbott.

Under the guardianship of the gracious Mrs. Abbott the sisters thrived. A governess taught Maude at home until she was sent to a private school in 1884. Eager to learn, Maude yearned to go to college even though most young women at that time in conservative Quebec did not have such an opportunity. In September of 1884 Sir Donald A. Smith announced he would be giving $50,000 to support the higher education of women, and in the fall of that year female students were permitted to enroll in the Faculty of Arts at McGill for the first time. Maude registered in 1886, in the third class that allowed women. On graduating in 1890 with the Lord Stanley Gold Medal, she was also Class Valedictorian. Maude received a Bachelor of Arts and a teaching diploma.

When Maude had asked her grandmother if she could become a doctor, Mrs. Abbott responded with "Dear child, you may be anything you like."[5] Despite Maude's considerable efforts she was not able to gain acceptance to study medicine at McGill, due to the opposition to teaching mixed classes of men and women. One person who wrote about the controversy explained that certain terms could not be used in lectures for risk of embarrassing the young ladies, and added another reservation: "And can you think of a patient in a critical case, waiting for half an hour while the medical lady fixes her bonnet or adjusts her bustle?"[6]

After becoming a medical doctor in 1894, Maude spent three years in Europe taking post-graduate training with distinguished medical teachers — most notably in Vienna, where she spent two years. She received particularly good training in pathology and internal medicine. Her sister Alice accompanied her on the trip and required considerable support, as she was a manic-depressive who became an invalid.

On returning to Montreal, Dr. Maude Abbott began practising medicine and started doing research in pathology and a clinical problem related to heart murmurs. An important scientific paper she wrote about her research was presented to the Medico-Chirurgical Society by a male doctor, since women were not permitted to be members. It was because of this impressive research that Maude was elected to the Society despite the rules. A subsequent research paper was presented on her behalf before the Pathological Society in London in January 1900 — the first time that a paper from a woman had been presented there.

Dr. Maude Abbott had begun to carve a name for herself and became known as an authority on congenital heart disease. In 1905 the noted physician and medical teacher Dr. William Osler asked her to write a chapter on this subject for a medical textbook he was preparing. This was a significant honour, and Dr. Osler said the paper she produced had "extraordinary merit ... It is by far and away the best thing ever written on the subject in English — possibly in any language."[7]

Osler also encouraged Maude Abbott to become heavily involved in her work at the McGill Medical Museum, and she developed an important course in pathology that involved its collections. Maude then began organizing the International Association of Medical Museums. She served as its secretary for thirty years and edited its journal. Maude gained international recognition for her work with medical museums as well as congenital heart disease.

Reluctant to leave McGill, Maude finally accepted one of the many invitations she received from other universities. In 1923 she agreed to go to the Women's Medical College of Pennsylvania as Professor of Pathology and Bacteriology and Director of Clinical Laboratories. On her return to McGill two years later, Dr. Abbott became Assistant Professor of Medical Research. Despite her numerous entreaties requesting a promotion, Dr. Maude Abbott retired at age sixty-five with the title of assistant professor. Author Margaret Gillett speculates that this was because Maude "was an anomalous female scientist in a conservative male milieu."[8] McGill did, however, grant her two honorary degrees. Gillett reflects that Maude received important but relatively small opportunities, which she managed to transform into major accomplishments.

Despite the lack of recognition in the place where she particularly wanted it, Maude earned many honours and boasted a lengthy list of accomplishments. After Maude retired in 1936 she was elected an honorary member of the New York Academy of Medicine. She had written over 140 publications and her *Atlas of Congenital Heart Disease* (published in 1936 by the American Heart Association) was an important reference. Along with Dr. Helen MacMurchy, Dr. Maude Abbott worked to found the Federation of Medical Women of Canada; each year the group awards the Maude Abbott Scholarship in her honour.

Dr. Maude Abbott died on September 2, 1940. Colleague Charles Martin wrote that she was "a scholar at McGill who, with but few exceptions, had greater international repute and contacts than anyone in the Canadian profession," and a person with "vivid personality, with engaging traits of character to give an example to future generations."[9] In 1993 the Historic Sites and Monuments Board of Canada recognized Maude as a national historic person of Canada, and in January 2000 Canada Post released a commemorative stamp to celebrate her accomplishments.

Quote:

"I wonder what my life will be like and if I will have any opportunity to do something good or great with it."[10]

Diary of Maude Abbott, age fifteen.

A Lady of the Empire

Lady Aberdeen
(Ishbel Maria
Marjoribanks)
1857–1939

Dubbed one of the
brainiest women to tread
Canadian soil, she created
a big stir.

Lady Aberdeen.

Lady Aberdeen loved Canada, even before she and her husband moved here when he served as Governor General. The couple had travelled across the country on vacation, purchasing a scenic ranch in the Okanagan. Lady Aberdeen called it Guisachan after her father's estate in the Scottish highlands.

Ishbel Marjoribanks was born in London, England, in 1857 to a wealthy and politically influential family. Her stern father was a banker from the Scottish gentry. She grew up in the exclusive Mayfair area of the city, overlooking Hyde Park. As a young girl she enjoyed times spent in the more relaxed atmosphere of the highlands, where she could ride ponies. Forbidden by her father to enter university, Ishbel welcomed her mother's invitations to deliver food and medical supplies to isolated residents of the Scottish highlands near Guisachan, and a Lady Cavendish involved Ishbel in helping the needy of London. The religious young woman believed in Christian charity — her vocation would be to help others.

There were, of course, still obligations for young women in her position. Wearing a beautiful white satin gown with a ruffled train, she was presented to Queen Victoria on reaching her eighteenth birthday. Ishbel socialized with the most powerful people in the land, including British Prime Minister Gladstone — who became a close friend. Then of course a suitable marriage had to be arranged. At the age of twenty, Ishbel wed John Campbell Hamilton Gordon, the seventh Earl of Aberdeen. He spent his life as a public administrator, most notably as Lord Lieutenant of Ireland in 1886 and from 1906 to 1915, and Governor General of Canada from 1893 to 1898.

When the Aberdeens moved to Canada with their four young children, Ishbel was thirty-six years old. She was energetic, intelligent, knowledgeable, and articulate. Despite initial nervousness about her responsibilities, Lady Aberdeen plunged in with her usual enthusiasm. She soon earned a reputation as a charming hostess who organized extremely popular social events, such as costumed balls. Lady Aberdeen took a very active role in behind the scenes political manoeuvring, including some very delicate discussions, since Lord Aberdeen was involved with four prime ministers during his term in Canada.

Lady Aberdeen provided her husband with valuable political advice and by all accounts was a primary confidant. Her frequent travels across the country provided the Governor General with useful information about what was happening. Ishbel was a true partner. John T. Saywell, editor of a published version of her journals, remarked on the extent of the power she held: "While both the law and the conventions of the constitution are silent on the point, Lady Aberdeen might well be graced with the title of Governess-General. Like Victoria's Albert she was a power that could not be overlooked."[11]

Ever the reformer, Lady Aberdeen also played a significant role in many social projects. The year that she moved to Canada, Lady Aberdeen was elected president of the International Council of Women, a federation of women's groups created "to best conserve the highest good of the family and of the state." Except for a brief break she held this post until her death in 1939. Some women approached Lady Aberdeen about organizing a Canadian group, so she eagerly helped found the National Council of Women (NCW) and became its president.

Through the leadership of the NCW, Lady Aberdeen and her colleagues created the Victorian Order of Nurses to improve health care for Canadians in remote areas. Lady Aberdeen worried about the suffering of settlers and was inspired by the national nursing service in England. Despite strong protests from doctors and the Aberdeens' political opponents, Lady Aberdeen launched a successful public relations campaign — including talks given by a prominent American doctor — to quell the opposition. In December 1898, the Victorian Order of Nurses was established by royal charter, with Lady Aberdeen as president.

Touched by the loneliness of isolated pioneer farmers in the wheat fields of Manitoba, the irrepressible Ishbel also developed the Aberdeen Association for Distribution of Good Literature to Settlers in the West; the pioneers soon began receiving welcome parcels of books and magazines. Ishbel helped female Ottawa teachers organize an educational union. She created the May Court Club, a group of young women socialites in Ottawa, whose members committed to do community work. The list of charitable work went on and on.

In 1898 Lord Aberdeen completed his term as Governor General of Canada and his family returned home. The *Chicago Record* remarked on Ishbel's contribution to Canada:

> She is particularly interested in the intellectual advancement of women, and during the last five years has roused the women of Canada in all social classes to improve their conditions. The wife of no Governor-General within recollection has created so much of a stir. The working girls, the shop-clerks, the servant class, the farmers' wives, the trained nurses, the schoolteachers, and every other class have received a share of her interest...[12]

Many farewell banquets, receptions, and other social events marked the departure of the Aberdeens. The Senate and House of Commons presented Ishbel with a gift of two hundred pieces of Royal Doulton china, on which Canadian subjects had been painted by sixteen women from the Women's Art Association of Canada. By delivering a speech of appreciation for the "splendid gift," Lady Aberdeen became the first woman to speak in the House of Commons. The *Globe* newspaper reported her speech "...was grand as a piece of oratory, and her voice was simply thrilling. She brought tears to the eyes of all who were around her. I never saw an audience so captivated by a woman."

Another tribute to Lady Aberdeen came from the *Brockville Recorder*: "Her excellency is one of the brainiest women that ever trod Canadian soil, and sympathy of soul and breadth of thought are the prominent features of her every public word and act..."[13]

Lady Aberdeen was a born leader. Biographer Doris French comments that the accepted notions of the appropriate role of women confined Ishbel to the backrooms of power. "Her acumen, generosity, zeal and loyalty would have carried her far in the first instead of the second rank of public affairs."[14]

The Historic Sites and Monuments Board of Canada recognized Lady Aberdeen as a national historic person of Canada in 1979.

Quote:

"In the towns, they will go to those who cannot now afford the care of trained nurses and often die for lack of it; on the prairies, in the forests, in mining districts, everywhere throughout the country they will go hither and thither amongst our brave pioneers and bring help to those who are building up the future of this beautiful country amidst many hardships and privations."

Lady Aberdeen, referring to the Victorian Order of Nurses.

Superstar
Emma (Lajeunesse) Albani
1847–1930

Emma Albani.

One of the world's great sopranos, she moved Brahms to tears when she sang his Requiem.

Emma Albani was the first Canadian singer to become an international celebrity but is not well known today. During her forty-year career as an opera singer she performed in forty operas and was praised for her oratorios and recitals. She enchanted audiences in the musical capitals of the world.

Emma Lajeunesse was born in Chambly, Quebec. Her father, Joseph, was a professional musician who began teaching her how to play the harp and piano at an early age — and demanding she practise four hours per day. After the death of Emma's mother in childbirth, Joseph became a music teacher at a convent in Montreal, so Emma received a good education free of charge. The Mother Superior encouraged the talented girl to pursue a career in music, but the family didn't have the money to pay for her training. In 1865 they moved to Albany, New York, where the citizens were more supportive of the idea of women on the stage. Thanks to a number of benefit concerts Emma soon had the money to head to Europe to continue her studies.

Emma trained with prominent teachers in Paris and Milan while taking singing engagements to pay her bills. She made an impressive operatic debut in Messina, Italy, in 1870 at the age of twenty-two with the stage name Albani. The singer was then contracted by Frederick Gye at the prestigious Covent Garden opera house in London, where she was a principal artist from 1872-1896. Emma Albani also performed throughout Europe, Russia, North America, Mexico, Australia, New Zealand, South Africa, India, and Ceylon. For one season she was engaged as the leading soprano at the Metropolitan Opera in New York. At thirty, the popular prima donna married Ernest Gye, son of Frederick Gye, and gave birth to a son the following year.

Adored around the globe, Emma Albani became a favourite of Queen Victoria. The monarch enjoyed concerts as well as private meetings with Emma, whom she presented with many gifts. The talented singer cherished the pearl cross and necklace given to her by the Queen and was honoured to sing at her funeral — in response to written instructions by Victoria before her death. Royalty, political leaders, society figures, fellow musicians, and the press admired the dazzling Emma Albani for her extraordinary musical abilities as well as her charming personality and professionalism. Renowned composers Gounod, Von Flotow, Dvorak, and Sir Arthur Sullivan wrote music for her. The famous Canadian entertainer received many honours throughout her life, including the title of Dame Commander of the British Empire from King George V.

Emma Albani died in London in 1930. The Historic Sites and Monuments Board of Canada recognized Emma Albani as a national historic person in 1937 and installed a commemorative plaque in Chambly. Canada Post issued a postage stamp in honour of the celebrated diva to commemorate the fiftieth anniversary of her death. But as columnist Paul Gessell noted, "Albani's memory in the collective Canadian psyche has largely faded."[15]

Quote:

"I have married an Englishman, and have made my home in England, but I still remain at heart a French-Canadian."[16]

Flames for Freedom
Marie-Joseph Angélique
ca.1709–1734

An imaginary portrayal of Marie-Joseh Angélique by artist Richard Horne.

She rebelled — and paid with her life.

The young Black woman was just twenty-five years old when she was executed in Montreal in 1734. Marie-Joseph Angélique's body was then burned. The crime: arson. What had driven her to set the fire that blazed through the settlement? Was she guilty?

Marie-Joseph Angélique lived her last years as a slave in what is now Canada. The first complete record of a Black person being sold as a slave in New France dates back to 1629, though it was not until about 1671 that slavery became common. Marie-Joseph was one of the more than four thousand slaves known to have been kept in New France during the next 125 years, until slavery gradually disappeared. About a third of the slaves were Black people, with the remainder being Native people. The slave owners included people from all ranks of society and the professions.[17]

About half of the slaves in New France lived in Montreal, as did Marie-Joseph. Taken from her native Portugal to what is now the United States, she later became the property of François Poulin de Francheville.[18] He was a wealthy French seigneur, fur-trader, and merchant, whose businesses included the Saint-Maurice ironworks. Like other slaves in the colony Marie-Joseph presumably lived with the family and was taught Catholicism, though she remained unable to read or write. In June of 1730, when she was about twenty-one years of age, Marie-Joseph was baptized and Francheville was named her godfather; owners often served as sponsors for the baptism of their slaves.

In January of the following year Marie-Joseph gave birth to a son called Eustache. In May 1732, the young woman gave birth to twins Louis and Marie-Françoise. A Black slave called Jacques-César, owned by another Montreal seigneur called Igance Gamelin, fathered her three children. All of the offspring were listed in early records as belonging to slave owner Francheville. We can only imagine Marie-Joseph's sorrow when her three babies died soon after they were born.

Francheville died in November 1733 and his wife, Thérèse, inherited his slaves. Marie-Joseph apparently learned that she was to be sold by her new mistress. The young woman seems to have fallen in love with a white man called Claude Thibault and decided to flee with him towards New England. To cover her escape Marie-Joseph allegedly set fire to her owner's house in the evening of April 10 or 11, 1734, hoping to create a panic. A blaze erupted and quickly spread from house to house, burning both the church and convent of l'Hôtel-Dieu. The fire destroyed forty-six buildings.

Captured as she tried to escape the scene, Marie-Joseph was thrown into prison.[19] When a slave was charged with a crime, the individual was to receive the same treatment as a free person. While it is not certain how Marie-Joseph fared in jail, she was tried in a Montreal court and convicted of setting the fire. As the town continued to smoulder, she received her sentence: Marie-Joseph Angélique would have her hand cut off and then be burned alive.

As in all cases of condemnation to death, there was an appeal to the higher court in Quebec City (where the frightened slave was taken for her trial). The verdict was the same: guilty of arson as charged. But the sentence was changed. Her hand would not be cut off and she would not be burned alive: she would be hanged first, and then her corpse would be set afire.

The young slave was taken back to prison in Montreal. She was tortured four times, until she finally confessed to setting the fire but courageously refused to name an accomplice. The clerk of the court appeared to read her final sentence and a priest heard the condemned woman's confession. She was turned over to the hangman, believed to be a Black slave called Mathieu Léveillé. Marie-Joseph was loaded in a rubbish cart and taken to the parish church to give a public apology — and to ask the forgiveness of God, the King, and the courts.

She was paraded through the streets of Montreal, past the site of the blaze, then to the gallows in the public square. The hangman's noose extinguished her last breath. Her corpse was set on fire and the ashes of Marie-Joseph Angélique cast in the wind.

The noted historian Marcel Trudel, who conducted a comprehensive study on slavery in French Canada, related the experiences of Marie-Joseph in a chapter about crimes and punishments.[20] He indicates that the Montreal fire was the most spectacular crime committed by a slave during the years of slavery in Canada. Trudel suggests that her crime was not against society, but rather that of an individual against the widow of Francheville to enable a love affair. But is it even clear that Marie-Joseph started the blaze? Did she intentionally put the lives of others at risk? Was she severely mistreated by her mistress?

Many now view Marie-Joseph Angélique as a Canadian heroine, a desperate rebel credited with a dramatic act of resistance against slavery. A martyr. As noted by Dr. Esmeralda Thornhill on receiving an Honorary Doctorate of Laws, "In honoring me, you honor forebears and icons like Marie-Joseph Angélique of Nouvelle-France, who struck a defiant blow against slavery back in 1734."[21]

In a tribute to her tragic life, the story of Marie-Joseph was brought to the screen in the short 1999 film *Angélique* (by Michael Jarvis) and presented on the stage in a play of the same name by Lorena Gale. The young slave is portrayed as a desperate woman forced to have sex with her master and then to submit to abuse by his widow — her only hope for dignity and a better life was to escape. Another powerful commemoration to the young slave is the modern ballet *Marie-Joseph Angélique*, choreographed by Dr. Zelma Badu-Younge.

Quote:

"Said that she never spoke to Thibault or to anyone else about doing such a thing [as setting the fire]."[22]

Court transcript of testimony by
Marie-Joseph Angélique at her trial.

Murder of a Mi'kmaq Activist

Anna Mae Maloney Aquash
1945–1976

She fought for the rights of Native people, until someone shot her in the back of the head.

Photo courtesy Mary Rebecca Julian and Anna Mae Justice Fund

Anna Mae Pictou Maloney Aquash, ca. 1974–5.

On February 24, 1976, a rancher in South Dakota discovered a decomposing body on the Pine Ridge Indian Reservation — a young Indian woman curled up at the base of a cliff. She carried no identification.

Within a few hours the site was swarming with sheriff's deputies, police from the Bureau of Indian Affairs (BIA), and the FBI. A pathologist from the BIA soon concluded that the woman died of exposure and took the unusual step of chopping off her hands — placing them in a jar and giving them to FBI observers. Curiously, the BIA ordered the local mortician to arrange a quick burial despite the absence of an official death permit or death certificate. The woman was buried in an unmarked grave, apparently without genuine attempts to identify her.

On March 3, 1976, a fingerprint analysis by the FBI showed that the corpse was that of Anna Mae Aquash, a Canadian who was the most prominent woman in the American Indian Movement.[23] Anguished friends and family demanded a second autopsy, which showed that the thirty-year-old activist had been killed by a .32 caliber bullet shot at close range. Who murdered Anna Mae?

Anna Mae Pictou grew up poor on a Mi'kmaq reserve near Shubenacadie, Nova Scotia. She spent many years at the Pictou Landing reserve, where her family lived in an abandoned army house — with no electricity, running water, or heat. Suppers of turnips and potatoes were common. Because of their poor diet, the three Pictou sisters and their younger brother, Francis, were often ill. In early childhood Anna Mae was diagnosed with tuberculosis.

She grew up wearing poorly fitting, and sometimes moth-eaten, clothes provided by the federal Indian agent. Anna Mae attended church on Sundays and classes in a one-room school. At the age of eleven she was bused to a Catholic school off the reserve, where she soon discovered Indian children were not welcome. Her grades dropped even before her mother suddenly remarried and abandoned Anna Mae and her two young siblings. They were taken in by her older sister Rebecca and her husband, but there were too many mouths to feed. Anna Mae dropped out of school in grade nine, joining the annual migration from the reserves down to Maine.

She spent the summer picking blueberries and sleeping on a bed of straw. In the fall Anna Mae helped harvest potatoes, then headed down to Boston. She started working as a packer in a factory and began a relationship with Jake Maloney from Shubenacadie. At the age of nineteen Anna Mae gave birth to their daughter Denise. Their second child, Deborah, was born the following year on a trip to New Brunswick, during which Anna Mae immersed herself in Mi'kmaq culture and traditions. Anna Mae and Jake married in Richibucto, then settled down to an urban lifestyle in Boston.

Anna Mae worked in a sewing factory for a couple of years but grew increasingly interested in finding a way to help her people. In 1970 Jake and Anna Mae divorced, and she helped organize the Boston Indian Council. Her life took a new direction as she developed a greater appreciation of Native heritage and a commitment to helping other Indians through community work.

Anna Mae began teaching at an Indian cultural center in Maine called TRIBE: Teaching and Research in Bicultural Education. She studied teaching methods and Native history and enrolled in the New Careers program at Wheelock College in Boston. Anna Mae was offered a scholarship at Brandeis University but declined because of financial constraints, responsibilities to her daughters, and her growing desire to work for Native causes.

Now involved with Nogeeshik Aquash, a Chippewa artist from Ontario, Anna Mae and her new partner helped create an employment service for Indians in the Boston area. They also assisted with a Native fashion show at the National Arts Centre in Ottawa. In November 1972 she participated in the occupation of the Bureau of Indian Affairs building in Washington, organized by the American Indian Movement's Trail of Broken Treaties protest.

Anne Mae believed such demonstrations were needed to draw attention to issues affecting Indians. When the occupation of Wounded

Knee began in South Dakota on February 27, 1973, Anna Mae and Nogeeshik decided to join this protest against reservation grievances related to treaty rights. They were married during the occupation and spent about a month there. The couple faced only minor charges for their involvement, but Anna Mae Aquash was now branded as an AIM sympathizer — a supporter of a group that the FBI would attempt to disrupt and discredit.

As she discovered the traditional ways of Aboriginal people Anna Mae became increasingly spiritual, participating in traditional ceremonies and learning from elders. Her life now revolved around the American Indian Movement. Jake Maloney gained custody of their two daughters and raised them in Nova Scotia. Anna Mae's marriage to Aquash failed.

The idealistic and energetic young woman became heavily involved with AIM as an organizer, becoming a widely respected member closely connected to leaders Leonard Peltier and Dennis Banks. She worked and travelled across the United States, participating in protests, developing fundraising operations, creating education programs, arranging media relations, and security. She organized benefit concerts that involved enter-tainers such as Harry Belafonte, Kris Kristoferson, and Canadian folk singer Buffy Sainte-Marie. Anna Mae dreamed of having AIM schools that would train students to create reservation histories for Native people across Canada and the United States.

In 1974 the young activist joined the occupancy of Anicinabe Park in Kenora, Ontario. Anna Mae was now dodging the FBI, as they believed she could have knowledge about the killings of two FBI agents shot in South Dakota. The FBI file on her was apparently code-named the Brave Hearted Woman.

AIM members such as Anna Mae Aquash began moving to South Dakota to help defend community members who could not depend on police protection in an increasingly violent situation on the Pine Ridge Reservation. Traditionalists were trying to impeach tribal chairman Richard Wilson, whom they accused of everything from vote buying to allowing uranium leases on the reservation. In 1974 there were twenty-three murders on the reservation, and the reign of terror continued throughout 1975.

Anna Mae was arrested twice in the fall of 1975 and went under-ground. Rumors spread that Anna Mae was an FBI informant, and she was questioned by AIM in December of 1975.

Then she disappeared.

Events following the discovery of Anna Mae's body in February 1976 suggest a conspiracy to prevent an investigation of her murder.

Some speculated she'd learned too much about AIM and could possibly identify members that were spying for the FBI, or spill information about its operations. Others suggested the FBI arranged her killing because she wouldn't cooperate with them. It was only in March 2003 that two men were indicted for the murder of Anna Mae Aquash: Arlo Looking Cloud and John Graham, security guards for AIM events in the 1970s.[24]

Anna Mae Aquash was a courageous Canadian activist who dedicated her life to helping other Native people, most notably through her work for the American Indian Movement. Tributes to her heroism include the play *Annie Mae's Movement* by Yvette Nolan, which premiered at the Native Canadian Centre of Toronto in 2001, and the song *Bury My Heart at Wounded Knee* by Buffy Sainte-Marie. Tragically, it is her death that brought great attention to the causes Anne Mae lived and died for.

Quote:

"After I realized how you people live, I didn't want the things I had before. I left everything because I wanted to show you I love you people and want to help you."[25]

Anna Mae Aquash explaining to Roslyn Jumping Bull why she was determined to assist the women on the Pine Ridge Reservation.

The Cow Bay Saloon Raider

Edith Jessie
Archibald
1854–1936

Her secret weapon was
Parlour Meetings —
where society ladies
politely drank tea and
plotted reforms.

Edith Archibald.

Fuelled by her opposition to what she called "the coiled serpent of the liquor traffic," Edith Archibald led a group of Women's Christian Temperance Union (WTCU) members on raids of three illicit saloons in Cow Bay, Nova Scotia. Edith lived in this remote mining town for eighteen years while her husband managed the Gowrie Colliery.

An influential leader in the Canadian women's movement, Edith Archibald played important roles in many organizations, working to improve the lives of women and ensure they had a voice in society. Born in St. John's, Newfoundland in 1854, Edith Archibald belonged to a very prominent family with a history of public service. She received some of her early education in London and New York, where her father was British

Consul General. At the age of twenty Edith married her second cousin Charles Archibald, a mining engineer posted to Cow Bay and then Halifax — where he became vice-president of the Bank of Nova Scotia.

While living in Cow Bay the Archibalds enjoyed the luxury of a large house overlooking the sea. With the help of servants and boarding school, Edith raised four children. As a woman of means with relatively few housekeeping and childcare duties she had ample free time — and used it productively as a social activist. Edith Archibald became involved in the WCTU in the 1880s and served as Maritime Superintendent of the Parlour Meetings Department, which encouraged social events in members' homes as a method of organizing temperance activities and educating women. Enthusiastic about the benefits of Parlour Meetings, Edith surveyed the fifty-four local unions to find their assessment of the meetings, published a circular letter in the official national paper of the WCTU, and also printed it as a leaflet. Edith Archibald realized that local action was necessary to achieve the national goals of the organization. What better way than a tea party to plan revolt!

Wherever she was located Edith got involved in women's organizations — at the local, regional, and national level. In addition to her work in the Women's Christian Temperance Union, she also served as a leader in the National Council of Women of Canada and the Victorian Order of Nurses (VON). She was president of the Halifax Local Council of Women from 1896-1906 and president of the Halifax VON from 1897-1901. Edith battled for decades for women's right to vote and led a 1917 delegation of women to convince Nova Scotia Premier Murray not to block the suffrage bill; the legislature finally granted this right in 1918.

Edith Archibald's interests were varied and wide-ranging. She served as first president of the Halifax Ladies Musical Club, which provided opportunities for female musicians, teachers, and composers; she even composed some patriotic tunes. During the First World War she served as vice-president of the Nova Scotia Red Cross, where her efforts focused on assisting Canadian prisoners of war. She also helped establish the Children's Hospital of Halifax and supported a summer camp for poor children.

Edith was a passionate orator who used such evangelical phrases as, "Come out with me on the watch tower, O discouraged sisters! and, as you look over the battle-field of the world, see how the blood-stained banners of the Cross are ever increasingly victorious over the hosts of sin and darkness!"[26] After the war she put her writing skills to good use, publishing works such as a war history of the Red Cross, a biography of her father, and a three-act play that was published as a novel as well as performed at the Majestic Theatre in Halifax.

Dedicated to creating a better world, Edith Archibald played an important role in gaining the vote for women and increasing their opportunities to participate in Canadian society. Through her involvement in a multitude of organizations she worked throughout her life as a reformer. When Edith Archibald died in 1936 her death was front-page news in all five Halifax newspapers. She was praised as an outstanding woman in her province, a leader in the social and economic advancement of women, who lived a life of "wide and varied interests, of splendid achievement and great usefulness."[27] Not bad for a socialite.

The Historic Sites and Monuments Board of Canada recognized Edith Archibald as a national historic person of Canada in 1997.

Quote:

"The voice of the disfranchised portion of the people goes up to God in strong crying and tears night and day and enters into the ears of the Lord of Hosts. How long, oh Lord, how long?"[28]

Pitseolak Ashoona.

Inuit Life in Art

Pitseolak Ashoona
1904–1983

Art became her salvation, as it did for countless others whom she inspired.

Pitseolak realized how phenomenal her journey had been: "I know I have had an unusual life, being born in a skin tent and living to hear on the radio that two men have landed on the moon."[29]

A renowned Inuit artist, Pitseolak was born about 1904 in the Canadian Arctic on Nottingham Island, where her family was wintering. She grew up living from the land, hunting and fishing, travelling in sealskin boats, and learning the traditional ways of her people. Her father, Ottochie, still hunted with bow and arrow and her mother, Timungiak, sported the customary tattoo markings on her face. The family moved from camp to camp.

Pitseolak married Inuit hunter Ashoona when she was a young woman. She wore clothes of caribou skins when they were wed at Cape Dorset. The couple moved frequently, sometimes ten times a year, since Ashoona wanted to live far from other people. Pitseolak was content and particularly enjoyed the times when she and her husband would play the accordion and dance. In the early years of their marriage Pitseolak had a baby every year, seventeen in total though just six lived. Pitseolak wondered if it would be easier to give birth in a hospital!

When Pitseolak was in her early forties Ashoona died suddenly, leaving her alone with the responsibility of providing for the children. She moved her family to the growing community at Cape Dorset, where they suffered some hard times until the arrival of an influential fellow whom locals dubbed "The Man." He was James A. Houston, a federal civil servant working for the Department of Indian and Northern Affairs. He introduced the residents of Cape Dorset to drawing and printmaking in the late 1950s.

Pitseolak credited Houston with being the first man to help the Inuit. Desperate to support her children, the young widow was among the first at Cape Dorset to take up drawing as a means of augmenting the income she was making from sewing parkas and duffel socks. Houston encouraged her to depict the old ways of her people, so Pitseolak developed imaginative pictures of the traditional culture of the Inuit. Her graphic designs appeared in the annual Cape Dorset print collections from 1960 until 1984 (the year following her death). Pitseolak's work included more than seven thousand original images, some of which were displayed internationally. She prided herself on becoming a real artist.

Pitseolak gained considerable recognition for her art during her lifetime. In 1971 she left her familiar surroundings to fly to Ottawa, where the Honourable Jean Chrétien formally presented a book about her life to the National Library of Canada. That same year the National Film Board released a film about her, and Pitseolak attended the opening of a solo exhibit of her work in Montreal at the Canadian Guild of Crafts. The Inuit artist was elected to the Royal Canadian Academy of Arts in 1974. In 1977 Pitseolak Ashoona was awarded the Order of Canada in recognition of her contribution to Canadian art.

An influential role model, Pitseolak inspired many others in Cape Dorset — including four of her children — to become artists. She continued to draw until she died. In 1993 Canada Post paid tribute to this notable Canadian artist by issuing a commemorative postage stamp in her honour. Pitseolak Ashoona's artwork is held in permanent collections across North America.

Quote:

"After my husband died I felt very alone and unwanted; making prints is what has made me happiest since he died. I am going to keep on doing them until they tell me to stop. If no one tells me to stop, I shall make them as long as I am well. If I can, I'll make them even after I am dead."[30]

Was She or Wasn't He?

James Miranda
Barry
1795–1865

Dr. James Miranda Barry.

Dr. Barry was quite likely a heroic woman who disguised herself as a man in order to serve as a medical doctor.

It was a shocking revelation. Throughout Dr. Barry's adult life she presented herself as a male medical surgeon; but after her death a charwoman who examined the body revealed that the deceased was actually a woman. Newspapers spread stories of the supposed discovery. If indeed a woman, Dr. Barry was the first female doctor to practise medicine in Canada.[31]

It is not certain where James Miranda Barry was born or who her parents were — presumably part of the plan to conceal her true identity. Extensive research conducted by biographer Rachel Holmes[32] suggests that Barry was born Margaret Bulkley, the daughter of a destitute woman in Ireland who begged her brother James Barry for assistance. He was a well-know painter, a member of the Royal Academy of Arts and a supporter of the feminist Mary Wollstonecraft. The girl seems to have become the protégée of her uncle before he died in 1806, leaving his estate to his sister and making it possible for his young relative to receive a good education. Margaret disappeared and a young man called James Miranda Barry appeared, presumably in a bid to follow a path that was not open to women.

The student enrolled at the University of Edinburgh's prestigious medical school in Scotland, with the support of some of her uncle's illustrious friends — most notably Lord Buchanan (also a pro-feminist) and the famous revolutionary General Francisco de Miranda who liberated Venezuela. Barry, Buchanan, and Miranda all strongly influenced the life of James Miranda Barry. After graduation Dr. Barry continued studying medicine in London with the famed surgeon Astley Cooper before joining the Army Medical Department in 1813. The distinguished career of Dr. Barry included stints in South Africa, Mauritius, Jamaica, St. Helena Island, Trinidad, Malta, Corfu, and then Canada. Throughout her life she travelled with a Black manservant and a series of small white dogs — all named Psyche.

Dr. Barry's professional career was marred by conflicts that led to many transfers — even arrest and a duel. She was, however, a brilliant doctor with an impressive career, the recipient of a series of promotions as she worked round the globe. Dr. Barry was a notable medical reformer who championed improvements that would help women, lepers, prostitutes, prisoners, the poor, slaves, and the insane. In 1826 she completed one of the first successful Caesarean section deliveries in the world. Dr. James Barry also penned some valuable scientific papers regarding hernias and treatment of syphilis and gonorrhea.

For the last posting of her career, the hot-blooded doctor was assigned to one of the coldest places in the world. "So I am to go to Canada to cool myself after such a long residence in the Tropics and Hot Countries,"[33] wrote Dr. Barry. Over sixty when she arrived, Dr. Barry served in Canada from 1857 to 1859. Dr. Barry held the important post of Inspector General of military hospitals and introduced many reforms. She supervised hospitals and barracks in Montreal, Quebec, Kingston, and Toronto.

A vegetarian attentive to good nutrition, the doctor worked to improve soldiers' rations and recommended the installation of ovens in their quarters so they would be able to vary their diet. Appalled by the unsanitary conditions at the Quebec barracks, Dr. Barry wanted changes made to the sewage and drainage. She also campaigned for separate quarters for married couples and better bedding for the troops — the doctor demanded that straw be replaced by hair mattresses and hair or feather pillows.

Based in Montreal, Dr. Barry enjoyed the privilege of belonging to the St. James Club and whizzing through the winter streets in a fine red sleigh. The slender doctor, wearing her dark-blue military uniform and gold-braided cap, would be bundled in furs. Now sporting dyed red hair, she was a dapper figure. After suffering from a series of chest infections during the long winters, Dr. James Barry came down with a severe case of bronchitis and was sent back to England in the spring of 1859. Despite her protests and a plea to return to Canada, Dr. Barry was directed to retire — ending a remarkable career of more than forty years as an army medical doctor.

Following a few lonely years in a London lodging house, Dr. James Barry died in 1865. The feisty medical pioneer had attained the most senior ranking of Her Majesty's Inspector General of Hospitals. Known throughout the British Empire, she became one of the most influential physicians of the nineteenth century because of her innovative medical reforms in various areas of the world. She had infuriated Florence Nightingale by her criticisms and received a diamond ring as a gift from the Hapsburg archduke Maximilian. Count de Las Casas, a close friend of Napoleon, had considered the doctor "an absolute phenomenon." Charles Dickens noted that Barry was "unique in appearance, and eccentric in manner," and developed a creative account of the inspector's life for his popular magazine.[34]

The mystery about the true sex of Dr. James Miranda Barry may never be solved, but speculation about this remarkable individual makes for fascinating reading. Who was the fiery five-foot redhead?

Quote:

"I have certainly striven to do my duty towards God and Fellow men."[35]

First Lady of the Yukon

Martha Black
1866–1957

She climbed the Chilkoot Pass to seek her fortune in the Klondike gold rush, becoming one of the most celebrated sourdoughs in the north.

National Archives of Canada/C-081812

Martha Black.

Martha Munger Purdy was a wealthy Chicago socialite, settled in a comfortable middle-class life with her spouse and two sons, until news broke of the Klondike gold rush. When her husband Will Purdy got gold fever, Martha was determined to join him in his trek to the gold-fields. He arrived safely in Seattle but suddenly decided to go to the Sandwich Islands (Hawaiian Islands) instead of north. Martha refused to change plans and convinced her brother George to head up to Skagway, Alaska, with her.

In the summer of 1898 George and Martha climbed the Chilkoot Pass along with thousands of other gold seekers. She wore a fashionable "outing costume" — a brown corduroy velvet skirt that was five yards around the bottom, brown silk bloomers, boned corsets, a blouse with a high collar, a pleated Norfolk jacket, and high boots made of Russian leather. The stylish outfit soon proved impractical, as Martha set out on the dreaded trail.

> With staff in hand, at last I had taken my place in that continuous line of pushing humans and straining animals. Before me, behind me, abreast of me almost every man toted a pack of 60 to 80 pounds, in addition to driving dogs and horses harnessed to sleighs and carts, herding pack ponies and the odd cow, while one woman drove an ox-cart.[36]

Cursing her clothes and hitching up her bloomers, she slogged to the summit and descended on shaky legs. With torn boots and bleeding hands she tripped over tree roots, staggering along until her brother carried her for most of the last mile of the Trail of '98.

Martha and George continued on to Dawson. Finding the price of lots sky-high, the siblings squatted about a mile and a half from the town and built a cabin. George began working the claim he had staked while Martha fulfilled a promise to check out the will of a miner who had supposedly left a million dollars in gold dust; she was eagerly expecting to receive half of the latter if she recovered the inheritance. She found nothing and was terror-stricken to discover she'd been pregnant while hiking the Chilkoot Trail. There was no way for her to leave the North before winter, and the distraught young woman prayed to God to let her die.

Martha Purdy was alone in her wilderness cabin in the long dark days of winter when her third son was born on January 31, 1899. She was touched when "miners, prospectors, strange uncouth men called to pay their respects,"[37] bringing gifts of ptarmigan, moose meat, chocolates and cakes, gold nuggets, and gold dust. The visitors dubbed the new babe the little chechako. Martha survived a wild winter in Dawson, having soon realized she and George had squatted above the red-light district. She had a ringside seat to observe the gaiety and despair of life in the gold rush, the saloons, and the dance halls, the gambling rooms, the drinking, and debauchery.

Martha fell in love with the land of the midnight sun and became one of the most notable pioneers in Yukon history. She divorced her husband, raised her boys, formed a gold-mining partnership, and efficiently operated a sawmill that made her a lot of money. In 1904 the enterprising lady married criminal lawyer George Black, who was appointed Commissioner for the territory in 1912. The dynamic new mistress of Government House in Dawson City transformed it into a charming mansion where the Blacks hosted many social events. As one guest noted, "A visit to Government House was a trip to another country so far as the rest of us were concerned and did much to keep up our morale."[38]

When George Black resigned his position to lead a Yukon contingent in World War I, Martha insisted on accompanying him across the Atlantic — the only woman on a troop ship with over three thousand men. In 1921 George Black was elected as a federal member of parliament. Martha Black became an accomplished amateur botanist, wrote magazine articles, and did some public speaking. When George Black resigned as House Speaker in 1935 due to illness, Martha ran in his place in the federal election. She won the seat, becoming the second female member of

Parliament at the age of sixty-nine, and served a five-year term. George Black later returned to federal politics, retiring in 1949. Years later the remarkable couple was still referred to as "Mr. and Mrs. Yukon."

Martha Black lived until she was ninety-one. During her lifetime she was awarded the Order of the British Empire for her volunteer work during World War I and made a Fellow of the Royal Geographical Society in recognition of her research on Yukon flora. The Historic Sites and Monuments Board of Canada commemorated the legendary pioneer as a national historic person, and the Commissioner's Residence where the Blacks lived from 1912 to 1916 is part of a national historic site in Dawson. Black Street in Whitehorse and two mountain peaks in the Yukon are named in honour of Martha and George Black.

Quote:

"What I wanted was not shelter and safety, but liberty and opportunity."[39]

Yukon Archives: Martha Louise Black Fonds, 82/218, #16.

Martha with son Lyman and brother George, in their cabin near Dawson.

Statue of Marguerite Bourgeoys in Montreal.

René Chartrand photo

We Shall Teach
Marguerite Bourgeoys
1620–1700

This sister was no pushover. She even battled with a bishop in her fight to create the first Canadian religious community — whose members would travel around the wilderness to teach children.

When she was thirty-three years old Marguerite Bourgeoys set sail for New France, intent on setting up a school in the recently established Ville-Marie (now Montreal). She became a respected leader in the struggling settlement, a notable figure in Canadian history, and eventually a saint.

Marguerite came from a region of France where women had played important roles in public life since the Middle Ages.[40] Born in Troyes on April 17, 1620, Marguerite was the daughter of Guillemette Garnier and Abraham Bourgeoys, a candle-maker and official in the Troyes Mint. When she was twenty the young woman was suddenly inspired when gazing at a statue of the Virgin Mary, and decided to enter an external congregation of the Congrégation of Notre Dame. This group of young women lived in their own homes but attended classes in religion and pedagogy in the monastery, unlike the religious sisters who were cloistered and could not go into the community. On joining the group Marguerite helped with charity work such as teaching young girls.

Marguerite heard stories of Canada from the group's director, Louise de Chomedey de Sainte-Marie — sister of Maisonneuve, who was one of the founders of the colony at Ville-Marie. Unwilling to bring a religious order to Montreal, Maisonneuve accepted Marguerite's offer to join him there if she agreed to be a teacher. Marguerite arrived in New France in 1653 but there weren't enough school-age children to warrant a school until 1658. She welcomed her first students in the only available building: a large stone building that had served as a stable.

Known as the "Mother of the Colony," Marguerite helped establish the growing community in many ways. She organized the construction of the chapel of Notre-Dame-de-Bon-Secours. She chaperoned and educated young orphan girls brought over as brides (known as the daughters of the king or *filles du roi*), and screened the men who wanted to wed them. With teachers she recruited from both France and Canada Marguerite opened a boarding school for young girls in Ville-Marie, and her "sisters" taught in more remote areas. She established a school for Aboriginal girls on the Sulpician Reserve of La Montagne and a domestic training school at Saint-Charles point. To support the many activities of the congregation Marguerite Bourgeoys also set up a farm.

For many years Marguerite Bourgeoys struggled to get official recognition of her religious community in order to ensure its continuance. She met resistance because her "sisters" were not cloistered, as was customary at this time, and church officials were reluctant to approve an order that might become a financial burden. In 1669 Bishop Laval authorized the sisters to teach anywhere in Canada. On a trip to France Marguerite managed to meet Louis XIV and obtain letters of patent from him in May 1671. She showed impressive independence in resisting the desire of her bishop, Monsignor de Saint-Vallier, to amalgamate her group with the Ursulines in Quebec, and on July 1, 1698, the Congrégation de Notre-Dame was officially endorsed. Marguerite Bourgeoys and her colleagues were able to make simple vows, and the sisters became part of the first non-cloistered religious community in Canada.

Today it is perhaps difficult for us to imagine how innovative this was. Many of the sisters travelled extensively, by foot, horseback, or canoe, teaching the inhabitants along the shores of the St. Lawrence River. Guaranteed only "bread and soup" by their founder, the sisters lived poorly in order to provide free education. Reflecting the principles of teaching she had learned in France, Marguerite insisted on such novel practices as intensive teacher-training and minimal use of strapping in the classroom — at a time when it was a common form of discipline.[41]

Her contemporaries regarded her with the highest esteem. Among them was Marie Morin, the first nun born in Canada, who wrote of her in glowing terms:

> My sister Bourgeoys can do anything; she is equally suc-
> cessful in temporal and spiritual matters, because her love
> of God guides her actions and gives her wisdom. She has
> all the character of the proverbial wise woman and it
> would be very difficult to find another like her.[42]

In January 1700 one of the young sisters, Soeur Catherine Charly, became very sick. Marguerite prayed that God take her own life instead, and she was suddenly overtaken by a strong fever. Sister Charly recovered, and Marguerite Bourgeoys died several days later.

Canada Post issued a commemorative stamp in her honour, and the Historic Sites and Monuments Board of Canada recognized Marguerite Bourgeoys as a national historic person. When Pope John Paul II canonized her on October 31, 1982, she became the first Canadian woman to be sainted. Sisters of the Congrégation of Notre-Dame now serve in Canada, the United States, Japan, Latin America, Cameroon, and France.

Quote:

"We are asked why we prefer to be vagabonds rather than cloistered nuns, since the cloisters offer protection to persons of our sex. We reply that the Blessed Virgin was never cloistered but she never refused a voyage which allowed her to carry out some good or charitable deed. Because we see her as our teacher, we are not cloistered, although we live in a Community. In this way, we can go everywhere we are sent to educate girls."[43]

A Mohawk Diplomat

Molly Brant
(Gonwatsijayenni)
ca.1736–1796

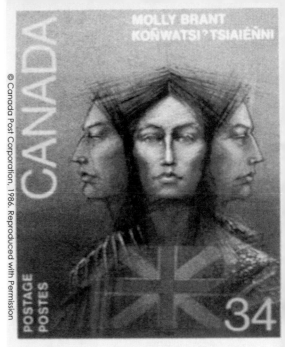

She was a bridge between two worlds — Whites and Natives.

Molly Brant.

Molly (Mary) Brant was a powerful Mohawk woman: head of the Six Nations matrons. She played a key role in the American Revolutionary War by ensuring the support of the Iroquois for the British. By the time she moved to Canada Molly had become a respected diplomat and stateswoman.[44]

A member of the Wolf clan of the Mohawks, her birth name was Gonwatsijayenni — meaning "someone lends her a flower." Molly Brant was probably born on the Mohawk River in New York about 1736 to Christian parents. She grew up in the Indian town of Canajoharie, now Upper Castle, in an area already surrounded by settlers. The colonists were anxious to have good relations with the Mohawks, who were members of the powerful Iroquois confederacy of Six Nations, which also included the Cayuga, Oneida, Onondaga, Seneca, and Tuscarora. Molly belonged to a matrilineal culture in which women played influential roles.

Molly Brant's position among her people as well as European colonists was enhanced by her long-time intimate relationship with Sir William Johnson — the most prominent and powerful person in the early development of the Mohawk Valley. Johnson was a shrewd Irish landowner who became a successful businessman and Superintendent of Indian Affairs. A prestigious leader, he worked closely with the Iroquois to ensure their support of the British in North America.

They lived together as man and wife from 1759 until his death in 1774, during which time Molly raised their eight children. She skillfully managed the household at Fort Johnson and later Johnson Hall with a large staff of servants and slaves. One English woman described the gracious hostess:

> Her features are fine and beautiful; her complexion clear and olive-tinted ... She was quiet in demeanour, on occasion, and possessed of a calm dignity that bespoke a native pride and consciousness of power. She seldom imposed herself into the picture, but no one was in her presence without being aware of her.[45]

Molly Brant was extremely influential in Johnson's political life, as outlined by a frequent visitor (Judge Jones): "through her means he was always enabled to gain the most authentic intelligence, and to counteract every scheme undertaken by his enemies to set up the Indians against him."[46]

When Sir William Johnson died in 1774, Molly Brant's life quickly changed. She returned to Canajoharie with her eight young children aged one to fifteen. In the following years she struggled to ensure that they continued to receive a good education and that each received the inheritance left to them by Johnson. The eldest son, Peter, learned French, English, and Mohawk and could play the fiddle; his parents were grooming him to be a great landlord and merchant, a man who would play an important role with both Mohawks and Whites. The family lived in a European-style house and had some of the belongings from their previous home — including fine ceramics and silver.

Molly Brant assisted British loyalists once war broke out in the colonies. After she sent Indian runners to warn of a planned attack on Fort Stanwix by American forces in 1777, Molly and her children were forced to flee their home. The British recognized Molly's strong commitment to their cause and her potential power in the conflict, knowing that "one word from her goes farther with them [the Iroquois] than a thousand from any white Man without Exception."[47] Major John Butler invited Molly to come to Fort Niagara, where she worked hard to ensure Iroquois loyalty to the British. In recognition of her support, General Haldimand (commander of the British forces in Canada) arranged for a house to be built for Molly and also sent some money.

In the late summer of 1779 many Iroquois lost their villages and their crops after American forces moved in to deter their continued involvement in the war. Many homeless Indians were forced to winter on Carleton Island, at the head of the St. Lawrence River, where Molly Brant joined them and again successfully encouraged loyalty to the King. She spent the remainder of the war there while her younger children attended school in Montreal. Her son Peter had joined the military and died fighting for the British.

After the American Revolution Molly moved to Cataraqui (Kingston, Ontario), where she lived for the remainder of her life in a home that Governor Haldimand had ordered for her. He also arranged an annual British pension of one hundred pounds per year because of her valuable assistance during the war. The family eventually received compensation for their losses in the years of conflict.

During the 1790s Molly and her daughters held an important position in their new home and were highly respected in the community. Molly was very involved with the Anglican Church and was the only woman listed in the founding charter of 1792. A visitor was surprised at seeing Molly in church: "...we saw an Indian woman, who sat in an honourable place among the English."[48]As was her custom, Miss Molly — proud of her ancestry — dressed in a mixture of traditional Mohawk clothing with English accessories. The elderly woman enjoyed frequent dinners as the guest of John Simcoe, Lieutenant-Governor of Upper Canada, and his wife, Elizabeth.

Molly Brant died in Kingston on April 16, 1796, and was buried at what is now St. Paul's Church. Considering the status of women in the eighteenth century, she had been a woman of significant influence — a heroine of the Revolutionary War and a notable British loyalist recognized for her war service. But, as historian Ian Wilson outlined in 1976, "Posterity has done scant justice to this remarkable woman. In her lifetime she commanded respect from Indian and white alike. Soldiers, statesmen, governors and generals wrote her praise. Her life from the Ohio and Mohawk Valleys to Kingston was not easy. It was fraught with danger and uncertainty and little seemed settled. She survived this turmoil with dignity, honour and distinction as a mother and a leader."[49]

A number of tributes have been given to this extraordinary woman in recent years. In 1986 Canada Post recognized the important contribution of Molly Brant by issuing a commemorative stamp in her honour on the 250th anniversary of her birth. In 1994 the Anglican Church of Canada added her name to the church calendar, with April 16 being the day that special prayers are given to commemorate her.

Miss Molly would no doubt have been flattered that on August 25, 1996, the citizens of Kingston honoured her as a respected pioneer: on Molly Brant Celebration Day. A commemorative plaque was dedicated in recognition of her designation by the Historic Sites and Monuments Board of Canada as a national historic person. A bust of the Mohawk matron, sculpted by local artist John Boxtel (using a distant Brant relative as a model) was unveiled at the site of Molly Brant's home in Kingston — now the location of the Rideaucrest Home for the Aged. In April 2003 the Cataraqui Archeological Research Foundation presented a new opera at St. George's Cathedral in Kingston. Composer Augusta Cecconi-Bates wrote *Molly Brant: A One Woman Opera* to celebrate a woman she considers "a true Canadian heroine."

Quote:

"...the Indians are a Good dale dissatisfied on Acc't. Of the Colo's. hasty temper which I hope he will soon drop Otherwise it may be Disadvantageous I need not tell you whatever is promised or told them it Ought to be performed."[50]

From a letter Molly wrote to Col. Daniel Claus on October 5, 1779.

Forgotten Physicist?

Harriet Brooks
1876–1933

A brilliant scientist, she became the first female nuclear physicist in Canada.

Miss Harriet Brooks, nuclear physicist, Montreal, Quebec, 1898.

Born in Exeter, Ontario, Harriet grew up in a family of eight supported by her father, George Brooks — who struggled to feed and clothe the brood from his earnings as a travelling salesman for a flour company. Harriet managed to attend McGill University only because she was an outstanding student who won many scholarships. On graduation in 1898 she joined a research group under the prominent physicist Ernest Rutherford.

Harriet conducted some important research on radioactivity, providing the first evidence that one element could change into another. She became a fellow in physics at Bryn Mawr College while studying for her Ph.D., and then accepted a fellowship to study at Cambridge University in England. The young scientist returned to McGill without completing her Ph.D., perhaps in fear of losing her research job there. She discovered the recoil of the radioactive atom before accepting a job as a tutor in physics at the women's college of Columbia University in New York.

When Harriet became engaged to a university professor there, she was advised that marriage would mean her termination from the college. Dean Laura Gill wrote, "I feel very strongly that whenever your marriage does take place it ought to end your official relationship with the college ... The College cannot afford to have women on the staff to whom the college work is secondary."[51] Harriet Brooks was outraged. Her engagement broke off and she resigned from the college.

Harriet travelled to Europe and ended up working with the famous Marie Curie at the Curie Institute. Professor Rutherford once noted in a reference for Harriet Brooks that: "next to Mme Curie she is the most prominent woman physicist in the department of radioactivity."[52] While waiting to hear about another prestigious fellowship, Harriet decided to marry a suitor called Frank Pitcher and abandon her career.

Harriet Brooks was a remarkable Canadian scientist who made important contributions to nuclear science in the relatively short time she pursued her career. Curiously, she often showed little self-confidence in her abilities or those of women in science in general — a sad reflection of the society she lived in and the pressures on a talented woman whose gifts led her on a path where few Canadian women had travelled.

Quote:

"I think also it is a duty I owe to my profession and to my sex to show that a woman has the right to the practice of her profession and cannot be condemned to abandon it merely because she marries. I cannot conceive how women's colleges, inviting and encouraging women to enter professions can be justly founded or maintained denying such a principle."[53]

Harriet Brooks, on being told that if she married she could no longer work at Barnard College.

Arctic Bound

Agnes Deans Cameron
1863–1912

The New North, 1910

Agnes Deans Cameron during her Arctic trip.

She was an original, proving women could succeed in the professions and follow their dreams. Even those who dared to defy the establishment.

A trip to the Arctic? Why not.

Agnes Deans Cameron was an adventurer, as well as an educator, writer, and lecturer. In 1908 she and her niece Jessie Brown travelled sixteen thousand kilometres from Chicago, across the continent to the Mackenzie River Delta. They were among the first white women to journey overland to the Arctic Ocean. Agnes then penned a popular travelogue book entitled *The New North*[54] and showed her lantern slides of the trip on an extensive tour in the United States. The publication provided fascinating stories and images of the people of Northern and Western Canada, proving to be an effective promotional tool for Agnes' work as a journalist and publicist for the Western Canada Immigration Association in their Chicago office.

"Like most overseas girls, I was brought up to do something and to earn my living,"[55] Agnes remarked. Born in Victoria to Scottish immigrants who had followed the lure of gold from California to British Columbia, she was the daughter of a miner/contractor and a former teacher. She began a very successful teaching career and by 1894 was appointed school principal at South Park School in Victoria — the first woman in the province to hold such a position. An excellent teacher who was not shy about expressing her views on education or the rights of women, she felt the focus of education should be the development of strong analytical skills that would teach children how to live and become good citizens. She strongly opposed the introduction of training programs intended to prepare young students for specific jobs, fearing that "the crusaders would teach every boy to be a carpenter and every girl to cook."[56]

Agnes Deans Cameron was a feminist who believed in justice. She supported many causes — including pay equity, suffrage for women, and the elimination of age discrimination — and vigorously shared her views in public meetings as well as in articles in the local newspapers and journals. Outraged to learn that school trustees planned salary increases for male teachers only, Agnes called the action "retrogressive and demoralizing."[57] While her initial focus was the classroom and the educational system, Agnes was also active in organizations such as the Women's Christian Temperance Union, the Children's Aid Society, the Society for the Prevention of Cruelty to Animals, the Local Council of Women, and the Dominion Women's Enfranchisement Association.

Agnes became involved in a number of controversies with school trustees, and in 1901 she was suspended for insubordination. The outspoken teacher was reinstated following widespread community support, but in 1905 she was accused of allowing her students to cheat on an exam by using rulers rather than drawing freehand. Agnes was fired on December 15, 1905. Despite a public outcry, a Royal Commission, and the fact that three male principals were accused of the same offense and never lost their jobs, her career as an educator ended. The school board blatantly discriminated against this opinionated woman and finally managed to get rid of her.[58]

Agnes then focused on her writing career. She made some useful contacts by joining the Canadian Women's Press Club and soon began her work in Chicago, and then in the Arctic. During this expedition she met a Roman Catholic priest who was utterly amazed to learn that the enthusiastic adventurer had taught school for twenty-five years, and yet "you remain so glad!"[59] Building on the success of her lecture tour about the Arctic trip, she got a two-year assignment in England to promote Canadian immigration — giving over two hundred presentations at Oxford, Cambridge, the Royal Geographical Society, and to several other esteemed organizations. She was a splendid speaker who earned a reputation as a dynamic and witty woman.

The celebrated journalist Agnes Deans Cameron returned to Victoria at the close of 1911, where she was greeted as a local heroine at a reception hosted by the city. Now considered "one of the foremost women in Canada," she was invited to share the platform when the famous British suffragist Emmeline Pankhurst lectured there. A few months later Agnes was dead at the age of forty-eight, following the onset of pneumonia after an appendectomy.

The *Daily Colonist*, reporting on Victoria's largest ever funeral procession, noted that "It is possible that when the history of British Columbia comes to be written the name of Agnes Deans Cameron will be inscribed therein as the most remarkable woman citizen of the province."[60] A notable promoter of Western and Northern Canada and a determined educational reformer, she lived her life as she encouraged her students to: "to ring true and stand for something."[61]

Quote:

"A child's individuality is the divine spark in him. Let it burn."[62]

Emily Carr.

Painting with Passion
Emily Carr
1871–1945

One of the most talented artists in Canadian history, her powerful paintings evoke the wonders of the natural world and the Native culture of Canada's West Coast.

After watching her family dog for a long time, the little girl grabbed a charred stick from the fireplace and drew the pet on a brown paper bag. On seeing the picture her father bought her a paint box and arranged for art lessons. So began the long journey of Emily Carr: the agonizing search for the means of truly expressing herself through her art and her writing. It was only near her death that people identified Emily Carr as an important writer and were beginning to fully recognize her artistic greatness.

Emily was born in Victoria, British Columbia, in 1871, the youngest of five girls and a boy born to an English couple. She grew up in a strict household controlled by her stern and domineering father — a wealthy businessman. The quiet and gentle Mrs. Carr was able to balance the force of his personality somewhat, but she died when Emily was just fifteen. When Mr. Carr died two years later, Emily and the younger children were left in the hands of an authoritative elder sister, Edith.

This Victorian upbringing stifled the spirited Emily, who was an adventurous and curious girl often chided by her elder sisters for being naughty. After graduating from high school Emily managed to convince the gentleman whom her father had named guardian to permit her to attend the San Francisco School of Art. At the age of seventeen, the happy young woman headed for California (taking a beloved canary in a cage), where she spent six years.

After financial failures in the family estate, Emily had to return to Victoria. She taught art classes for children, fell in love, and in 1898 made her first sketching trip to the Ucluelet area on Vancouver Island. Here she would sketch the Native people and their villages. The Native people, who became a major inspiration for her art, loved the bubbling Emily and called her "Klee Wyck": Laughing One.

Emily felt she needed to go to Europe for more instruction. She studied at the Westminster School of Art in London, the Academie Colorossi in Paris, then worked with British artist Harry Gibb in the French countryside. Emily was beginning to find her own style, and Gibb was impressed by her paintings: "You will be one of the painters — woman painters — of your day."[63]

The periods of study were interspersed with significant periods of illness, as well as more teaching to earn a living and additional trips to visit Native communities on the west coast of British Columbia. Eager to document the disappearing totem poles, Emily painted and drew many before they decayed.

An attempt to show her works at an exhibition in Vancouver fell flat as both critics and public panned her paintings — paintings of a modern style they were unfamiliar with. A discouraged Emily set up a rooming house in Victoria to pay her bills, and occupied herself with breeding dogs and making pottery and rugs. She painted little between 1913 and 1928.

Emily Carr's life changed dramatically after the noted ethnologist Marius Barbeau discovered her canvases and suggested she show some at an exhibition of Canadian West Coast art at the National Gallery of Canada in 1927. For the first time the works of artist Emily Carr were shown in Eastern Canada. The Group of Seven welcomed her, and Lawren Harris in particular encouraged and supported her.[64]

An uplifted Emily Carr returned to Victoria, beginning the most prolific years of her life. She was fifty-seven. The artist began to paint the world of nature, the power of the forests and the land. In the next ten years her pictures were displayed at sixteen major exhibitions of international standing, including the Tate Gallery in London, the Stedelijk Museum in Amsterdam, and the Paris International Exposition. She became an honorary member of the Group of Seven, and the National Gallery of Canada bought six of her paintings. Her studio became a gathering place for artists and writers visiting Victoria.

Emily Carr also began to write. She enrolled in a short story course with a school in Los Angeles and began to vividly tell her stories.

Despite Emily's growing reputation in the art world, sales were few, and her financial situation was as precarious as it had always been. In 1937 she suffered a severe heart attack. Friends pleaded with Eric Brown at the National Gallery to help alleviate her financial stresses, and he asked the English art critic Eric Newton to visit Emily and select fifteen pictures to be sent east for prospective buyers. Newton saw Emily Carr in hospital and helped set her on the road to recovery again. He later wrote, "Emily Carr is not merely a good woman painter, she is the greatest woman painter who has yet lived."[65]

It was not until 1941 that Emily Carr managed to get her first book published, and the preparations lifted her spirits. The book *Klee Wyck* soon brought accolades from across Canada, and Emily Carr was acclaimed as a great Canadian writer. The work won the Governor General's Gold Medal for general literature.

To celebrate the publishing of the book and the seventieth birthday of Emily Carr, the president of the University Women's Club of Victoria gave a large reception on December 12, 1941. The gala affair was attended by local notables as well as Emily's friends, and for the first time she was feted in her home town. A deeply moved Emily spoke to the crowd, thanking them and explaining: "I would rather have the good will and kind wishes of my home town, the people I have lived among all my life, than the praise of the whole world."[66]

The next year the still struggling artist created the Emily Carr Trust Collection, willing 170 of her best works to the Province of British Columbia on condition that they be exhibited at the Vancouver Art Gallery. She left an additional five hundred other works to be sold to benefit a scholarship fund that would assist young artists in British Columbia.

In the last few years of her life Emily was still trying to express herself creatively though her physical strength continued to decline. In 1942 she went to Mt. Douglas Park and painted fifteen large oil sketches in eight days, after which she was taken to hospital on a stretcher after suffering a near fatal heart attack.

Emily saw more of her books being published and pictures sold, and financial worries were finally disappearing. In Montreal, fifty-six pictures were sold within a couple weeks.

Emily Carr died just as she was beginning to be recognized as a significant figure in Canadian art. In 1950 the Historic Sites and Monuments Board of Canada recognized her as a national historic person of Canada.

Quote:

"This is my country. What I want to express is *here* and I love it. Amen!"[67]

Emily Carr writing of her feelings about Canada.

A painting by Emily Carr: *Gitwangak*, 1912.

The Dangerous Radical[68]
Thérèse Casgrain
1896–1981

Yousuf Karsh/National Archives of Canada/PA-178177

Thérèse Casgrain, ca. 1937.

A relentless social critic, she was the guiding spirit of the Quebec feminist movement for forty years.[69]

Thérèse Casgrain was born to the bourgeoisie but spent her lifetime speaking out for those who had no voice in society. Born in Montreal, she was the daughter of Lady Blanche MacDonald and Sir Rodolphe Forget — a wealthy lawyer, stockbroker, and long-time Conservative MP. At the age of nineteen Thérèse married Pierre Casgrain, a lawyer who became a Liberal MP, Speaker of the House of Commons, and Secretary of State.

Thérèse Casgrain raised four children and led an active social life, but plunged into politics in the early 1920s after the illness of her husband forced her to give a political speech on his behalf. Pierre was re-elected, and Thérèse accepted the invitation of some local suffragists to join the struggle for women's rights. The intelligent young woman proved to be witty and articulate, charming and outspoken, confident and inexhaustible in her support of political and social issues. She soon became a leading feminist reformer.

Throughout the 1920s and '30s Mme. Casgrain campaigned for Quebec women's right to vote and practise law and for improvements in their legal status. In 1926 she founded the Young Women's League to encourage involvement in social work. Through her Radio-Canada program *Fémina* Thérèse spread her radical ideas throughout the province. From 1928 to 1942 she served as president of the League for Women's Rights. A member of the National Health Council and the National Welfare Council, she helped found the French Federated Charities, the French Junior League, and the Montreal Symphony Orchestra Society. Thérèse

Casgrain was named an Officer of the Order of the British Empire in recognition of her World War II service in the Consumer Branch of the Wartime Prices and Trade Board.

In 1942 Mme. Casgrain decided the only way she could play a significant role in resolving social problems was to enter active politics by running for office in the next federal election. With her children grown up and her husband having left the House of Commons to become a judge, she announced her intentions. Opposition to electing a woman was widespread, and one newspaper editor suggested Thérèse should return to cooking and sewing.[70] From 1942 to 1962 she ran nine times in both federal and provincial seats — and was never elected. Despite these failures this remarkable woman still managed to have an incredible political impact, becoming the grande dame of Quebec politics.

Mme. Casgrain became disillusioned with the established political parties, concluding that "Canada needed a political party centred upon the common good rather than on the promotion of personal interests."[71] In 1946 she joined the Cooperative Commonwealth Federation (CCF), which later evolved into the NDP. When Thérèse was elected leader of the Quebec branch of the CCF in 1951 she became the first woman leader of a political party in that province.

Thérèse Casgrain devoted her considerable energy to many causes, including world peace, medical aid to Vietnam War victims, adult education, fair treatment of Japanese Canadians, consumer rights, the status of Aboriginal women, the participation of women in public life, human rights, and improved relations between English and French-speaking Canadians. Prime Minister Trudeau appointed her to the Senate in 1970, and she served nine months before reaching the mandatory retirement age of seventy-five. Adding the fight against forced retirement to her list of issues requiring attention, the passionate reformer continued to campaign for social reforms until she died at eighty-five.

A devoted feminist and humanist who contributed to significant reforms that benefited Canadians across the country, Thérèse Casgrain received a multitude of honours during her life and following her death. The recognition of her amazing contributions include the "Woman of the Century" medal from the National Council of Jewish Women of Canada (1967), a medal from the Society of Canadian Criminologists, the Order of Canada and Companion of the Order, the Governor General's Award in Commemoration of the Persons Case (1979), honorary doctoral degrees from twelve universities, the creation of the Thérèse F. Casgrain Fellowship for Research on Women and Social Change, a commemorative stamp from Canada Post (1985), and the Thérèse Casgrain Volunteer Award (2001).

Quote:

"The true liberation of women cannot take place without the liberation of men. Basically the women's liberation movement is not only feminist in inspiration, it is also humanist. Let men and women look at one another honestly and try together to give society a new set of values."[72]

Thérèse Casgrain, ca. 1915–1920, Montreal.

Dupras & Colan/National Archives of Canada/PA-127291

The Angel of Cassiar

Nellie Cashman
ca. 1844–1925

Gold!
She gave it away as fast as she found it.

Nellie Cashman, 1874.

"We tossed up a coin, heads for South Africa, tails for British Columbia. It fell tails up so we went North."[73] The thirty-year-old veteran stampeder Nellie Cashman, along with six other adventurers, headed for the newly discovered mines in the Cassiar District in 1874. The party sailed from San Francisco to Victoria, where they purchased provisions before taking a steamer to Wrangell, Alaska. After a boat trip up the Stikine River they arrived at Telegraph Creek. Nellie opened a combined boarding house and saloon on Dease Creek, grubstaked men with promising claims, and did her own mining and prospecting for gold nuggets and dust.

After making what one journalist referred to as a "comfortable pile," Nellie returned to Victoria in early November. But she soon received news that a severe winter storm had trapped hundreds of men at Cassiar without supplies. Scurvy had already hit the miners. Nellie immediately set out to prevent a disaster at the diggings, hiring six men to accompany her on a dangerous midwinter journey through some of the most rugged country on the continent. Friends considered her insane to risk the rescue trip, but challenge never stopped Miss Nellie Cashman.

Before taking a steamer out of Victoria she bought 1,500 pounds of supplies, including medicine, lime juice, and other foods thought to counter scurvy. Once on the trails of the Stikine the rescuers continued on snowshoes, each of the seven in the party pulling a heavily loaded sled through the deep snow. Often they could make just eight kilometres per day. One cold night Nellie was buried alive by an avalanche as she slept, but was already digging herself out by the time her companions rushed to her aid. By early March Nellie led her rescue team safely into Dease Lake, where she nursed the ailing miners before returning to her mining. They called her "The Angel of Cassiar."

Nellie Cashman was already a seasoned miner and shrewd business-woman by the time she trekked into the Cassiar District. A native of Ireland, she immigrated to the United States as a small girl with her sister and widowed mother. The trio settled in Boston before moving west, where Nellie was lured in the early 1870s to a mining boom in Nevada. For the rest of her life the enterprising women would race to each new strike, making mining claims and setting up restaurants, stores, hotels, and rooming houses. Then she moved on to a new frontier in her search for the big bonanza. Along the way she seemed to become modestly wealthy but spent much of her money helping other miners and supporting churches, hospitals, and other charitable causes.

When gold production began to drop in the Cassiar Nellie packed up and returned to Victoria in June 1876. Her success had enabled her to send her mother $500 in gold, and she was also able to give the Sisters of St. Ann in Victoria a welcome donation of $543 for their new St. Joseph's Hospital — thanks to the contributions she'd solicited from the Cassiar miners. Nellie decided to head back south for a new mining camp. By the late 1890s she had spent a quarter of a century in a dozen different places on the frontier, from Arizona to Montana, Idaho, Mexico, and Wyoming. Nellie also cared for five nieces and nephews orphaned after her sister died in 1884, though at one point nephew Mike Cunningham noted he left her because he couldn't keep up: "We were always on the move, looking for gold and silver."[74]

With news of the discovery of gold in the Klondike, Nellie was quickly packing for an expedition north. She slogged over the Chilkoot Pass with thousands of stampeders, arriving in Dawson in April 1898. During the next six years she operated many mining claims and ran a series of restaurants, though she seems to have spent most of her efforts on placer mining. She faced a number of legal problems with her claims, but apparently still managed to take out over $100,000 on her No. 19 claim below Bonanza. In 1904 Nellie, now about sixty years old, was also working some claims in the Alsek and Kluane areas of the Yukon, where at one point she walked about thirty-four kilometres when the temperature hovered at -61° F.

Within a few months of her arrival in the Yukon Nellie Cashman was already raising money for a three-storey addition to the local hospital and raising funds for the church. A newspaper article reported that "Miss Cashman is the pioneer woman in this country and is widely known for her good deeds." She was so generous with miners who couldn't pay their bills that they referred to her Dawson grocery store as "The Prospectors' Haven of Retreat."[75]

Nellie was a remarkable mining prospector. An attractive and intelligent woman who was as comfortable in civilized society as she was in the roughest mining camp, she was a daring adventurer and an aggressive leader. A devout Roman Catholic known for her Irish wit, Nellie Cashman enjoyed the company of religious people such as the sisters who operated the hospital in Dawson. They knew her well, and "with their knowledge of her true worth, her charity, her purity of life, her faith, her deep Catholicism, they ranked her among living saints."[76]

After gold production peaked in Dawson, Nellie headed north of the Arctic Circle in search of gold mines in the Koyukuk River basin of Alaska. She spent another twenty years there, still travelling by dogsled on five- hundred-kilometre trips when she was in her seventies. The legendary lady became ill on a trip to the outside in 1925. Though being well taken care of in a hospital in Seattle, Nellie wanted to go back to St. Joseph's Hospital in Victoria, British Columbia: to the hospital she helped build, and to her longtime friends the Sisters of St. Ann. "I am going home to die," she said.[77]

Quote:

"Every man I met up north was my protector, and any man I ever met, if he needed my help, got it, whether it was a hot meal, nursing, mothering or whatever else he needed. After all, we pass this way only once, and it's up to us to help our fellows when they need our help."[78]

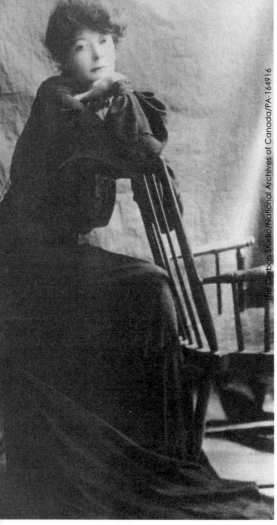

The Carbon Studio/National Archives of Canada/PA-164916

Woman's Kingdom
Kathleen Willis Watkins Coleman
1856–1915

Kit Coleman, ca. 1890s, Toronto.

She was a witty journalist with a string of firsts: first women's page editor of a Canadian newspaper, first accredited female war correspondent in North America, first president of the Canadian Women's Press Club, and Canada's first syndicated columnist.

Everyone called her "Kit." Her successful newspaper column "Woman's Kingdom" ran for twenty-one years, making her the most popular women's page writer of her generation.[79]

Kathleen Ferguson was a fiery redhead, born in 1856 to a family of modest means in Galway, Ireland. She was educated at a Roman Catholic boarding school, then married off to a prosperous Irish merchant named Mr. Willis, who was about forty years older. He apparently sent her to schools in Dublin and Belgium, and she had at least one child from their marriage. No offspring survived. When Willis died the family fortune went to his sister, so the destitute Kit sold the furniture in their house and immigrated to North America in 1884.

She arrived in Toronto, poor but bright and well-educated. The attractive widow began working as a secretary and soon married her employer, Edward Watkins. After moving to Winnipeg the couple had two children, a son, Thady, and a daughter, Patsy. Kit taught French and music, while her husband worked as a commercial traveller. Fed up with his womanizing and heavy drinking, Kit separated from Watkins after they moved back to Toronto.

Kit was determined to be a journalist, and the publisher of the magazine *Saturday Night* bought several of her articles. In 1889 the *Toronto Mail* hired her as a full-time women's page editor — a first in Canada. She began the weekly column that she wrote for more than two decades; when the paper merged with another in 1895 it became the *Mail and Empire*. Her column included advice to the lovelorn (another Canadian first), a bit about fashion, and a lot about life as Kit saw it — current events, interesting people, social mores, entertainment, the arts, politics, finances, whatever. She wrote with humour, wit, and punch, never shying away from controversy. Her editors didn't seem to mind, as her brash and provocative statements attracted attention and sold more copies.

Kit avoided writing about topics that would interest only the female sex. Men and women alike read "Woman's Kingdom" (even Prime Minister Wilfrid Laurier). When Kit was in London in 1897 to cover Queen Victoria's Diamond Jubilee celebration, she was the Prime Minister's guest at a Buckingham Palace medal-giving ceremony. He and his wife arrived in a fine carriage to pick her up at the seedy lodgings she was staying at, since Kit's employer could usually be convinced to let her travel off for a good story — but not to pay a lot for expenses.

Beginning in 1892, Kit had begun to do travel articles for her newspaper. By all accounts Kit was an adventurer, a hustler willing and eager to roam the globe to interview fascinating personalities and write about notable events. She became the first accredited war correspondent in North America through coverage of the 1898 Spanish American War, though she managed to get to Cuba only after the battles. Kit reported on the Chicago World Columbian Exposition and a sensational murder trial. She interviewed William Randolph Hearst, Sarah Bernhardt, and Lillie Langtry. She talked her way into a Cleveland jail to interview the famous swindler Cassie Chadwick and scooped the North American press corps. Kit loved to explore behind the scenes, disguising herself to experience other worlds — such as the time she went on a nighttime exploration of the opium dens of Chinatown in San Francisco, where she dressed as a man and dragged along a detective. Or when she used the same approach to wander through the underworld of London. Kit's colourful accounts of such stunt journalism gained wide audiences and approval. A London *Times* journalist wrote that "The *Daily Mail* is fortunate to have on its staff one of the smartest women writers in America."[80]

In 1898 Kit married for a third time, to Dr. Theobald Coleman. The kindly doctor was apparently somewhat easier to get along with than her previous spouses but never contributed greatly to the household income; he didn't like charging poor patients for his services.

In 1904 Kit Coleman helped form the Canadian Women's Press Club — intended to assist members in both their professional and personal lives. Kit and fifteen other women formed the group while en route to the World Exposition in St. Louis, Missouri — a free junket sponsored by the Canadian Pacific Railway. Kit became the first president of the new association and attended (with daughter Patsy) its first national conference in Winnipeg in 1906.

Kit left the *Toronto Mail and Empire* in 1911 due to disputes with the management. But her writing continued, and once established as a syndicated columnist (another Canadian first) she quite enjoyed the challenge of her new freelance career. She sold "Kit's Column" to dozens of daily and weekly newspapers across Canada.

In May 1915 Kit Coleman died of pneumonia. She was a respected journalist who paved the way for other women reporters in Canada. Colleagues either liked her or adored her. Her friend Jean Blewett, a columnist for the Toronto *Globe*, dubbed her "the Queen of Hearts." She wrote that Kit "not only writes of the affairs of the heart when she renders romantic advice, but she touches our hearts with everything she does. Whether in laughter, or sadness, or anger. She is the Queen of Hearts, the supreme monarch of all of our emotions."[81]

Quote:

"Old maids are the wise virgins of this earth. The married women took the terrible men they refused."[82]

Tale of a Broken Heart

Laure Conan
(pen name for
Marie-Louise-Félicité
Angers)
1845–1924

She dared to write a novel
when she had no female
role models to follow,
becoming the first French
Canadian woman novelist.

Laure Conan.

Félicité Angers lost the love of her life and withdrew into a world of her own: a world of introspection, rose gardening, and reading. She also decided to write a novel — the first woman in Quebec to do so. With its publication she created a new identity for herself, the author Laure Conan. The origins of her pen name are unknown.

Félicité Angers was born in La Malbaie, Quebec, in 1845. She was the daughter of blacksmith Élie Angers and his storekeeper wife Marie Perron. A well-established family in the Charlevoix area, the Angers family had settled in Quebec about 1667.

After attending school in La Malbaie, Félicité studied at the Ursuline convent school in Quebec City from 1858 to 1862. She was an excellent student, and on returning home she read voraciously, including writings by Bossuet, Chateaubriand, Veuillot, Silvio Pellico, the Jesuit priests, and Marie de l'Incarnation. She also read books about the history of New France and Canada.

Seventeen-year-old Félicité fell in love with Pierre-Alexis Tremblay. He was a land surveyor/geometrician about eighteen years older than she was. The two became fiancés, until he ended the engagement for unknown reasons around 1868.

The heartbroken Félicité became a recluse. Feeling the need to express herself, she decided to become a writer — a courageous act since she had no female models. Félicité wrote a lengthy story, *Un amour vrai* (A True Love), which was published by *La Revue de Montréal* in 1878. At the age of thirty-three the young woman become Laure Conan: author.

Her first real novel, *Angéline de Montbrun*, was published in serialized form in 1881-82. The book is the first psychological novel in the history of Quebecois literature. In 1891 Laure Conan's first historical novel was published: *A l'oeuvre et B l'épreuve*, which was awarded a literary prize by the French Academy in 1900.

During her lifetime Laure Conan wrote about love and the family, religion and history. In addition to writing novels she also worked as a journalist of sorts. She frequently contributed to *Le Journal de Françoise* (the first feminist publication in French Canada). From 1893-98 she lived in a monastery at Saint-Hyacinthe and prepared its religious journal. One of the sisters was a close friend of Laure, and according to author Roger Le Moine, Laure confided that three of her novels (*Un amour vrai, Angéline de Montbrun*, and *A l'oeuvre et B l'épreuve*) were varied expressions of her passion for the love of her life, Pierre-Alexis.

Returning home to care for a sick sister, Laure Conan continued writing historical novels and even tried creating a theatrical adaptation of her most popular novel, *L'Oublié*. In her late seventies Laure Conan moved to a rest house maintained by the sisters of Jésus-Marie in Sillery, now part of Quebec City. She completed her last historical novel before dying at the age of seventy-nine. Laure Conan was buried in the cemetery at La Malbaie, in the plot next to that of her beloved Pierre-Alexis Tremblay.

Throughout her life Laure Conan was daring behind the pen yet timid in the real world — reluctant to have any personal information about herself in the prefaces to her novels. As she explained to confidant Father Casgrain: "My personality is of such insignificance that it would be of no interest to the public. And if life has made me sad and bitter, I don't want to complain about it, nor have others do so."[83]

Laure Conan was a prolific author who wrote some interesting psychological novels. An important figure in the literary history of Canada, Laure Conan is not widely known today. In 1983 Canada Post recognized this notable woman in Canadian literature by issuing a commemorative stamp that illustrates her novel *Angéline de Montbrun*.

Quote:

"Nothing in love is small. Those who await grand occasions to express their tenderness do not know how to love."[84]

Taking H.G. Wells to Court
Florence Amelia Deeks
1864–1959

She was a brave woman with a brave idea: to write a history of the world that showed the influence of women.

Florence Deeks (right) and her sister, Annie, ca. 1880.

Florence Deeks dared to accuse one of the most famous authors in the world of plagiarizing her work — and was probably right. She was an aspiring Canadian author who launched a sensational international lawsuit against British novelist H.G. Wells, accusing him of stealing ideas from her manuscript for the first feminist history of the world. While Wells grew wealthy from sales of his book *The Outline of History*, Florence Deeks used every penny she could find to continue her legal action in Canada and finally in England. Florence lost every case and every appeal, though extensive research by Canadian historian A.B. McKillop strongly suggests that justice was not served.[85]

Florence Deeks grew up in a religious family in Morrisburg, Ontario, where she was strongly influenced by her mother, Melinda, and her belief in the importance of education. At age thirty she enrolled at Victoria College in Toronto, and after several years of study started teaching at Presbyterian Ladies' College. Active in a number of women's groups, Florence was the first historian for the Women's Art Association of Canada and recording secretary for the Toronto women's Liberal Club. She also wrote about a variety of topics that interested her, and decided to develop a history of the world that included the contributions of women.

For about four years Florence worked on her project, enthusiastically researching at the public library and then pounding away at her Remington typewriter. She strived to describe "the work and influence of woman in weaving up the story of the human race — the web of human history."[86] It was to be a history book that showed the prominent roles of women such as Lucrezia de Medici who helped rule France, Anne of Constantinople, Marguerite Luther (mother of Martin), Elizabeth I, Marguerite de Roberval of New France, and Queen Victoria. Caught up in Florence's passion for her project, her entire family (mother, sisters Mabel and Annie, even her brother George) shared in the excitement. In February of 1918 Florence Deeks completed her book manuscript, which she called *The Web of the World's Romance*.

While searching for a publisher Florence discovered astonishing similarities to her manuscript in a new book about world history published by the famous author H.G. Wells. Could someone from Macmillan Company in Canada, a publisher who had rejected her submission after keeping it for a curiously long period of time, possibly have shared Florence's manuscript with this British author? After years of analysis and consultation with experts, Florence concluded she had a strong case and sued H.G. Wells for $500,000.

With amazing determination, Florence Deeks spent years fighting for justice. She even appealed to the Privy Council in England, resorting to presenting her own case when funds ran out and she could no longer afford lawyers. Then in her late sixties, the feisty Florence did an admirable job of arguing her case, but lost again. Before sailing home to Canada she sent a personal letter of appeal to King George V and letters of complaint to members of the Judicial Committee of the Privy Council. But the case was dead, as was the spirit of Florence Deeks.

Quote:

"I shall undertake to show that the total of evidence, and the whole history of the case, is such as to vindicate fully my charge that the Macmillan company put to an illegal use the [manuscript] which I entrusted to their possession, that during the time the [manuscript] was in the possession of the MacMillan Company Mr. Wells wrote 'The Outline of History' and that in this task he made use of my [manuscript]. I shall undertake to show that all this was done, not only in violation of my proprietary rights and copyright but also at the cost to me of severe sacrifice and injury."[87]

Florence Deeks addressing four male judges in the
Ontario Court of Appeal on May 13, 1931.

An Imaginary World

Mazo de la Roche
1879–1961

Recognition from the United States launched the stunning literary career of this Ontario author, who soared to international success with the famous novels about the Whiteoaks of Jalna.

Mazo de la Roche.

The prolific author Mazo de la Roche was once one of the most widely read Canadian novelists, yet her talent as a writer seems never to have been fully appreciated in her home country. She lived most of her life as a recluse, in the company of her favourite cousin, and remains a mysterious figure in Canada's literary history — primarily due to her own efforts to remain out of the public eye and present inaccurate personal information.[88]

Mazo de la Roche was born on January 15, 1879, in Newmarket, Ontario. Despite the French-sounding name, her father, William Roche, was actually of Irish origin; she apparently modified the name to add some grandeur. Mazo's mother was Alberta Lundy, who was from a large family that seems to have provided some inspiration for her novels about the Whiteoaks.

Despite growing up with loving parents, Mazo's childhood was unsettled due to frequent moves required by her father's many jobs. An only child, she soon became inseparable from her cousin Caroline Clement. They loved creating characters and putting on plays, living in a fantasy world of theatre and books. Mazo wrote her first story at age nine and was frequently writing and drawing.

On graduation from high school Mazo attended the Ontario College of Art, and her first published story appeared in 1902 when she was twenty-three. The subsequent years were often difficult for her, with financial problems, dependence on relatives, the 1915 death of her father, and a nervous breakdown. Then Mazo's stories started to be accepted by the *Atlantic Monthly*.

Fame and fortune suddenly arrived in 1927, when *Atlantic Monthly* selected her manuscript for *Jalna* as best novel and awarded the newly acclaimed author a $10,000 prize. At the age of forty-eight, Mazo de la Roche gained international recognition. She wrote a total of seventeen volumes in her *Jalna* series, chronicling the fictional Whiteoaks family of Ontario for a century. More than 9 million copies of the books have been sold throughout the world, with 193 English and 92 foreign-language editions published. A popular play based on the series played in London, New York, and Toronto, and the CBC filmed a thirteen-hour-long television series entitled *The Whiteoaks of Jalna*. The latter was broadcast in various foreign markets through sales to Thames Television in the U.K. and other stations.

Mazo de la Roche's writings include twenty-three novels, more than fifty short stories, and thirteen plays. Some critics disparaged the *Jalna* books as sentimental romances, without recognizing the excellent writing in many of her works, particularly the early *Jalna* books.

Among her works were an autobiography, which seems to conceal more than reveal the true identity of Mazo de la Roche.[89] Until her death at age eighty-two, Mazo lived with her cousin Caroline Clement. The two lived primarily in Ontario, though they did spend some years in England. In 1931, when Mazo was fifty-two, she adopted two young children. Yet she would never explain the circumstances of the adoption — not even to the boy and girl, who were raised primarily by servants and in private schools.

As Joan Givner wrote in her excellent biography, "Mazo did something extraordinary for a woman of her generation: she seized power in what had hitherto been a masculine bailiwick. Not only did she amass a fortune, but she did it through her mastery of the language..."[90] Among Mazo's relatively few admirers in the literary world was author Robertson Davies, who dubbed her "a born story-teller." He wrote, "The creation of the *Jalna* books is the most protracted single feat of literary invention in the brief history of Canada's literature."[91]

The Historic Sites and Monuments Board of Canada recognized Mazo de la Roche as a national historic person in 1976. The Ontario Heritage Foundation has restored a Georgian-style brick home in Mississauga, Ontario, that apparently was a source of inspiration for the *Jalna* series. Sovereign House, a home where the Roche family lived from 1911 to 1915 in Bronte, Ontario, has been preserved as a heritage building and is open to the public on a limited basis; Mazo incorporated the house in the *Jalna* series and her first book, *Possession*. In West Wales, one can even stay in the Jalna Hotel — named for the famous series penned by Mazo de la Roche. Many of her books are still in print.

Quote:

"Telegrams, flowers, letters of congratulation deluged us. The warmth, the feeling of goodwill toward me was, as I remember, universal. Even critics who had not been very kind to my books joined in the praise. The general feeling seemed to be that of rejoicing that a Canadian (not this Canadian in particular) had achieved distinction in the United States, a country which heretofore could scarcely have shown less interest in Canadian letters."[92]

Mazo de la Roche referring to *Jalna* being selected
as best novel by *Atlantic Monthy*.

The Professor
Carrie Derick
1862–1941

Miss Carrie M. Derick, Montreal, Quebec, 1890.

She was appointed the first woman university professor in Canada. Too bad it was a token gesture.

Carrie Matilda Derick had the curious honour of being one of the few women to be listed in *American Men of Science* (1910) — acknowledgment of her status as a distinguished scientist. She earned international recognition for her research on heredity and became a pioneer in the study of genetics, but her impressive academic credentials weren't enough to land the job that many felt she deserved: Chair of Botany at McGill University.

Born in the Eastern Townships of Quebec, Carrie started teaching school at the Clarenceville Academy at age fifteen and became the principal after completing teacher training in Montreal. A few years after McGill University began accepting female students, Carrie Derick earned a Bachelor of Arts there — graduating with the highest average in the school. She also won the Logan Gold Medal in natural science and prizes in classics and zoology. In 1892 Carrie became the first female instructor at McGill, where she taught part-time in the botany department.

The respected scholar earned her M.A. and, after considerable struggle, gained an appointment as lecturer in the botany department. She then studied at Harvard, Wood's Hole Biological Station in Massachusetts, the Royal College of Science in London, and the universities of Munich, Berlin, and Bonn. At Bonn she met the research requirements for a Ph.D., but at the time the institution would not grant this award to a woman. Carrie Derick broke new ground by publishing many scientific papers and joining professional associations not previously open to female academics.

Carrie Derick also became a notable reformer, a feminist who contributed to a multitude of social causes in hopes of improving women's lives. She was involved in organizations such as the Montreal Local Council of Women, the National Council of Education, and the Federation of University Women in Canada.[93] She participated in the suffragist movement, played an important role in a project that provided meals for working-class women, supported individuals seeking to practise in their chosen field, presented a brief on women wage-earners, and lectured Quebec's Prime Minister Sir Jean-Lomer Gouin on the merits of birth control. After which the shocked man exclaimed, "How she made me blush, that old maid from McGill!"[94]

Carrie served as the acting chairperson of the botany department at McGill for three years, but when the Board of Governors filled the position on a permanent basis they picked a younger American man. To soften the blow, McGill decided to appoint Miss Carrie Derrick as a Professor of Morphological Botany in 1912. While the nomination appeared to be an important step for the aspiring academic as well as for Canadian women, it brought no increase in salary and no seat on the faculty. Furthermore, morphological botany wasn't Carrie's area of expertise. The principal at McGill advised her she'd been given a "courtesy title" and was not actually a professor. When the new Chair of Botany arrived he began assigning Carrie work suitable for a demonstrator. "Miss Derick was not amused."[95]

Despite her frustrations and disappointments, Carrie Derick persevered at McGill, and a new demonstrator was hired so she could return to teaching and research. Professor Derick retired in 1929 after a career of significant accomplishments. McGill designated her as its first woman emeritus professor. When Carrie Derick died in 1941 she had fulfilled her personal vision of a trailblazer: "Without aggression, without any noisy obtrusiveness, a few Canadian women by deep thought, by clear vision, or by honest service have prepared the way for those who will follow, and have proved the right of all to work as they are able."[96]

Quote:

"...the country is too young and too thinly populated to afford an adequate field for the exercise of unusual gifts. In consequence, Canada's most celebrated singer is seldom heard at home; the best Canadian pictures are hung in foreign salons; the best books are published first in London and New York."[97]

Marie Dressler.

An Unlikely Hollywood Star

Marie Dressler
1868–1934

In a world that idolizes youth and beauty, she proved that a homely, overweight woman in her sixties could be the queen of cinema — more popular than the glamorous Greta Garbo.

A green-eyed redhead who stood five feet seven inches tall, Marie Dressler often weighed two hundred pounds and some said she had the face of a bulldog. But she also had incredible talent and determination that brought her dazzling success.

In 1933 the aging star, dying of cancer, was at the height of her success. Eight hundred guests attended a lavish gala in Los Angeles to celebrate Marie Dressler's birthday. She'd won the 1930–31 Academy Award for Best Actress, been the first female actor to grace the cover of *Time*, won a gold medal from Britain after fans voted her their favourite movie performer of the year, and her recent movies were all smash hits. Marie Dressler also earned the distinction of being the top box-office attraction in a 1932 poll and would win again in 1933. The unlikely star was a bigger draw than Hollywood beauties Joan Crawford, Jean Harlow, Mary Pickford, and Greta Garbo.[98]

The party's host, Louis B. Mayer of MGM, joked that the tributes to Mary Dressler could even be heard by radio in her birthplace of Cobourg, Ontario. The star began her life there as Leila Maria Koerber, the daughter of devoted mother Anna Henderson and Austrian-born music teacher Alexander Koerber. The family was supported by Koerber's work teaching music and playing the organ, but his quick temper resulted in frequent moves throughout Ontario after he lost each successive job. Despising her father and anxious to earn money to help support her mother, Leila left home at age fourteen with her older sister.

In the early 1880s the gutsy young sisters started performing with a theatre group called the Nevada Stock Company. To avoid embarrassing her family Leila adopted the stage name of Marie Dressler. A natural singer, she spent three years with the George Baker Opera Company before debuting on Broadway in 1892 and becoming a celebrity. Marie Dressler became a well-known vaudeville comedian. As the performer remembered from her childhood, "I soon learned to be just as happy when folks said, 'Isn't she funny!' as if they had ah-ed and oh-ed and exclaimed, 'Isn't she beautiful!'"[99]

In 1914 Marie Dressler starred with Charlie Chaplin and Mabel Normand in *Tillie's Punctured Romance,* a silent picture many consider to be the first feature-length movie. It was a hit, but Marie's career in the movies was derailed by World War I (during which she sold an incredible amount of Liberty Loan bonds and entertained troops) and a 1919 strike by actors on Broadway. Remembering her days as an $8-a-week chorus girl, Marie jumped into the battle as a union negotiator — elected as first president of the Chorus Equity Association of America. Marie emerged as a heroine in the successful fight that won better wages and working conditions for the girls. Some historians suggest Marie was subsequently blacklisted by producers because of her involvement in the strike.

The following years were a nightmare for Marie Dressler: her career fizzled and her husband became ill and died. She had married James Dalton in Monte Carlo in 1908, but discovered only years later that her dear spouse had staged a fake ceremony. It turned out that he had never divorced his first wife so couldn't legally wed Marie. The actress and Dalton continued to live as a married couple despite his weakness for chorus girls and strong drink, and he worked as Marie's manager. But when James died in 1921 Mrs. Lizzie Dalton claimed the body and buried him.

A 1927 offer from director Allan Dwan to play in his next film rescued the depressed actress from obscurity and launched an incredible comeback. Screenwriter Frances Marion then convinced MGM to hire Marie for the movie *The Callahans and the Murphys.* Marie moved to Hollywood and became a major star in "the talkies," which allowed millions of moviegoers around the world to both see and hear this incredibly talented performer. Now billed by MGM as "the world's greatest actress," Marie Dressler became an internationally acclaimed performer: a beloved star adored by audiences who could relate to her tough but enduring characters such as Tugboat Annie. Marie Dressler made three films in the year before she died.

In Marie's birthplace of Cobourg, Ontario, flags flew at half-mast following her death in 1934. As a tribute to the talented entertainer, the Ontario Heritage Foundation later erected a commemorative plaque there. Cobourg is also the location of the Marie Dressler Foundation, which has collected many of the star's early movies and presents them in a summer film festival.

Quote:

"Never shall I forget those naked, clean-swept little Canadian towns one just like the other. Before I was twelve years old, I must have lived in fifty of them."[100]

Marie Dressler (centre) with Charlie Chaplin and Mabel Normand in a scene from *Tillie's Punctured Romance*, 1914.

Novels of Newfound-land

Margaret Duley
1894–1968

She was a Newfie who described her home as a country she both loved and hated.[101]

Margaret Duley.

When the outside world had little knowledge of the craggy coast of Newfoundland and its desolate outport communities, Margaret Duley evoked powerful images of a harsh yet splendid island in the Atlantic. As the *Globe and Mail* noted when her novel *Highway to Valour* was released in 1941, "the Newfoundlanders are folk of whom, we realize, we have not heard nearly enough."[102]

Margaret Duley, born and raised in St. John's, became the first Newfoundland author to gain international acclaim. Her mother, Tyrphena Soper Chancey, was from Carbonear, Newfoundland, and was the daughter of a fisherman and his wife. Raised in St. John's by more prosperous relatives, Tyrphena gained a reputation as a domineering snob. She married Thomas Duley, a gentle fellow who had emigrated from Birmingham, England, and owned the finest jewellery store in St. John's. Margaret was brought up in a strict Congregationalist family.[103]

Margaret was an imaginative child who loved books and performing. She graduated with the equivalent of grade eleven from the Methodist College, then studied at the Royal Academy of Drama and Elocution in London, England, in 1913. Fear of war apparently sent her back home.

Duley became involved in the suffragist movement in the early 1920s; women gained the right to vote in parliamentary elections in 1925. Margaret joined several clubs and became a member of the Women's Franchise League. She also participated in many social activities in St.

John's, and regularly attended garden parties, dances, and dinners at Government House. Margaret never married, despite many romantic relationships throughout her life and a yearning to be a wife and mother. She was secretive about her personal life, even with close friends, but biographer Alison Feder suggests that Margaret probably never found the strong mate that would have suited her independent nature. So Margaret wrote books — which she referred to as her brain-children.

As a young woman from an affluent family, Margaret was able to read extensively and travel in the United States, England, and Europe — and explore Newfoundland and Labrador. Inspired by the land and people around her, Margaret penned a novel about a young girl yearning to escape her life by the sea; *The Eyes of the Gull* was published in England in 1936. Margaret also wrote four other novels and some short stories, magazine articles, and radio presentations. Her books were popular — receiving good reviews abroad and to some degree in Canada, but little praise from home.

Margaret Duley's novels were peopled with independent women and addressed issues such as abortion, divorce, and female sexuality that were not discussed openly at the time.[104] In addition to her involvement in the suffrage movement, in 1928 she also participated in a public debate as an advocate of equal pay for women. Her niece Margot Duley remembers her as "a free thinking, free spirited, outspoken and charismatic personality in a society where this was not encouraged."[105] She was an intelligent and imaginative woman.

Margaret Duley wrote a fifth novel, *Octaves of Dawn*. When her publisher rejected the work, the discouraged author destroyed the manuscript. Greater problems overtook her life — death and illness in the family, financial failures, and another war. Her short career as a novelist ended, though she published a few short stories.

After World War II Margaret released a small non-fiction book, *The Caribou Hut*, about a hostel for servicemen where she did volunteer work for the Red Cross. She worked in freelancing and broadcasting, and then became Director of Publicity for the Red Cross. While on a trip to England for the 1953 coronation of Queen Elizabeth she made some programs for the British Broadcasting Corporation. Diagnosed with Parkinson's disease in 1955, Margaret suffered for many years before her death in 1968.

A 1976 report from the Department of English, Memorial University of Newfoundland, noted that Duley was "forgotten by her own compatriots and virtually unknown now on the mainland," but "deserves to be nationally recognized as a Canadian author of high quality."[106] Because of Margaret Duley's significant contribution to Canadian literature she was recognized as a national historic person by the Historic Sites and Monuments Board of Canada. As the author herself once wrote, "I have left them a heritage. In their library will be a little corner of Margaret Duley's works."[107]

Quote:

"Whatever Newfoundland has been she was never trivial."[108]

Painting for a Purpose
Henrietta Muir Edwards
1849–1931

Henrietta Muir Edwards.

She was a remarkable redhead reputed to know more about women and the law than the Chief Justice of Canada. Not bad for someone who wasn't a lawyer.

Henrietta Muir Edwards used income from the sale of her paintings to help others with the many projects in which she was involved — including work with women prisoners, the homeless, mothers, and children. In Montreal she and her sister founded the Working Girls' Association, a forerunner to the YWCA. The pair edited a periodical called *The Working Woman of Canada*, which was the first magazine for working women in this country. The energetic reformer and feminist activist was also one of the Famous Five women who made legal history in Canada through the Persons Case.

Born in Montreal, Henrietta grew up in a wealthy religious family. She married Dr. Oliver Cromwell Edwards in 1876 — with the future Sir William Osler as best man — and had three children. An artist who studied in New York and Europe, she exhibited paintings at the Royal Canadian Academy. Henrietta was particularly skilled in painting china and miniatures, and a set of china she painted at the request of the Dominion Government was exhibited at the 1893 World's Fair in Chicago. Among her notable miniatures were representations of Lord Strathcona and Sir Wilfrid Laurier.[109]

With the assistance of her father, Harriet first became involved in social work by converting a Montreal home into a boarding house for working girls. While living in Ottawa she helped Lady Aberdeen create the

Victorian Order of Nurses (1897) and the National Council of Women (1893). For the latter organization Henrietta served thirty-eight years as convener of the committee on laws affecting women and children. She also served as President of the Ottawa YWCA, worked with the Women's Christian Temperance Union, and supported the Baptist Women's Missionary Society.

In 1903 Dr. Edwards accepted a post as medical health officer for the Blood and Peigan Indians in Alberta, where the family lived on a reserve near Fort Macleod. Henrietta wrote many law articles and headed numerous delegations to both the Alberta and Dominion Governments in support of laws protecting women and children. She developed an important handbook on the legal status of women in Alberta and another related to the Dominion.[110]

Despite her lack of formal legal training, Henrietta Edwards earned national recognition as an expert in laws that affected women. She made a significant contribution in influencing changes to provincial and federal legislation. The seasoned activist was seventy-eight when Emily Murphy invited her to join a group of five women in a legal petition to challenge the interpretation of the term "persons" in the British North America Act. Henrietta did most of the legal research for the presentations to the Supreme Court of Canada and then the Privy Council in Great Britain. On October 18, 1929, Canadian women were declared to be persons with the right to be appointed to the Senate.

The Historic Sites and Monuments recognized Henrietta Muir Edwards as a national historic person in 1962, and Canada Post issued a commemorative stamp in her honour in 1981. The City of Edmonton named a park after this passionate defender of women's rights, and she is included in a number of group tributes to the Famous Five.

Quote:

"The woman is queen in her home and reigns there, but unfortunately the laws she makes reach no further than her domain. If her laws, written or unwritten, are to be enforced outside, she must come into the political world as well — and she has come."[111]

Rose Fortune.

Policing the Port
Rose Fortune
ca. 1774–1864

A former slave, she became the first female police officer in North America.

Rose Fortune is believed to have been born in Virginia during the American Revolutionary War period. She was a slave owned by the Devone family, who emigrated to Nova Scotia after the war along with other Loyalists — including about three thousand Black refugees. Rose was about ten years old when she arrived in Annapolis Royal with her parents in 1783.[112] Here they were free.

Despite British promises of land and protection in the North, the Black Loyalists struggled to survive in their new surroundings. As a young woman Rose Fortune showed considerable initiative and determination in setting up a successful cartage business in order to earn a living. Soon renowned for her strength, the legendary entrepreneur transported people and goods in her trusty wheelbarrow or wagon. Whenever a ship from Saint John or Boston arrived in the busy port town, Rose was on the wharf to carry trunks, boxes, and carpet bags to hotels and homes. She also offered a wake-up service to customers like the visiting Judge Haliburton, who liked to sleep in but counted on Rose to make sure he didn't miss the boat to his next town.

An authoritative individual, Rose Fortune appointed herself to keep order in Annapolis Royal and became the town's sole police officer. Her word was law, and she ensured smooth operations on the docks. The colourful character imposed curfews and kept the youth of the seaport town in line. She even resorted to spanking disobedient youngsters. Rose is often described as the first female law officer on the continent. She also played a significant role in the Underground Railroad by transporting escaped slaves to safe locations.

A single mother with two daughters, Rose Fortune lived an unusual life for a woman of her time — particularly a Black woman who might have faced considerable prejudice. Yet she managed to support her family with a career that was certainly not traditional for a woman and became an influential person in her community. Rose Fortune was a trailblazer: an inspiring one. One of her descendants, Dr. Daurene E. Lewis, was elected mayor of Annapolis Royal in 1984. Dr. Lewis became the first Black female mayor in North America.

The remarkable life of Rose Fortune has been depicted in a film called *Rhythm Stick to Freedom*, helping to ensure that she is not forgotten as a Canadian heroine.[113] The Association of Black Law Enforcers created the Peter Butler III-Rose Fortune Scholarship Program in recognition of Canada's first Canadian Black law enforcers.

Quote:

"You come right along, jedge. No time to be sleeping now. Yo'all got to hold co'at in Digby, and yo'know right well you got to ketch that boat."[114]

Rose Fortune urging Judge Haliburton to hurry up
so he wouldn't miss his boat.

A Union Militant
Laure Gaudreault
1889–1975

Laure Gaudreault at the celebration of her sixty-year career, 1966.

More than a great teacher, she was an inspirational leader who brought reluctant school mistresses together in a powerful union.

Laure Gaudreault refused to suffer in silence. As a young school mistress in rural Quebec in 1906 she earned $125 per year, about a tenth of the wages of a city teacher.[115] Of course she paid for the school workbooks, chalk and brushes, wood supply, and cleaning materials — which she used herself to do the janitorial chores. Deductions were also made for every day that the she was ill. Laure was a dedicated teacher but would not accept the deplorable working conditions in country schools.

Born in La Malbaie, Quebec, she grew up in a family that placed high value on education. Since there was no schoolhouse in the area, Madame Gaudreault taught her ten children at home. Five of the six girls became school mistresses, following the example of their mother and many aunts. Laure first attended school at the age of thirteen, when she began studying with the Grey Nuns. Thanks to a scholarship the keen student was able to attend the Normal School of Laval in Quebec City. She then began teaching a class of forty-eight girls in a rural school.

During a stint as a journalist Laure Gaudreault used her writing talents to create awareness of problems faced by school mistresses in the country. On returning to the classroom in 1931 Laure realized that there had been no improvements for her colleagues, so she decided to create an association of female elementary school teachers in rural Quebec. It's hard to imagine today how frightening such a plan would be to some of the school mistresses — many of whom were young, isolated, and terrified of losing their jobs by showing any signs of rebellion.

Laure convinced the teachers that through solidarity they could attain justice and respect for their profession. In 1936 she organized a meeting that resulted in the creation of a union called the Association catholique des institutrices rurale, then worked to create thirteen regional associations with more than six hundred members. A 1937 congress of teachers resulted in the establishment of the FCIR (the Fédération catholique des institutrices rurales de la province de Québec), with Laure Gaudreault as president. The passionate unionist subsequently devoted twenty years of her life to winning better salaries, pensions, and working conditions for female rural teachers.

Laure Gaudreault wrote a newsletter for members, facilitated professional development, and played a key role as a union organizer in all of the battles fought by Quebec teachers. She helped consolidate Quebec teaching associations into a union now known as the CIC, for which she served as vice-president from 1946 to 1965. Beginning in 1961 she focused her energy on helping retired teachers, and founded an association which became the AREQ (Association des retraitées et retraités de l'enseignement du Québec). Thanks to her efforts pensions were raised and indexed to the cost of living.

As a teacher, journalist, and unionist, Laure Gaudreault made a significant contribution to the development of unionism and the improvement of the teaching profession in Quebec. During a remarkable career of more than sixty years, she was a firm and unrelenting advocate of teacher's rights and their important role in society. Laure Gaudreault continues to be remembered by the unions she built. Though a mountain in Quebec has been named after the headstrong pioneer and a documentary film records her many achievements, the French language paper *Le Devoir* notes that this admirable figure is unfortunately unrecognized for her role in history.[116]

Quote:

"No, they weren't the good old days. We tore out our hearts to change them."[117]

Militant Mother

Marie Lacoste Gérin-Lajoie
1867–1945

Marie Lacoste Gérin-Lajoie.

Convinced that married women shouldn't have to hand over their wages and property to their spouses, she spent a lifetime changing the law.

Marie Lacoste Gérin-Lajoie had a double career: militant and mother.[118] At the age of twenty she agreed to marry lawyer Henri Gérin-Lajoie on the condition that he give her the freedom to continue to work for women's rights. He accepted only with the assurance that Marie would not neglect her family responsibilities.[119] She raised four children and became a prominent feminist in Quebec.

Born into a wealthy Catholic family in Montreal, Marie was one of the thirteen children of Lady Lacoste and Sir Alexandre Lacoste. Lacoste was a brilliant lawyer, judge, and senator with an impressive legal library. After Marie completed her convent education at fifteen she decided to continue her studies by reading her father's law books. Amazed to discover the inferior status of married women in the province, she became a self-taught legal expert bent on improving the situation. To help educate women about their legal status, she published a popular work about civil and constitutional law in 1902, *Traité de droit usuel*, which became an important reference manual for decades.

Marie Gérin-Lajoie agitated for women's rights by becoming an author, educator, reformer, and organizer. She joined the Montreal Local Council of Women (a primarily Anglophone association), conducted legal research, wrote many articles about the status of women, lectured at universities, and established links with feminists in other countries. At the beginning of the twentieth century, the militant feminist played a major role in a movement to provide French-Canadian women access to university education in their own language. In 1908 the Catholic clergy in Quebec finally agreed to the establishment of the first classical college for women.

In 1907 Marie co-founded the Féderation nationale St-Jean-Baptiste, which brought together many francophone associations inspired by Christian feminism. Serving as president from 1913 to 1933, she established a monthly publication called *La Bonne Parole* and directed campaigns to fight infant mortality, alcoholism, tuberculosis, and other circumstances that affected women. Active for decades in the battle to gain the vote for women in Quebec, Marie gave up on that cause in 1922 and focused her energies on women's rights. She continued to lead the battle for improved legal rights and testified before the Dorion Commission (1929). The resulting amendments made to the Quebec Civil Code in 1931 finally brought in the changes she fought for throughout her life. Marie Gérin-Lajoie felt her work was completed.

Marie Lacoste Gérin-Lajoie was a remarkable feminist who fought for women's rights in Canada. In 1906 the Government of the French Republic awarded her the Palmes académiques, and in 1924 the Saint-Jean-Baptiste Society gave her a medal in recognition of her work for French Canadian women. For her role in the latter organization Marie Gérin-Lajoie also received a medal from the Pope in 1933. The Historic Sites and Monuments Board of Canada has recognized her as a national historic person of Canada.

Quote:

"...you guessed it, my treatise on rights was written for women. I do not pardon them for their ignorance in these matters."[120]

Around the World
Helen Smith Grant
1853–1943

Helen Grant.

A daring seafarer, she navigated a ship from Shanghai to the other side of the globe.

Helen Mary Smith was a bluenose. Born by the sea in Maitland, Nova Scotia, she was the daughter of shipbuilder George Oxley Smith.[121] She was teaching school when the dashing Captain William Grant arrived in port to pick up his new barque in 1873. When it was ready they sailed away on the *George* as newlyweds, bound for Montreal to pick up cargo, then off to South America on a working honeymoon. After stops in Montevideo and Valparaiso, the Grants rounded Cape Horn and sailed across the Atlantic to Antwerp.

For the next thirteen years Helen Grant led a vagabond life on the great oceans of the world, making major shore visits only to give birth to her two sons. She loved the adventures of seafaring despite the hazards of raising small children on a ship. Many a night she nursed them through illnesses with limited medical supplies, praying that an ailing boy would live to see the morning.

In the winter of 1879 the young mother faced the most terrifying ordeal of her life, when their heavily laden ship, the *Thomas E. Kenny,* ran into a raging storm. After a week of fighting the mountainous seas, the second mate and a sailor were swept overboard and never seen again. Pumps were useless against the rising water. When a hurricane-force gale struck, Captain Grant was finally forced to abandon his sinking ship. A Portuguese brig managed to rescue the family and remaining crew and land them in Lisbon.

During her years at sea Helen Grant had learned to navigate from her husband. A keen mathematician, she pored over the charts and studied the ocean currents, constellations, trade winds, and the barometer. The eager student soon excelled at taking observations and making calculations to establish positions. She acquired an impressive knowledge of rigging, sailing, and steering a ship. Helen had an unexpected opportunity to show her superb navigational skills when the barque *George* was on a voyage to the Orient in 1883.

Captain Grant spent several weeks in a Shanghai hospital, where he was critically ill with appendicitis and peritonitis. As his condition improved somewhat he decided to begin the trip back to Montreal. When William suffered a complete relapse at sea, Helen took over as captain and commanded the crew of seventeen. For five months, as her husband lay helpless and often delirious, Helen Grant navigated the *George* across the Indian Ocean and along the coast of Africa. She guided the ship safely round the Cape of Good Hope and over the Atlantic Ocean to Montreal.

Helen had sole responsibility for charting the course of the barque, as William was too ill to provide any assistance and no one else on board understood navigation. Throughout the dangerous trip she nursed her husband, cared for her two young boys, and took her share of watches on the ship. Helen's skills, as well as her incredible bravery and determination, saved the *George*, its crew, and her family.

Captain Grant recovered from his illness, and the family settled in Victoria, B.C., in 1886. They built a fine home overlooking the Pacific and invested in the sealing industry. Helen Grant owned the sealing schooner *Beatrice* and became a prominent suffragist. Serving on the Victoria School Board for six years, she won a better rate of pay for teachers and in 1901 was presented to the Duke of York as the first and only woman school trustee in Canada. Active in many causes to help orphans, the aged, and the sick, she received a gold medal from the city in recognition of her services to the community.

Helen Grant died at the age of ninety-one. She was a notable woman in maritime history and a true heroine of the sea, but seems to have been forgotten.

Quote:

"...I was young and quick on my feet so I landed safely in the dory. The older boy came next — he was only four. I heard his father calling for a loose rope, the end of which was tied around the child, who after a few moments of suspense was tossed into the outstretched arms of a sailor in the boat. Then came the baby..."[122]

Helen Grant recounting the Grant's escape from a shipwreck.

An Orkney Lass Called Fubbister
Isobel Gunn
Late 1700s–?

She convinced everyone she was a man, until she suddenly gave birth.

Isobel Gunn as depicted in the film *Through Her Eyes: The Orkney Lad*.

Isobel Gunn dreamed of adventures in the wilds of Canada — and made her dream a reality by disguising herself as a boy. She is believed to be the first European woman to venture to Western Canada.

Isobel was an Orkney lass, a resident of the isolated islands north of mainland Scotland where the Hudson's Bay Company (HBC) often recruited labourers to serve in what is now Canada. Her brother returned home with fascinating stories of life with the fur traders, and Isobel apparently decided to follow his example rather than accept what might befall her as a poor woman, still single despite being in her late twenties. Another version of events suggests she was following a lover.[123]

Dressing in men's clothes, Isobel somehow managed to be hired by the HBC in 1806 as John Fubbister. She would have experienced the hardships and highlights of long days paddling the heavy canoes, the challenges of the portages, and the thrills of riding the rapids of wild rivers. Isobel travelled with a brigade across the country to the Red River — to the Pembina post. Reports showed that Fubbister "worked at anything & well like the rest of the men."[124]

Isobel's life of adventure came to an abrupt end with an arrival that shattered the myth of her male identity: a baby boy, whom she gave birth to on December 29, 1807. Speculation about the events that resulted in pregnancy range from suggestion of a love affair with an older trader called John Scarth, to the idea that he may have raped or seduced Isobel. And perhaps promised to keep her secret in return for sex.

As a white woman requiring support to feed and clothe herself as well as a son, Isobel was no longer considered an asset to the HBC. She worked for a while as a washerwoman, but on September 20, 1809, was shipped back home to the Orkneys, to family and a community that would have shunned her for the sin of sex without the sanctity of marriage. John Scarth never accepted any responsibility for mother or child.

The details of the remainder of her days are uncertain, but Isobel apparently died a vagrant.[125] We can only wonder if any of her contemporaries realized what a remarkable woman she was and what courage she had to cross an ocean in pursuit of her goals.

Quote:

"...he stretched out his hands toward me, and in piteous tones begged me to be kind to a poor, helpless, abandoned wretch, who was not of the sex I supposed, but an unfortunate Orkney girl, pregnant, and actually in childbirth. In saying this she opened her jacket, and displayed a pair of beautiful, round, white breasts; ... In about an hour she was safely delivered of a fine boy, and that same day she was conveyed home in my cariole, where she soon recovered."[126]

An account by fur trader Alexander Henry when he discovered the true identity of John Fubbister.

Founder of the Ursulines

Marie Guyart (Marie de l'Incarnation)
1599–1672

Sacrificing home and family, she set out for the New World to teach young girls in the wilderness.

Marie de l'Incarnation.

She obeyed the calling of God to become a nun, leaving behind a young son who stormed the convent crying, "Give me back my mother, give me back my mother."[127]

Marie Guyart was born in Tours, France, in 1599, the daughter of a master baker and a woman of noble ancestry. Marie received a good education and by the age of fourteen was interested in becoming a nun. At the insistence of her parents she married a silk-worker called Claude Martin. His death two years later ended the apparently troubled marriage, and left Marie a nineteen-year-old widow with a son just six months old.

She then lived with her sister and brother-in-law — the owner of a carrier business that Marie eventually managed. Unable to resist her divine calling, Madame Martin left her son in the care of her sister and became an Ursuline nun. She took her vows in 1633 with the name Marie de l'Incarnation. When the Lord called her in a dream to go to Canada, she resolved to go to New France and educate French and Native girls.

Arriving in Quebéc in 1639, Marie de l'Incarnation founded the Ursuline order in New France. Using her expertise in business, she proved to be an efficient administrator in establishing and managing the religious order. An intelligent woman full of dreams for New France, she became a confidant and advisor to men of power and influence in the colony — governors, intendants, and notables.

Marie de l'Incarnation also fulfilled her goal of educating the girls of the colony by establishing a boarding school, which parents could pay for in kind rather than money — perhaps with a barrel of salted eel, a fat pig, or a pot of butter. Marie also tried to educate adult Indians, and began studying their languages. She created an Iroquois catechism and dictionary, as well as French-Algonkin and Algonkin-French dictionaries.

Marie de l'Incarnation played an important role in the building of New France. She was a respected leader who faced the challenges of Iroquois raids, a fire that destroyed the nuns' dwelling, unscrupulous businessmen, and a harsh climate. The good works of the Ursuline order continue in Quebec today.

Marie's beloved son, Claude, joined the Benedictines and became one of the superiors of that order. She sent him a fond farewell message before passing away on April 30, 1672, at the age of seventy-two. Following her death Marie de l'Incarnation was venerated as a saint, but she was not beatified.

Quote:

"My very dear son, the ships are about to weigh anchor, so I cannot open my heart to you as you would like. I am extremely tired because of the number of letters I have written. I think I have written more than two hundred. One must do all this along with our other duties while the ships are here."[128]

Letter from Marie Guyart to her son on September 5, 1644.

Frank Craig/National Archives of Canada/C-001549

The arrival of the Ursulines in Quebec.

Mary Riter Hamilton.

The Battlefields
Mary Riter Hamilton
1873–1954

Determined to leave a memorial to those who fought in World War I, she refused to sell her battlefield paintings despite her poverty.

"It is fortunate that I arrived before it was too late to get a real impression," said Mary Hamilton. "The first day I went over Vimy [Ridge], snow and sleet were falling, and I was able to realize what the soldiers had suffered. If as you and others tell me, there is something of the suffering and heroism of the war in my pictures it is because at that moment the spirit of those who fought and died seemed to linger in the air."[129]

After the end of the First World War artist Mary Hamilton left for Europe with a small commission from the Amputations Club of British Columbia to paint the battlefields. From 1919 to 1922 she strived to capture the devastation of war in France and Belgium. Living alone in a tin hut and subsisting on meager food supplies, Mary survived the threats of roving bands of deserters and looters, land mines, and booby traps. And she completed three hundred haunting paintings of the horrors of war.

Mary Riter Hamilton was already an accomplished artist when she began her mission in Europe. Born in Teeswater, Ontario, she spent her childhood in Clearwater, Manitoba, where her parents had moved to become pioneers. Mary Riter married storekeeper Charles W. Hamilton when she was sixteen but was widowed just four years later. She decided to follow her dream of becoming an artist and began supporting herself by teaching the painting of china and watercolours in Winnipeg. Mary studied briefly in Toronto with the respected artists George Reid and Mary Heister Reid, who encouraged her to develop her considerable talent by studying in Europe — where all serious students trained.

Mary Hamilton went to Europe in 1901, where she travelled and studied with renowned teachers such as Franz Skarbina in Germany, and Mereon and Gervais at the Vitti Academy in Paris. By 1905 Mary had the honour of exhibiting three of her works at the prestigious Salon of the French Academy in Paris, and she regularly showed her paintings there in future years. The artist also painted and displayed her work in Canada, with exhibits in Toronto, Ottawa, and Montreal in 1911 and 1912. But it was the battlefield art of Mary Ritter Hamilton that brought the greatest recognition, particularly in France and England.

Mary's powerful paintings were exhibited at many prestigious locations in the 1920s, including the Salon, the Foyer of the Paris Opéra, and Surrey House in London. In 1922 Mary Hamilton became the only Canadian artist to be awarded the purple ribbon of Les Palmes Académiques by the Minister of Beaux-Arts. By 1923 she was ill and had lost the use of one eye. Mary no longer had the zeal to pursue her earlier style of painting and turned for a time to creating dress accessories, for which she won a gold medal in 1925 at the International Decorative Arts Exhibition. Having earned enough money to bring herself and her pictures home, Mary returned to Canada.

Despite her need for money, she gave away some of her battlefield work to veterans and refused all offers to sell her collection. Eager to leave a legacy of battlefield art to the people of Canada, Mary Hamilton donated 227 of her paintings to the Public Archives of Canada. She continued to paint, teach, and exhibit her works in subsequent years until she passed away in Vancouver in 1954. The gifted artist was poor, nearly blind, and largely forgotten while thousands of dollars worth of her pictures "[lay] discarded in the dust and darkness of a public library."[130] It is only recently that her notable contribution to Canadian art has been recognized, most notably when the University of Winnipeg hosted the first Mary Riter Hamilton exhibition, *No Man's Land*, in 1989.[131]

Quote:

"I came out because I felt I must come, and if I did not come at once it would be too late, because the battlefields would be obliterated, and places watered with the best blood of Canada might be only names and memories."[132]

Letter to Dr. Arthur Doughty, Dominion Archivist, 27 July 1926.

ATA pilot Helen Harrison stepping into the cockpit of a Spitfire.

At Home in a Spitfire
Helen Harrison
1909–1995

"What are you doing driving a cab?" asked the World War II ace when he recognized pilot Helen Harrison. Good question.

Despite her extensive flying experience Helen Harrison couldn't land a job as a pilot after World War II. She ended up driving taxis at Dorval Airport near Montreal, where she picked up the famous flyer Buzz Beurling. He arranged for her to demonstrate Percival Proctor planes across Canada.[133] The stint as a cab driver was just one of the many bumps in Helen Harrison's lengthy career in aviation.

Helen was born in Vancouver, where her francophone father worked as a waiter on the Canadian Pacific Railway and her English mother played the piano for silent movies.[134] Her parents soon bought a small café in Steveston, leaving Helen and her brother Jim alone much of the time. The children ran wild and Helen's schooling suffered. The family moved to England when she was a teenager, after her grandfather died and left a significant inheritance in trust for Helen and Jim.

Sent off to a prestigious boarding school at Wiltshire and then a finishing school in Brussels, Helen resented the strict rules and couldn't catch up in her studies. She returned to England. Smitten with a soldier, the young woman married and within a few years became a mother of three. By the age of twenty-four she was divorced and took her mother's maiden name of Harrison. Helen was spending money like crazy, having inherited her fortune when she married. After a thrilling plane ride in 1933 she decided to make flying her life.

Helen bought herself several aircraft after earning her private pilot's licence. The adventurous pilot became qualified to fly a seaplane while visiting friends in Singapore, then obtained her commercial licence in England. She became the first Canadian woman to get her instructor's, multi-engine, and instrument ratings. On moving to Cape Town, South Africa, with her family, Helen's flying skills were readily appreciated and she was hired by the Royal South Africa Air Force to teach reserve pilots. Helen became the first female flying instructor in South Africa and the first woman in the British Empire to fly and teach on military planes such as the Avro Tutor and Hawker Hart. In looking back at her career, Helen later remarked: "South Africa was the only country where I didn't have to battle to get ahead. I was accepted as a pilot."[135]

When Helen returned to Canada in early 1940 she was an experienced pilot with 2,600 hours of flying on civilian and military planes. She taught flying, and at this time she was the only female pilot in Canada who managed to get paid work as an aviator. After the outbreak of World War II, Helen applied for the Royal Canadian Air Force — and was furious at being rejected because she was a woman. However, if Canada didn't want her services, Great Britain did.

Helen Harrison helped out the war effort by working for the Air Transport Auxiliary (ATA) in Great Britain — becoming the first Canadian woman to join. The ATA had been created to deliver aircraft to the Royal Air Force and Royal Navy, usually from factories or repair sites. Helen loved flying the fast military planes and during her years of service flew thirty-four different types — including Spitfires, Beaufighters, Barracudas, and Defiants. She also co-piloted a Mitchell bomber across the Atlantic in 1943.

Helen once flew a loaded Spitfire to a fighter squadron and was "sure tempted to give just a little burst." She logged about five hundred hours flying with the ATA, a considerable amount of time since most flights were only twenty or thirty minutes long. "My time with the ATA was the most exciting and interesting of my career," said Helen in later years.[136]

After the war Helen was broke. Following her jobs driving a taxi and the short assignment demonstrating planes, she and her three sons moved to Vancouver in 1947. A logging company hired her to transport staff in a Cessna 170 and she did a lot of "sweeping snow off the floats and flying drunks."[137] When this job ended Helen Harrison spent decades teaching flying and acting as temporary manager at clubs — until the clubs prospered under her guidance and new male managers were hired to carry on her work. "It was frustrating, always having to step back and let a man do the job when I had already shown that I could handle it."[138]

Helen acquired the reputation as the best floatplane instructor in British Columbia and was dubbed "Floats Harrison." She flew thousands of hours in floatplanes and heavy twin-engines, but the airlines wouldn't hire her to actually fly. The reasons? She was told that she might be too weak to handle the controls, that the public wouldn't accept a female pilot, and that a woman couldn't be hired to work in the bush. A bitter Helen reflected, "I couldn't overcome my sex."[139]

When she ended her amazing career in 1969 Helen Harrison had logged fifteen thousand hours of flying. She is believed to be the first woman in the world to hold commercial flying licences for four countries: Canada, the United States, Great Britain, and South Africa. A notable pioneer pilot, she is a Canadian heroine in the field of aviation. In 1974 Helen Harrison was inducted into Canada's Aviation Hall of Fame and named to the Order of Icarus, an award to honour individuals who have made outstanding contributions to Canadian aviation.

Quote:

"When I applied to the RCAF I was rejected because I wore a skirt. I was furious. I just couldn't believe it. I had 2,600 hours, an instructor's rating, multi-engine and instrument endorsements, a seaplane rating, and the experience of flying civil and military aircraft in three countries. Instead they took men with 150 hours."[140]

Helen Harrison (fourth from left) and students with DH82C "Tiger Moth" aircraft of the RCAF.

Heroine of Isle aux Morts

Ann Harvey
1811–1860

In a daring rescue attempt, she risked her life to save the passengers of a sinking ship.

School children on the Harvey Trail.

Thousands of ships have wrecked on the rugged southwest coast of Newfoundland, many along the well-named Isle aux Morts — island of death. Among the most notorious wrecks was that of the brig *Despatch*, bound for the port of Quebec in the summer of 1828 with about two hundred Irish emigrants.[141]

Ann Harvey was the eldest child of Jane and George Harvey, a fisherman who had lived all his life on the rocky island east of Port aux Basques. George spotted distress signals from the *Despatch* during a summer storm after strong winds had driven the vessel onto rocks a few miles from the Harvey's home.[142] The passengers were stranded on the rocks and on the remains of their sinking vessel.

As George Harvey prepared to launch his small fishing boat into the stormy seas, seventeen-year-old Ann volunteered to join him. Without her help it would have been impossible for the lone man to have any hope of reaching the brig. Ann's twelve-year-old brother, Tom, and their fearless Newfoundland dog also leaped into the twelve-foot punt. Despite their best efforts rowing for several hours through the raging waves, the rescuers couldn't reach the doomed *Despatch*.

George ordered their dog to swim to the ship. He eventually returned carrying a line that they used to haul a heavy rope to shore. Once the rescuers secured the rope on land, the crew rigged up a breeches-buoy to ferry people, one by one, to safety. After three days the Harveys managed to rescue about 160 people before the ship disappeared into the ocean. Captain Lancaster and many others drowned, including two infants who were swept from their mother's breasts as they huddled on the rocks. The Harveys then shared their meager food supplies and small shelter with the survivors.

The bravery of the Harveys came to the attention of King George IV of England, who rewarded them with one hundred gold sovereigns, an engraved medal, and a handwritten note. George Harvey insisted that his daughter Ann take the medal because it was her determination that was key in saving so many lives. She was later dubbed the "Grace Darling of Newfoundland" after the famous British woman who rowed with her father to rescue survivors of a shipwreck.

Ann Harvey married Charles Gillam at the age of nineteen and settled in Port aux Basques, where they raised six children. In 1838 the young mother and George Harvey again risked their lives, this time to save passengers of the ship *Rankin* from Glasgow — and rescued twenty-five people. This courageous woman died at forty-nine and was buried in an unmarked grave.[143] In 1987 the Canadian Coast Guard launched an ice-breaker named the *Ann Harvey* in her honour. The Harvey Trail in Isle aux Morts was opened in 1999 to commemorate the heroic Harvey family and their daring sea rescues.

Ah Kamouraska!

Anne Hébert
1916–2000

Anne Hébert.

She rebelled against the stifling conservatism of Quebec and helped usher in the Quiet Revolution.[144]

Anne Hébert was a reserved woman who cherished her privacy; hence much of her personal life remains a mystery. She often said she would have loved to have had children but could not be both a mother and writer. Writing was her passion — her life.

Born in the village of Sainte-Catherine-de-Fossambault near Quebec City where the Héberts had a summer home, Anne belonged to a notable family with illustrious ancestors. Her father, Maurice, a civil servant who was also an author and literary critic, greatly influenced her education and the rigour of her writing style. She attended several schools in Quebec City and as a child began entertaining her younger siblings with stories she invented. During summers at Ste.-Catherine she was inspired by watching her cousin Hector de Saint-Denys Garneau develop as a poet and produce plays in the parish hall; she also adopted some of his symbolism in her writings and picked up feelings of alienation in Québécois society.[145]

Encouraged to write by both Hector and her father, Anne created poems and stories that were published by literary magazines. Her first book of poetry was published in 1942 and won the Prix David. Hector's sudden death in 1943 shattered Anne, and her writings became dark and violent, burning with rebellion and images of repression. It was difficult to find publishers for such material in a province whose social and intellectual lives were strictly controlled by the Catholic clergy and the Duplessis government, so she self-published several works.

Anne Hébert worked for Radio-Canada and the National Film Board from 1950-54, when she was awarded a grant from the Royal Society of Canada to write in Paris. The author spent most of her adult life in self-imposed exile in France. Removed from her homeland, she found it easier to write about the country and the people that inspired much of her writing.[146] With the passage of time her work moved toward light, freedom, and awakening. The writer's impressive legacy includes ten novels, five poetry collections, and four plays. Her famous novel *Kamouraska*, published in 1970 and later made into an acclaimed film by Claude Jutra, was a romantic tragedy inspired by a nineteenth-century murder. The book evoked powerful images of Anne's native Quebec, bound by traditions and the burden of history.

Anne Hébert was an active writer for about sixty years, and her last novel was as fine as her first, "like the work of a young writer at the height of her powers ... each word set down like a jewel and every page infused with light."[147] The gifted poet, playwright, and novelist won countless awards during her career — including the prestigious Prix Femina, Prix des Librairies, Gilles-Corbeil Award, and three Governor General's Awards for literature.

When Anne Hébert learned she had cancer she came home to die. The death of Quebec's literary giant in January 2000 brought a stream of tributes to an elegant lady with a dazzling smile. A woman who helped define Quebec and served as an example for other female writers.

Quote:

"Poetry is no Sunday recreation. It is hunger and thirst, bread and wine."[148]

Of Farm and Field

E. Cora Hind
1861–1942

Cora Hind.

Despite being told that journalism was no job for a woman, Cora managed to get hired at the *Winnipeg Free Press* — about twenty years after she applied. Along the way she became a prominent journalist, renowned agriculturist, and women's rights activist.

It was a difficult start for a child. Her mother passed away when she was two, and before her fifth birthday her father died of cholera. Aunt Alice Hind mothered Ella Cora Hind and her two orphaned brothers and became a close friend when the two women headed to Western Canada — and the unknown challenges of the frontier.

Cora Hind was born in Toronto on September 18, 1861, but grew up with Aunt Alice on her grandfather's farm in Artimisea, Grey County, Ontario. The little girl loved the farm, and the world of agriculture became the focus of her life. It wasn't until she was eleven that there was a one-room schoolhouse to attend, so Cora received her early education on the farm. Her grandfather taught her about the livestock, the crops, and the challenges of successful farming.

Aunt Alice had hoped Cora would be a school teacher, but when some cousins visited with tales from the west of the country the two women decided to move there. Cora was just shy of her twenty-first birthday when they boarded a train for Winnipeg in 1882. They set off with more hope than money. Aunt Alice wanted to make a living by dressmaking, while Cora wanted to be a journalist. She had a letter of introduction to W.F. Luxton, editor of the *Manitoba Free Press*.

Luxton, astonished at Cora's request to be accepted on trial as a reporter, explained that the work was not suitable for a woman. A determined E. Cora Hind had to wait twenty years before she was finally asked to be a reporter at the newspaper, which later became the *Winnipeg Free Press*. In the intervening years she had proved beyond a doubt that she was an exceptional woman of many talents.

Faced with the immediate need of earning a living, Cora rented what was then a new piece of equipment that few knew how to use: a typewriter. After becoming a skilled two-finger typist, she was hired by a good law firm. In 1893 she set up her own public stenography business, which was the first such establishment west of the Great Lakes. Through her business and personal interests, Cora made sure she gained a comprehensive knowledge of all aspects of agriculture in the west. She began contributing articles to the *Manitoba Free Press*, and probably began her career as an agricultural journalist when she submitted her minutes from the Manitoba Dairy Association. She served five years as their secretary-treasurer, reported on dozens of conventions, circulated market reports, and attended livestock shows.

Cora got a big break in 1898 when a Colonel Maclean (whose publishing empire gave birth to *Maclean's* magazine) wired from Toronto to ask if she would take an all-expenses paid trip to survey the state of the crops in the west; eastern financiers were concerned about the possibility of major failures. Cora's excellent report provided the necessary reassurances, and other agricultural publications began asking her to contribute articles.

The *Winnipeg Free Press* finally hired Cora Hind in 1901, when the new editor, J.W. Dafoe, invited her to join the staff. According to Dafoe, "she became the paper's expert authority on agricultural and marketing questions, and the advisor in these fields in shaping editorial policies."[149] Not only did Cora Hind write about agricultural issues; she was actively involved.

Cora attended agricultural shows and conferences throughout North America and frequently visited scientists in the Department of Agriculture in Ottawa. She took an active role in dairy, beef, and sheep-farming associations, and stockmen appreciated her contributions. At the 1916 gathering of the Western Canada Livestock Union they paid tribute to her with a gift of $1,300 in gold and an accolade: "Your record is one of faithful and invaluable service at all times ungrudgingly given to the interest of the Farm and the Farmer."[150]

For thirty years she contributed her crop inspection reports based on her own inspections by railway, buckboard, and, later, car. She commonly wore "high laced boots, riding breeches, long duck coat and soft khaki shirt," and perhaps her Stetson hat and the beaded buckskin coat given to her by the Calgary Stampede board.[151] Cora made amazingly accurate predictions of actual crop yields. When the *Free Press* ceased crop inspections in 1933, an announcement showed that Cora Hind's twenty-nine estimates had the highest rate of accuracy in comparison with government reports.

In addition to her important role as an agriculturist, Cora became heavily involved in a variety of groups working to obtain equal rights for women. Soon after arriving in Winnipeg, she joined the Women's Christian Temperance Union and conducted legal research for the group. In 1893 Cora debated in a mock parliament in Winnipeg about a bill granting the vote to women. Cora soon discovered her ability as a public speaker, and in 1894 went on a speaking tour of the province to support equal suffrage for men and women.

She was involved in many clubs and helped found the Quill Club (for writers), the Political Equality League, the Women's Canadian Club, and the Winnipeg Branch of the Canadian Women's Press Club.

Through a lifetime of involvement in agricultural activities, E. Cora Hind acquired impressive expertise in the field. Eager to learn about modern agriculture and foreign markets, she began to travel more and set off on a world tour at the age of seventy-four. On returning home, Dr. Cora Hind (having been awarded an honorary doctorate from the University of Manitoba) spoke about her experiences to a standing-room-only crowd in Winnipeg's Walker Theatre. For two and a half hours she spoke to an enthralled audience of 1,100 people.[152]

Cora continued to submit regular articles to the *Free Press* until her death at the age of eighty-one. In 1997 the Historic Sites and Monuments Board of Canada recognized her as a national historic person. But perhaps the tribute that would have pleased Cora Hind the most was Agriculture Canada's 1993 issuing of a new variety of Red Spring Wheat called AC Cora.

Quote:

"...it was a shock to find laws on the Statute Books of this province (Manitoba) that would have been a disgrace to heathendom. For example, a man could, if he so wished, will away his unborn child to other guardianship than that of its mother. The age of Consent was ten years. At the same time a woman or girl was not considered of sufficiently mature judgement to sell a piece of land or a horse or a cow until she was twenty-one."[153]

Homemaker with a Mission
Adelaide Hunter Hoodless
1857–1910

Adelaide Hoodless.

She turned personal tragedy into a life of helping others.

When her infant son John died from drinking contaminated milk at eighteen months, Adelaide Hoodless decided on her mission in life. On learning the cause of the tragedy she decided to help educate other mothers. She would later say, "Apart from my family duties the education of mothers has been my life work."[154]

Adelaide grew up on an Ontario farm. She was born on February 27, 1857, in a modest two-storey house called "The Willows," in South Dumfries, Brant County. Adelaide was the youngest of twelve children. One can only imagine the hardships faced by her mother, Jane, when Adelaide's father died just a few months after her birth. From this difficult childhood Adelaide would learn about the problems of farm women.

At the age of twenty-three Adelaide Hunter wed John Hoodless, the son of a prosperous furniture manufacturer who had become a full partner in the family business. She gave birth to four children: Edna, Joseph, Muriel, and John.

In the same year that her baby John died (1889), Adelaide saw an opportunity to become involved in helping women learn more about sanitation and nutrition. At this time knowledge of such topics was rudimentary at best; ice boxes were few, flies swarmed around kitchens, milk was delivered in open cans, and wells were not covered. When a Young Women's Christian Association (YWCA) was established and began giving cooking classes, Adelaide convinced the Hamilton School Board to send students.

In 1893, Adelaide Hoodless was one of sixty Canadian women who attended the Columbian Exposition in Chicago. She headed the YWCA delegation. A Woman's Building included exhibits about the work of women, and a Women's Congress brought together women from associations throughout the world. Many women's activities began through this unique opportunity to meet and share experiences. The idea of a national organization of YWCAs grew out of the gathering, and on her return home Adelaide began writing letters to cities and towns across Canada. Her efforts culminated in the first national conference of YWCAs in Toronto in December 1893. Participants elected Adelaide as the first vice-president, and in 1895 she became the second president of the national YWCA.

In Chicago Adelaide had met Lady Aberdeen, wife of Canada's new Governor General and a leader in creating women's groups in Great Britain. Adelaide and Lady Aberdeen organized a meeting in Toronto that was attended by 1,500 interested ladies. Such a gathering was indeed unusual, as shown by the comments of a writer for *The Empire* newspaper: "Hitherto it has not been the correct thing, from a Canadian society standpoint, for a woman to speak on a platform. But now for the first time a Governor General's wife has given a public address."[155]

The women organized the National Council of Women, with Lady Aberdeen serving as president and Adelaide as the treasurer. The organization decided to support Adelaide's goal of introducing domestic training (a home economics course) for girls in public schools across Canada. She was directly involved in the establishment of household science courses in many provinces.

As teachers would have to be trained for the new course, Adelaide and the National Council pressed for more teacher training facilities. Among the centres established through her involvement were the Macdonald Institute at Guelph and the Macdonald College at Ste. Anne de Bellevue. A publisher invited Adelaide to write a textbook on domestic science, and her work was published in 1898.

Adelaide Hoodless also helped Lady Aberdeen create the Victorian Order of Nurses in 1897 to help provide nursing assistance to women and children.

Adelaide still felt that the wives of farmers needed an association to help them become better homemakers. In 1897 she co-founded the world's first Women's Institute in Stoney Creek, Ontario, to promote knowledge of household science and to broaden and enrich rural life. The movement spread through the province, and Adelaide persuaded the Ontario Department of Agriculture to provide grants to fund lecturers. By 1907 there were five hundred Women's Institutes across the country.

The Women's Institute became the "largest organization of Canadian women." The movement spread to other countries, and an international organization was formed in Stockholm in 1933 called the Associated Country Women of the World.

Her work took Adelaide to many conferences, and she frequently gave lectures. In 1899 she attended the International Congress of Women in London and was presented to Queen Victoria — just one indication of the international recognition she attained as one of the most prominent women in Canada.[156] Through her countless activities, Adelaide Hoodless contributed much to improving the quality of life for women and their families. Household and public sanitation improved, and women's organizations provided social opportunities, continuing education, and greater involvement in society. Adelaide was a conservative feminist, in that she wanted to help women fulfill their traditional role — of homemaker and mother.[157]

While addressing members of the Federation of Women's Clubs at Toronto's Massey Hall in 1910, Adelaide Hunter Hoodless collapsed and died. She was fifty-two.

Many institutions and groups have recognized her contribution to Canadian society. In 1959 the Ontario Archaeological and Historic Sites Board placed a commemorative plaque at the homestead where she was born. The Historic Sites and Monuments Board of Canada recognized her as a national historic person in 1960 and designated the Adelaide Hunter Hoodless Homestead as a national historic site in 1995. The Federated Women's Institutes of Canada own and operate a small museum at the latter near Brantford, Ontario. Canada Post issued a stamp in honour of Adelaide Hunter Hoodless in 1993.

Quote:

"The management of the home has more to do in the moulding of character than any other influence, owing to the large place it fills in the early life of the individual during the most plastic state of development. We are, therefore, justified in an effort to secure a place for home economics or domestic science in the education institutions of this country."[158]

Frances and the Voyageurs

Frances Anne Beechey Hopkins
1838–1919

At a time when women were relatively invisible, she literally painted herself into the picture.

Mrs. Edward (Frances Anne) Hopkins, artist, Montreal, Quebec, 1863.

Frances Anne Hopkins painted many famous scenes of voyageurs travelling by canoe in the Canadian wilderness during the last days of the fur trade. Many of us will recognize the images, but too few may know they were painted by this talented woman who made some journeys with the voyageurs in the 1860s. If you look carefully at some of her canvases you'll note that she even painted herself into the scenes — a sophisticated lady wearing a hat.

Frances Anne Beechey was born in England. Among the accomplished artists in her family were her father, who painted watercolours and was a hydrographer and rear-admiral in the Royal Navy, and her grandfather Sir William Beechey — a famous painter and a notable geographer who had journeyed to the Arctic with explorers Parry and Franklin.[159]

Frances Anne's life changed dramatically after she married Edward Martin Hopkins, a widower with three children who worked as secretary to George Simpson — governor of the Hudson's Bay Company. In 1858 the newlyweds settled in Hopkins's home at Lachine, Lower Canada. Within a few years Frances was caring for her two young boys as well as her step-sons. She eventually gave birth to five children, though two died as infants. Despite her family responsibilities she found opportunities to sketch and paint watercolours, and some of her work was exhibited in London in 1860.

In 1861 Edward Hopkins became a Chief Factor based in Montreal, where the family lived for the remaining years of his service for the Company. During the twelve years that Frances lived in Canada she made a number of canoe trips with her husband and the voyageurs — on the Great Lakes as well as the Ottawa and Mattawa Rivers. Presumably she was accompanying

Edward on inspection trips of areas for which he was responsible. Her impressive oil paintings of the paddlers and their disappearing way of life became powerful pictoral records of the fur trade in Canadian history.

During their years in Canada the Hopkins family made a number of trips to England, but it is not known if Frances attended the opening of her first exhibition at the Royal Academy in London on May 3, 1869: her oil painting *Canoes in a fog, Lake Superior* was displayed. Research conducted by archivist Alice M. Johnson suggests that Edward and Frances may shortly afterwards have made a final canoe trip, somewhere into Rupert's Land.[160]

The Hopkins family moved back to England in 1870 — the year that some of Frances' work was exhibited by the Art Association of Montreal. In the following years Frances Anne Hopkins displayed her artwork dozens of times in London, including eleven showings at the Royal Academy. The images were frequently scenes inspired by her adventures in the wilds of Canada.

Frances Anne Hopkins made a notable contribution to Canadian history by vividly and accurately capturing on canvas the country's first major transportation system and the people who travelled it. Though a number of Canadian institutions have some of her works in their collections, it is doubtful that many people know about the woman who painted them. If you ever visit the Canadian Museum of Civilization in Gatineau, Quebec, be sure to look above the ticket counter at the massive canoe suspended there: a recreation of one of the artist's paintings. Amid the voyageurs sits Frances.

Quote:

"I have not found Canadians at all anxious hitherto for pictures of their own country."[161]

Frances Anne Hopkins writing about the poor sales of her paintings in a letter to Mr. McCord, July 12, 1910.

An 1869 oil painting by Frances Anne Hopkins: *Canoe Manned by Voyageurs Passing a Waterfall.*

National Archives of Canada/C-002771

Race Through Labrador

Mina Hubbard
1870–1956

A Woman's Way Through Labrador, 1908

Mina Hubbard cooking breakfast at a camp on Lake Michikamau.

She explored some of the wildest country in Canada in an incredible race.

In the early twentieth century just one area of North America remained unknown to European explorers: the interior of Labrador. An adventurous Canadian woman set out to change that.

A tragic expedition to the area in 1903, led by writer Leonidas Hubbard Jr., ended with his death by starvation. One of Hubbard's two travelling companions, New York lawyer Dillon Wallace, penned a best-selling book about the expedition. Hubbard's widow resented the impression given in the publication that her husband was a weak leader who was responsible for the failure of the trip. She was determined to finish his work and clear his name. Both Mina Hubbard and Wallace decided to complete the trek through Labrador to Ungava Bay. The bitter rivals organized competing expeditions in "the great race of 1905" and the press hyped up the battle. Who would win the race?

Born in 1870 on a farm near Rice Lake, Ontario, Mina Benson was the daughter of immigrants struggling to support a large family on poor land.[162] Like many young girls of the day she taught school, but moved to New York to attend the Brooklyn Training School for Nurses. After graduating in 1899 Mina worked in the Staten Island Hospital, where she nursed journalist Leonidas Hubbard Jr. through a bout of typhoid fever. Following his recovery Hubbard landed a job with the noted outdoor magazine *Outing,* and the couple married in New York City in 1901.

In an incredible turn of events, four years later the young widow canoed into the Labrador wilderness from Northwest River on June 25, 1905.[163] Sporting a sweater and short skirt over knickerbockers, she had a revolver, cartridge pouch, and fishing knife attached to her belt. A novice explorer, Mina had the good sense to hire an experienced crew of four. George Elson, who had served on the earlier Hubbard expedition, organized the group and engaged Joe Chapies (Cree), Joseph Iserhoff (Russian-Cree), and Gilbert Blake (Inuk). The expedition team of expert woodsmen brought knowledge of the country and the Native people. They brought along a good stock of food and supplies so they weren't dependant on the land. Hoping to be picked up by a Hudson's Bay Company steamer at the end of their journey, the team planned to travel more than nine hundred kilometres through the wilderness to reach their destination in two months.

Mina's team followed the Naskaupi River Valley, Lake Michikamau, and then the George River up to Ungava Bay. They reached their destination on August 27, 1905. Upon returning home Mina Hubbard completed a comprehensive book about the successful expedition: *A Woman's Way Through Unknown Labrador*. It included good maps (later accepted by the American Geographical Society and the Geographical Society of Great Britain)[164] that accurately depicted areas of the Labrador interior. Mina's work corrected previously erroneous geographical information, proving that Seal Lake and Lake Michikamau were in the same drainage basin and that the Northwest and Nascaupee were the same river. The book also included information about her deceased husband (along with his diary from the Labrador expedition), flora and fauna, geology, topography, and the Native residents of Labrador.

Mina Hubbard's expedition won the race. The rival group led by Wallace reached its destination six weeks later. The party was slowed down by the failure to engage Natives, the need to hunt for food along the way, problems finding an old portage route, and dividing the team to preserve supplies. Wallace's account of his expedition outsold Mina's, though his book couldn't match the wealth of material and accurate maps she presented.

Mina Hubbard presented public lectures about her expedition in the United States and England, where she met a wealthy Quaker called Harold Ellis. The pair married in 1908 and raised three children before divorcing. Mina frequently returned home to Canada and at the age of sixty-six made one last canoe trip with her crew chief and friend George Elson.[165]

Quote:

"Rugged, barren mountains rose in all directions ... I did not feel far from home, but in reality less homeless than I had ever felt anywhere, since I knew my husband was never to come back to me."[166]

Mina Hubbard's memories of the Labrador journey, as her expedition headed off for Lake Michikamau.

A Woman's Way Through Labrador, 1908.

Mina Hubbard "in the heart of the wilderness" in Labrador.

Marie de La Tour.

Heroine of Acadia
Françoise-Marie Jacquelin (Marie de la Tour)
ca.1602–1645

With a rope around her neck, she survived the shock of seeing her men hanged.

Françoise-Marie Jacquelin, commonly referred to as Marie de la Tour, was the first European woman to settle in what is now New Brunswick. She valiantly commanded Fort La Tour with forty-five soldiers, in the face of bombardment from both land and sea — losing control only when a traitor helped attacker Menou d'Aulnay.

Born in France, she accepted a marriage proposal around 1640 from Charles de La Tour, a lieutenant-governor of Acadia.[167] At the time of her arrival in Acadia he was in control of Fort La Tour at the mouth of the St. John River, while rival Lieutenant-Governor Charles de Menou d'Aulnay was established on the other side of the Bay of Fundy at Port-Royal. Françoise-Marie Jacquelin found herself living in a primitive dwelling inside a palisade of logs, and was soon involved in a fight for her new home as the rivalry turned violent.

To ensure that her husband's side of the conflict was heard in the French court, she sailed back to La Rochelle in the fall of 1643 with a load of furs. She managed to arrange for a ship to send back provisions to Fort La Tour, but the court sided with d'Aulnay and forbade her from returning to Acadia or sending aid. A defiant Marie escaped to England, where she hired a ship to take her back to her husband's fort with trading goods and supplies. She was not reunited with her husband and baby son until December 1644.

Marie found the fort in such dire need of supplies that she convinced her husband to head to Boston for help. He had not returned by the springtime, when d'Aulnay decided to attack. Marie took command of her fort and the forty-five remaining men — as she could not trust any of them to be in charge. D'Aulnay lost twenty men in the battle and another thirteen were wounded, but he eventually managed to invade Fort La Tour. Marie agreed to surrender only because of his promise to spare their lives. But he hanged the soldiers and apparently forced her to watch with a noose around her neck. Marie survived three weeks of imprisonment before dying, and rumours circulated that d'Aulnay had poisoned her. The fate of her young son is unknown.

For her courageous behaviour in trying to save Fort La Tour, Françoise-Marie Jacquelin is known as the heroine of Acadia. Fort La Tour has been commemorated as a national historic site of Canada, and a statue of the remarkable Marie de La Tour has been erected in Saint John, New Brunswick.

Cochran/National Archives of Canada/C-085125

Pauline Johnson, ca. 1895.

The Mohawk Poet
E. Pauline Johnson
1861–1913

At a time when respectable women didn't perform on the stage, Pauline made a career of enchanting audiences in Canada and abroad. She also raised awareness of Aboriginal culture.

E. Pauline Johnson was as comfortable wearing buckskin while giving a poetry recital in a miner's camp as she was garbed in a stylish ball gown while socializing in a salon in England. But it was in the image of a Mohawk princess that she gained international fame, while touring Canada, the United States, and England, giving dramatic readings of her poetry.

A striking woman, she appeared on stage in a buckskin dress with red broadcloth trim, a beaded belt with two scalps at her waist, bracelets of wampum beads, silver broaches, a bear claw necklace, and an eagle feather in her long curly dark brown hair. Pauline usually travelled with a male entertainer who complemented her theatrical performances and managed their tours.

Pauline was born at Chiefswood, her family's home on the Grand River in the Six Nations Iroquois Reserve, near Brantford, Ontario. Her mother, Emily Howells, was an Englishwoman raised in the United States. Her father, George H.M. Johnson, was a prominent Mohawk chief respected for this status as well as the government positions he held on the reserve and his ties with the Anglican Church. Pauline grew up in an upper-middle-class household, receiving much of her education at home from her mother and a governess. She was technically just three-eighths Native, yet it was her Native heritage that fascinated and inspired Pauline.

Her grandfather John Smoke Johnson was very knowledgeable about Iroquois history and culture and provided much of the information Pauline would use in her writings.

After some success in getting her poems published, Pauline's career as a performer was launched when she drew praise for a recital of her work for the Young Men's Liberal Club of Toronto. Customarily billed as an Indian princess, Pauline soon gained popularity in the entertainment circuit at a time when many famous writers toured to give readings. Her unique presentations and oration skills kept Pauline on the stage for much of the time from 1892 to1910, and also helped her to get publishing contracts for some of her poems, essays, and short stories about Native culture and history, Canada, and the wonders of the natural world.

Her 1898 engagement to a Winnipeg businessman was apparently called off because his family objected to her occupation as a stage performer and her Native blood. Pauline never married.[168]

Pauline Johnson retired to Vancouver, where she continued struggling to pay her bills. In 1913 she died of breast cancer. At her request, Pauline's ashes were placed in one of her special places — Stanley Park.

In her day Pauline Johnson was a legend, a cultivated and respected writer, and stage performer. A woman who was immensely proud of her Native ancestry and raised awareness of Native heritage. Her publications include collections of poems called *White Wampum* (1895), *Canadian Born* (1903), *Flint and Feather* (1912); a volume of Native stories, *Legends of Vancouver* (1911); and a novel entitled *The Shagganappi* (1913).[169]

The Historic Sites and Monuments of Canada recognized E. Pauline Johnson as a national historic person in 1945, and on the hundredth anniversary of her birth Canada Post issued a commemorative stamp. Pauline Johnson continues to be a popular figure in Canadian history.[170]

Quote:

"My aim, my joy, my pride is to sing the glories of my people. Ours was the race that gave the world its measure of heroism, its standard of physical prowess. Ours was the race that taught the world that avarice veiled by any name is crime. Ours were the people of the blue air and the green woods, and ours the faith that taught men to live without greed and to die without fear."[171]

Dr. Leonora King.

A Mandarin in Imperial China

Leonora Howard King
1851–1925

In a life described as "something out of *The Arabian Nights*,"[172] a determined Canadian devoted herself to China.

Move over Norman Bethune! What about Dr. Leonora King, the first Canadian to practise medicine in China[173] — where she stayed for forty-seven years despite wars, famines, and floods? The Empress Dowager of Imperial China recognized King's contributions to her adopted homeland by appointing her a Mandarin — akin to a knighthood. Dr. Leonora King became the first woman to achieve such an honour.[174]

Born in Farmersville (now Athens), Ontario, Leonora Howard became a teacher but wanted to become a doctor. Unable to study medicine in Canada because of her gender, Leonora graduated as an M.D. from the University of Michigan Women's Medical College and set sail for Shanghai in 1877 with the backing of the Woman's Foreign Missionary Society (WFMS). She began working as a doctor in Imperial China more than sixty years before the famous Dr. Norman Bethune. Stationed at a Methodist mission in Peking for two years, Leonora was soon the sole physician managing its small hospital for women and children. She also travelled by Peking cart or mule to treat poor Chinese patients in villages up to hundreds of kilometres away.

In 1879 Dr. Howard was summoned to attend the seriously ill wife of Li Hung-chang, Viceroy of Chihli province, in Tientsin. Leonora cured Lady Li, gaining the support and protection of the influential couple. Lady Li provided her healer with part of Tseng Kuo-fan's memorial temple, where Dr. Howard opened the first Chinese hospital for women and children. Thanks to some wealthy sponsors in Baltimore, she was able to open a larger and more modern facility several years later: the Isabella Fisher Hospital for Women and Children. In 1884 Leonora married a widowed Scottish missionary, Rev. Alexander King of the London Missionary Society. She became Dr. King and had to resign from the WFMS, as it was expected that wives should assist the missions of their husbands. Leonora also had to leave the hospital she had developed.

Lady Li decided to build a new hospital for Leonora. Opened in 1885 under the direction of Dr. Leonora King, the Government Hospital for Women and Children in Tientsin was the first such facility financed with Chinese funds. With the outbreak of the Sino-Japanese war, the hard-working doctor devoted herself to treating those wounded in the conflict. In 1889 she was awarded the Imperial Chinese Order of the Double Dragon, making the courageous Canadian a Mandarin. Leonora received a ceremonial umbrella used to announce important people and was now entitled to wear ermine, as were Chinese royalty.

In later years Dr. King operated three free clinics as well as her hospital. In 1908 she opened the Government Medical School for Women, a Chinese-sponsored facility that trained doctors and nurses. During decades of working in China Leonora never charged for her services. It is a reflection of her abilities that she worked primarily independently of the missions — with impressive support from her host country. Recognized as a strong but gentle doctor who genuinely cared about the people of China, she refused to leave even when her city was under siege, missionaries were being murdered, and her home was attacked. The Kings officially retired in 1916, and in 1923 they visited relatives in Ontario. The couple planned to move there but Leonora died of flu before final arrangements were completed.

At the time of her death Leonora was hailed as a heroine in both Canada and China.[175] The significant accomplishments of Dr. Leonora King were forgotten until author Margaret Negodaeff-Tomsik wrote a book about this outstanding doctor in 1999. Previously unknown to the Canadian Medical Association, Dr. King was soon after inducted to the Canadian Medical Hall of Fame.

Quote:

"I am much stronger than was the case one month ago, and shall be satisfied to do the best I can alone, if you can only get a physician for Pekin [sic]."[176]

A report by Leonora Howard King to the WFMS
following her recovery from malaria.

Ride 'em Cowgirl
Flores La Due
1883–1951

Flores La Due.

She was a talented rodeo star — a world champion known to millions.

Grace Bensell ran away from home to join the circus. After her father left for work one day she disappeared in a stagecoach, making sure to sweep away the tracks with a broom to ensure she wasn't followed. The runaway adopted the stage name Flores La Due.

Grace Maud Bensell was born on an Indian reservation near Montevideo, Minnesota, where her father, Charles Bensell, was an Indian Agent.[177] An only child, whose mother died when she was young, Grace learned to ride horses at an early age and was an expert rider and roper. She spent a lot of time on the ranches owned by her father in Minnesota and South Dakota. Charles Bensell, who became a wealthy lawyer and then a prominent judge, strongly disapproved of his daughter's plans to become a performer.

After a few seasons in a travelling circus, Flores joined the Col. Fred T. Cummin's Wild West and Indian Congress as a trick rider and roper. While touring with these vaudeville shows she met a handsome, sweet-talkin' cowboy called Guy Weadick. The pair married in Memphis, Tennessee, in 1906, when Flores was twenty-three. She later had a stint working with the famous cowboy Will Rogers. The talented Weadicks performed together in vaudeville for nearly twenty years and also toured with Wild West shows, including the renowned Miller Brothers 101 Ranch Wild West. The couple lived like gypsies, showing their tricks to enthusiastic audiences across North America and Europe — including London, Glasgow, Berlin, St. Petersburg, Moscow, Odessa, Vienna, and Paris.

Flores La Due is reputed to be the "greatest woman trick and fancy roper of all time" and the first woman to perform the challenging Texas Skip — in which she jumped from side to side in a spinning loop of rope.[178] She shone as a horsewoman, doing trick stunts on her horse while performing rope tricks. As one observer reported:

> The most impressive of the cowgirls is Miss Florence La Due ... Florence is distinctly accomplished in prairie pastimes. She can "rope" [lasso] a running horse, steer, or even a man with the best cowboy going, and she can make the lariat do all sorts of twists, loops, and turns, and she can shoot "some."[179]

Flores was also an accomplished rodeo competitor. When her husband, Guy Weadick, produced the first Calgary Stampede in 1912, Flores earned the title of World Champion Trick and Fancy Roper. She earned two more championships in the event and retired undefeated. The petite cowgirl, barely five feet high, was a tough and talented athlete who made rodeo history.

In 1920 the Weadicks decided they needed to establish a home base. They purchased the Stampede Ranch in the Alberta foothills along the Highwood River, where they raised cattle and horses, operated a dude ranch, and provided the set for some movies. Mrs. Weadick, as she was always called on the ranch, managed the operation while Guy looked after other projects. The couple would spend the winters on the vaudeville circuit and the remainder of the year at their ranch. They welcomed visitors from around the world, including the Prince of Wales, who had purchased a nearby ranch. Flores taught the man who became King Edward VIII some rope tricks and reported that "Despite all the talk about his falling off horses, the King is a very good horseman."[180]

Flores La Due died of a heart attack in 1951 and was buried in High River, Alberta, beside her father, who had long ago forgiven the independent girl who joined the circus. A successful rancher, dazzling performer in Wild West shows, and champion competitor, the remarkable cowgirl played an important role in the development of rodeo in Western Canada and was widely known for her amazing skills in the art of trick and fancy roping. In 2001 the pioneer rodeo star was inducted into the National Cowgirl Museum and Hall of Fame in Fort Worth, Texas — which honours extraordinary women with the cowgirl spirit.

Quote:

"I wanted to ride so I started when I was four. They said a rider had to clean the stables. So I did."[181]

Flores La Due performing fancy rope tricks at the Calgary Exhibition and Stampede.

Landing in the Forbidden City

Mrs. Kwong Lee
(Mrs. Lee Chong)
18__ – ?

Her life is a puzzle with most of the pieces missing. We do not even know her first name.

This portrait was taken in Victoria in the 1870s, when there were few Chinese women there. Note her bound feet and particularly long nails. Could she possibly have been Mrs. Kwong Lee?

Mrs. Kwong Lee was the first Chinese woman to come to Canada and was not soon followed by many others.[182] She was a notable pioneer in a migration that has changed the face of Canada, where Chinese people are now the largest visible minority.

Mrs. Kwong Lee arrived in the town of Victoria on February 29, 1860.[183] Travelling from San Francisco with her two children, she came to join her husband — a prominent merchant who was one of the few Chinese men who could afford to bring his family to join him.

Mrs. Kwong Lee landed in the crown colony of British Columbia, where the Hudson's Bay Company had established Fort Victoria as a coastal trading post in 1843. Her husband was among the early arrivals after the discovery of gold in the Fraser River transformed the frontier settlement into a bustling centre of commerce that served miners bound for the interior.[184] Victoria's first Chinese immigrants were goldseekers, but there was also an important group of businesses from San Francisco that dominated the Chinese economy during the gold rushes.

By 1861 the biggest Chinese import and export company in Victoria was Kwong Lee & Co., whose branch office was operated by Lee Chong and Tong Fat. Lee Chong apparently played a key role in the business and became the face most commonly associated with it. Hence he was popularly known as "Kwong Lee."

Mrs. Kwong Lee and her two children would presumably have settled in Chinatown — a collection of tents and shacks on mud flats along the north bank of the Johnson Street ravine. Outsiders knew the community as Forbidden City, since few non-Chinese were likely to venture there. As Chinatown developed it included opium joints and gambling dens, secret hideouts and hidden passageways, stores, cafes, and tenements.[185] Considering Kwong Lee's situation as a merchant of means it would be expected that Mrs. Kwong Lee and the children would be housed in one of the best wooden structures in Chinatown.

Kwong Lee & Co. was based on Cormorant Street, where "Kwong Lee" and his associates arranged for the arrival of workers and goods. They served as bankers for the men working the goldfields or elsewhere, holding their money while they were working in the interior and sending back regular payments to family members still in China. The company was also involved in land speculation and development, as well as the lucrative importation and manufacturing of opium. The latter was legal in Canada until 1908. The Forbidden City's notorious Fan Tan Alley, named after a Chinese gambling game, was the site of both the Kwong Lee and Tai Soong opium factories.

As the lone woman in the Forbidden City, Mrs. Kwong Lee would likely have lived a fairly isolated life when she arrived. She was in a strange environment without support in a world where a Chinese woman was not usually seen outside her home. Living in a town where the Forbidden City was considered a slum, where Chinese men were often sneered at in the streets and called chinks, yellowbellies, and yellow pagans.

Mrs. Kwong Lee's husband was a notable exception in Victoria, though it is not certain how his status might have affected her life in the community. In the early 1860s Kwong Lee was the most influential leader in the Chinese community, a man respected in Victoria as well-educated, courteous, and highly intelligent. He was a reputable businessman who spoke English fluently — and "free from Yankee twang and slang."[186] Kwong Lee was frequently mentioned in local newspapers, and a few days after his wife arrived he and two other Chinese businessmen met with Governor Douglas to express concerns about a poll tax on Chinese immigrants to Canada.

By 1861 Mrs. Kwong Lee would have known one other Chinese woman in the Forbidden City: Mrs. Cumyow. She gave birth to son Won Alexander Cumyow, who was the first Chinese child born in Canada.[187] A decade later the Chinese population of Victoria was 211, with just 30 females.[188] If Mrs. Kwong Lee was still living there she would have had the company of other Chinese women in the community, though presumably at least some were prostitutes working in the brothels and therefore not likely involved in her life. It continued to be practically impossible for all but wealthy Chinese men to bring their families to join them, and the situation worsened when the federal government introduced the Act to Restrict and Regulate Chinese Immigration into Canada in 1885, with a $50 head tax for every new arrival.

Mrs. Kwong Lee made a notable contribution to Canadian history by becoming the first Chinese woman to settle in Canada. Sadly, this pioneer's story has not been preserved, and we may never know her impressions of life in the Forbidden City.

After the King of Siam
Anna Leonowens
1831–1915

Anna Leonowens, ca. 1862.

Whatever happened to Anna? Goodbye King Mongkut and hello Canada.

Many remember her tale — the glamorous governess in *Anna and the King of Siam*. Perhaps you saw the Rogers and Hammerstein Broadway musical or the more recent movie version with Jody Foster. These popular productions were adapted from the real life experiences of a woman called Anna Leonowens, who wrote about them with considerable embellishment. Audiences around the globe have been enthralled by her adventures in Siam.

Few may know that Anna moved to Halifax in 1878 and became a notable Canadian feminist. She spent most of the next thirty-seven years of her life in Canada, passing away in Montreal in 1915.

Born in India, Anna Harriette Edwards grew up in the barracks of the East India Company where her father served as a soldier.[189] At the age of eighteen she married Thomas Leon Owens, a clerk, and the couple apparently lived in England and Australia before settling in Malaysia. They had four children — two of whom died in infancy. When Thomas suddenly passed away ten years after their marriage, Anna was left to support two small children: Avis and Louis. It seems the widow taught school before landing a job at the Siamese Court three years later.

Anna sent her daughter off to boarding school in Britain, and she and Louis arrived in Bangkok in 1862. They entered an exotic world of shimmering temples and glittering mosaics, ornate gardens, saffron-robed monks, towering statues of Buddha, and ancient and unfamiliar Thai customs. Slaves, corruption, wealth, and intrigue — and the Grand Palace complex. Anna began her new position here as governess in the household of King Mongkut of Siam, teaching his many offspring — numbering more than sixty at the time — and some of the six hundred wives in his harem.

After her famous five years in Siam, Anna moved to New York City. She trained kindergarten teachers and wrote a variety of works about her experiences. Once establishing herself as a competent author, Anna Leonowens became a popular speaker on a lecture circuit. Throughout her life she was an aggressive self-promoter, not averse to changing the facts in her favour. Suggestions have been made that she was trying to conceal her relatively humble origins and possibly a mixed racial origin.[190]

When her daughter, Avis, and son-in-law, Thomas Fyshe, moved to Halifax, Anna joined them. In addition to devoting considerable attention to ensuring an exceptional education for her grandchildren, Anna continued to write: she travelled to Russia in 1881 on contract to report on the assassination of Emperor Alexander II.

Anna Leonowens was very active in the Halifax community, where she created the Pioneer Book Club and the Shakespeare Club for young women. After overseeing fundraising for a planned Victoria School of Art and Design, she became the institution's first director. The school now known as the Nova Scotia College of Art & Design includes the Anna Leonowens Gallery.

Beginning in 1894, Anna began to play an influential role in the Halifax Local Council of Women (which had been created by Edith Jessie Archibald and others). When the Women's Suffrage Association was established in March 1895, Anna Leonowens became president. An articulate woman with an international reputation as an author, she appeared as the most visible leader of Halifax feminists.[191] When the National Council of Women of Canada met for their annual meeting in June 1897 in Halifax, Anna, as always, drew considerable attention — though some called her a "regular Tartar." She worked on many campaigns, such as improving conditions for female prisoners, appointing a matron to assist with new immigrants, and gaining the vote for women.

Anna moved in 1901 to Montreal, where the Fyshe family had settled. Thomas was now employed by the Merchants' Bank of Canada and became general manager. The family lived in an elegant district on McTavish Street. Anna gave lectures in Montreal and became involved with the Baby and Foundling Hospital.

Tragedy struck when Anna's daughter died of food poisoning in 1902 and her son-in-law passed away in 1911. An aging Anna soon suffered a stroke and lost her sight. Relatively few noted the death of Anna Leonowens in 1915, following years of illness; but with the 1944 publication of the book *Anna and the King of Siam* by Margaret Dorothea Landon and the subsequent Broadway musical and films, the wonderful adventures of Anna the governess charmed a new generation of admirers.

Most of Anna's colourful life is relatively unknown, as are her contributions as an articulate and aggressive spokesperson for many worthwhile causes in Canada. *The Chronicle* newspaper in Halifax once reported Anna Leonowens was "one of the busiest women in the city ... never too busy to render assistance in every good work."[192] She was also an intrepid world traveller who could speak eleven languages, a powerful public speaker, and passionate promoter of freedom and equal rights — a woman who dared to speak her mind about injustice, whether it was to the King of Siam or anyone else.

Quote:

"...women have not only proved their capacity for governing great nations, but have shewn [sic] wonderful capacity for affairs and proved herself to be a true helpmeet and coworker, instead of a servant and plaything of a man!"[193]

Anna Leonowens referring to the achievements of Queen Victoria, in a speech supporting the vote for women.

Funniest Woman in the World
Beatrice Lillie
1894–1989

Beatrice Lillie.

She was the Queen of Comedy, a clown that Chaplin called "his female counterpart."[194]

Mumsie had great hopes for Beatrice Lillie's older sister Muriel, who was a talented pianist. But Beatrice was a prankster — prone to antics like running after fire engines, playing under a freight car, and doing tricks that got her expelled from the church choir. Despite Mrs. Lillie's expectations, it was Bea who became an international star.

Beatrice Lillie was born May 29, 1894, in Toronto at 68 Dovercourt Road, a home she described as "a red-brick house with a garden as big as a handkerchief in front and a yard the size of a postal card to the rear."[195] Her father was an Irishman from Belfast, while Mumsie (Lucie) came from England. Bea grew up loving the Canadian National Exhibition, summer trips to her grandparents' Muskoka cottage, and movies — which she earned money to attend by running errands, collecting old clothes for the rag man, and singing for shopkeepers. Beatrice reluctantly attended Gladstone Avenue School in Toronto (where Mary Pickford had been a pupil a few years earlier) and St. Agnes College in Belleville, Ontario. As Bea later wrote in her autobiography, "aspiration kept nudging me toward the stage; legislation demanded that girls of my age had to go to school. Of course, the law won..."[196]

Pushed towards a theatrical career by her ambitious mother, the young Bea was busy taking music and voice lessons, singing in Sunday school concerts, and performing in holiday shows. Mumsie chose the Rich Concert & Entertainment Bureau in Toronto to manage the careers of the three Lillie ladies: Lucie the star, Muriel the pianist, and Bea the singer. The proprietor, Mr. Harry Rich, also trained Bea in "dramatic gesture, elocution and mime."[197] A former concert comedian confined to a wheelchair after an accident, Rich taught her that every gesture had to have meaning. Beatrice Lillie later acknowledged Rich's great importance in developing her comedic genius: "I was brought up to do things his way, and now I confess I am grateful."[198]

After limited success touring as "The Lillie Trio" around Ontario, Mumsie and her two daughters headed to England — primarily so Muriel could prepare for a concert career. With the goal of becoming a singer, Beatrice Lillie was soon hired for a series of wartime revues produced by the celebrated Andre Charlot in London. She made her debut in October 1914 in Charlot's *Not Likely* and discovered she could make people laugh. She married into the British aristocracy in 1920, wedding Robert Peel and later giving birth to their son Bobbie. With the death of her father-in-law Bea gained the title of Lady Peel.

Beatrice Lillie debuted in New York in 1924 as one of the top performers in *Andre Charlot's Revue of 1924*, along with Gertrude Lawrence and Jack Buchanan. The show opened at the Times Square Theatre, bringing great reviews and making Bea a popular star on Broadway. By 1932 she had appeared in seventeen stage productions on both sides of the Atlantic, bringing her zany humour to thousands of enthusiastic fans. Critics dubbed her "the smartest female in Funnydom."[199]

During World War II Beatrice Lillie performed with her usual spunk for troops in France, Germany, Africa, and the Middle East. Glad to keep busy during these difficult years, Bea didn't mind being "jounced about in trucks and lorries, with and without springs, playing rain or shine, wherever there was an audience wanting to see us, in the sizzling heat of the day or the chill of the night."[200] In recognition of her contribution Bea later received the African Star from General de Gaulle.

Beatrice's son joined the Royal Navy during World War II and she was devastated to learn of his death in 1942; her husband had died in 1934, leaving her with significant debts and many unhappy memories.

Beatrice Lillie continued to be an incredibly popular performer following the war, gaining fame as "The Toast of Two Continents." During her career Bea starred in productions showcasing the works of her friends Noel Coward and George Bernard Shaw, as well as Cole Porter, Richard Rodgers and Lorenz Hart, Arthur Schwartz, and Howard Ditez. Charlie Chaplin was a friend and fellow buffoon whom she occasionally improvised with at parties.

Beatrice Lillie's notable performances on Broadway included the extravagant *Seven Lively Arts*, produced by Billy Rose at the Ziegfeld Theatre. One of her greatest successes was her show *An Evening with Beatrice Lillie*, which she began in 1952 and ended up touring until the fall of 1955. The show earned Lillie a Tony Award.

In addition to her stage work, Beatrice Lillie was also active in recording radio, television, and film. She sang as if "drunken fairies hit her over the head with a golden hammer" according to one critic, in a style deemed "utterly mad," and unique to Lillie.[201] She performed on radio shows with the likes of Bing Crosby and Milton Berle. On television she appeared frequently on programs hosted by Arthur Murray, Jack Paar, Merv Griffin, Johnny Carson, Bob Hope, and Ed Sullivan. Bea had a few films to her credit; from silent features to the 1967 movie *Thoroughly Modern Millie* starring Julie Andrews and Mary Tyler Moore, but Beatrice Lillie was at her best with a live audience.

Lady Peel appeared in her final stage production when she was approaching the age of seventy-one, playing Madame Arcati in the musical *High Spirits*. Theatre historian Stanley Green identified Bea as one of the top ten comic characters of Broadway. Critics around the world shared his views of the remarkably talented lady: "one of the greatest clowns of all time" (William Hawkins of *World-Telegram & Sun*). Both Brooks Atkinson (*Times*) and John McClain (*Journal-American*) gave her the title to which she was most commonly referred to: "the funniest woman in the world."[202]

Beatrice Lillie was a notable Canadian who earned international acclaim for her artistic genius in the field of comedy. As Bea noted in her autobiography, she was "a kid from the Canadian sticks"[203] who honed her skills in downtown Toronto and Ontario communities from Niagara Falls to North Bay. The only Canadian commemoration of this heroine of the entertainment world seems to be the 1989 naming of a Toronto public health office in her honour.

Quote:

"Television without an audience is like doing summer stock in an iron lung."[204]

A Chinese Voice

Jean Lumb
1919–2002

Jean Lumb.

A strong believer in the family, she lobbied to ensure that Chinese Canadians could bring over their loved ones from China.

If Prime Minister John Diefenbaker hadn't had trouble hearing in one ear, Jean Lumb might not have become an important spokesperson for Chinese Canadians. Jean was one of twenty people — and the only woman — selected by the Chinese community to present their concerns about immigration restrictions to the federal government in 1957. Fun Sing Wong, the leader of the group, happened to be seated beside Diefenbaker's bad ear and Jean was on the other side. The Chief kept asking Jean to repeat what Wong said in the brief. Since Jean had helped prepare the presentation and had memorized it, she easily repeated the plea for changes to the law, which would help reunite Chinese families. "The change to the immigration laws was my greatest accomplishment," said Jean.[205]

Jean was born in Nanaimo, British Columbia, in 1919 as Wong Toy Jin. As a child she had a registration card with her picture, as the 1923 Exclusion Act required all Chinese living in Canada to be registered. After arriving from China in 1899, Jean's father had worked as a labourer for a landowner who soon helped him bring over his wife and eldest son. Her father became a coal miner before settling the Wong family in Vancouver, where the parents and twelve children lived in a small apartment and operated a fruit store.

Jean was devastated at having to quit school at age twelve to work in the store. A few years later she moved to Toronto to work for her recently married older sister and at seventeen opened her own fruit store. As her business prospered the young entrepreneur moved her family from Vancouver to Toronto. Thanks to the efforts of a matchmaker, in 1939 Jean married Doyle Lumb — a determined Chinese emigrant who managed to enter Canada before the Exclusion Act by lying about his age and paying a $500 head tax. The happy couple raised six children while managing a grocery store for twenty years and then operating the successful Kwong Chow restaurant in Toronto's Chinatown.

Jean Lumb also became a prominent political activist and community volunteer, primarily because of the influence of her father — who had been so eager to be fully involved in his new homeland. In addition to lobbying for changes to immigration laws, Jean became president of the Women's Association in the Chinese community in 1940 and started the Chinese Community Dancers of Ontario. In the late 1960s Jean Lumb led a successful campaign to save Toronto's Chinatown, and was later involved in similar efforts in Vancouver and Calgary.

Jean supported many Chinese organizations before deciding to volunteer outside the Chinese community — a move she was encouraged to take by Pauline McGibbon, the future lieutenant-governor of Ontario. Jean Lumb became active in a multitude of organizations, serving on the governing boards of such groups as the Women's College Hospital and University Settlement House. Jean also worked as a Citizenship Court Judge.

"She is one of Toronto's greatest heroes," said former Toronto mayor David Crombie.[206] Because of her important contributions to her community and to Canada, Jean Lumb received many awards prior to her death in 2002. Jean was particularly proud to receive the Order of Canada in 1976 — becoming the first Chinese Canadian recipient. The annual Jean Lumb Awards of Excellence were created to honour the accomplishments of this remarkable Canadian.

Quote:

"What do I have to do to be accepted? I'm always looking in from the outside."[207]

Jean Lumb as a child.

Our Matron-in-Chief

Major Margaret C. Macdonald
1873–1948

Margaret Macdonald.

She cared for the sick and wounded on the major battlefields of her time.

Just call her Major. When Margaret Macdonald was promoted to Matron-in-Chief of the Canadian Nursing Service in 1914 she became the first woman in the British Empire to attain the rank of Major.[208]

Major Macdonald was an outstanding military nurse in a career that spanned nearly thirty years.[209] Born in her family's home at Bailey's Brook, Nova Scotia, Margaret graduated as a nurse from the New York City Hospital in 1895. During the Spanish-American War she cared for wounded soldiers on an American hospital ship and in military hospitals. After the outbreak of the Boer War in South Africa Margaret Macdonald served there with the Canadian Nursing Service, part of the Army Medical Corps, from 1900 to 1902. On completing some post-graduate training in New York City she spent eighteen gruelling months in Panama, where she had volunteered to serve during the building of the canal. Nurse Macdonald caught malaria, but insisted on returning to Panama after her recovery.

In 1906 Margaret Macdonald, along with Georgina Pope, was appointed to the permanent Army Medical Corps. Nurse Macdonald worked at military hospitals in Quebec City, Kingston, and Halifax. She also spent six months in England learning about the military hospitals there and the organization of the British military medical services. By the outbreak of the First World War, Margaret Macdonald was a well-trained military nurse with considerable field experience. She replaced Georgina Pope as Matron of the Canadian Nursing Service and began selecting the one hundred nurses to be sent to Great Britain in 1914 with the first Canadian troops.

Soon promoted to Matron-in-Chief, Margaret Macdonald proved to be a competent administrator who efficiently oversaw the expansion of a system of nurses that went from five in 1914 to about 1,900 at the time of the Armistice. Based in London, she was responsible for all Canadian military nurses overseas. Matron Macdonald deployed Canadian nurses to hospitals, hospital ships, and trains throughout Britain and worked closely with British Matron Maud McCarthy, who coordinated medical services in France. In recognition of Matron Macdonald's impressive wartime service King George V presented her with the Royal Red Cross in 1915. She later received the Florence Nightingale Medal.

Matron Macdonald returned to Canada in the fall of 1919 and participated in the reorganization of the Canadian Army Medical Service. All nursing sisters who had served in World War I were discharged by 1922 and Matron Macdonald retired the following year at age fifty-one. During the remainder of her life Margaret Macdonald travelled widely and received many honours, including an honorary degree of D.D.L. from Saint Francis Xavier University and an honorary lifetime membership in the National Council of Women of Canada. In 1926 the highly respected nurse participated in a moving ceremony on Parliament Hill. After a bugle sounded the last post, eight hundred nurses from across the country watched Margaret Macdonald unveil the Memorial to the Canadian Nursing Sisters. The sculpted marble panel depicts the history of Canadian nurses.

Major Margaret Macdonald died in 1948 in the house where she was born. The Historic Sites and Monuments Board of Canada recognized her as a national historic person of Canada and erected a commemorative plaque in Bailey's Brook, Nova Scotia, in 1983.

Quote:

"During the cruel bombing of the Canadian Hospitals came experiences of the most frightening, the recollection of which must ever remain painfully indelible. Yet at the time never was a complaint uttered by these valiant women who were conspicuously undismayed in remaining at their posts."[210]

Major Margaret C. Macdonald describing the courage of the Nursing Sisters during the repeated bombing of Boulogne, 1918.

Elizabeth Gregory MacGill, 1946.

Queen of the Hurricanes
Elizabeth Gregory MacGill
1905–1980

Crippled by polio, this extraordinary engineer couldn't fly the planes she designed.

Elsie was a pioneer: the first woman in the world to design and test an airplane, the Maple Leaf Trainer. She was also the first woman in Canada to receive an electrical engineering degree, and the first female in North America to earn a degree as an aeronautical engineer.

Elizabeth Gregory MacGill was born in Vancouver, the daughter of James MacGill, a lawyer, and Helen Gregory MacGill, a notable reformer and first juvenile court judge in B.C. Elsie and her sister attended public school in the coastal city, took drawing lessons from a then-unknown artist called Emily Carr,[211] swam in the ocean at English Bay just a few blocks from home, and proudly noted their mother's many reform activities. When Helen participated in a mock parliament staged to fight for suffrage, the girls appeared as parliamentary pageboys. Elsie grew up adoring her accomplished mother.

Elsie received an engineering degree from the University of Toronto in 1927 and began graduate studies in aeronautical engineering at the University of Michigan. Struck by polio, the young woman wrote her exams while in hospital. After being advised that she would never walk again, Elsie spent three years in a wheelchair before borrowing money to head back east to continue her engineering work. She completed her doctorate at the Massachusetts Institute of Technology, then did some innovative research on stress analysis of airplane wings while working at the Fairchild Aircraft Company in Montreal. For the rest of her life Dr. McGill walked with a cane; she was never able to become a pilot despite her love of flying.

Through her research, design, and construction of aircraft Elsie MacGill made a great contribution to aviation history in Canada. After the Canadian Car and Foundry Company hired her in 1938 as Chief Aeronautical Engineer, Elsie designed and tested the Maple Leaf Trainer aircraft. During World War II she supervised up to 4,500 workers in the production of about 2,000 Hawker Hurricane fighter planes — important in the Battle of Britain. Dr. MacGill earned the nickname "Queen of the Hurricanes" for this impressive accomplishment. The talented engineer also designed a winterized version of the aircraft and oversaw engineering work on the Curtiss-Wright Helldiver fighters for the United States Navy.

In 1943 Elsie married E.J. Soulsby, an aeronautics executive who was widowed with two children. The family lived in Toronto, where Dr. MacGill established an aeronautics consulting firm. After the war she became the first woman to serve as technical advisor for the (United Nations) International Aviation Organization. Elsie became the first woman corporate member of the Engineering Institute of Canada. Her engineering achievements were widely recognized by professional associations, and she received many honours: the Gzowski Medal of the Engineering Institute of Canada, the American Society of Women Engineers selection as Woman Engineer of the Year, the Order of Canada, the Julian Smith Award from the Engineering Institute of Canada, Associate Fellow of the Royal Aeronautical Society in England, and the Amelia Earhart Medal from the International Association of Women Pilots.

Elsie MacGill also took an active role in many campaigns intended to improve the status of women in Canada. A dedicated feminist, she served as president of the Canadian Federation of Business and Professional Women's Clubs and a member of the Royal Commission on the Status of Women.

Elsie Gregory MacGill died in 1980. In recognition of her outstanding career as an aeronautical engineer she was inducted into the Canadian Aviation Hall of Fame in 1983 and the Canadian Science and Engineering Hall of Fame in the 1990s.

Quote:

"I have received many engineering awards, but I hope I will also be remembered as an advocate for the rights of women and children."[212]

"Queen of the Hurricanes" comic.

Helen Gregory MacGill with daughters Helen and Elsie in Vancouver, ca. 1906.

Madam Judge
Helen Gregory MacGill
1864–1947

Millions of children — and their families — have benefited from her views on juvenile delinquency.

Helen Gregory MacGill was already an accomplished journalist and activist, as well as a mother of four, when she began her new career at the age of fifty-three. Helen became a prominent juvenile court judge, serving nearly three decades on the bench before reluctantly retiring.

Helen Gregory grew up in Hamilton in a prosperous family, where she was particularly influenced by her mother Emma's notions that women had a role to play outside the family. She was a maternal feminist who believed that "women's special role as mother gives her the duty and the right to participate in the public sphere."[213] Helen decided to become a concert pianist, and at age nineteen set off for Toronto to study music after her father was convinced that such training wouldn't make her unmarriageable. After becoming the first person to graduate with a Bachelor of Music from Trinity College she studied Arts there (the first woman allowed to attend lectures) and received an M.A.

By 1890 Helen was bound for Japan to report on political events for the *Atlantic Monthly* and *The Cosmopolitan,* with letters of introduction from family friend Sir John A. Macdonald. During her journey west the adventurous young woman explored the prairies for an assignment to do some articles for the Toronto *Globe* and secretly married a frontiersman called Frederick Charles (Lee) Flescher after a one-week courtship. The partners used the family name of Gregory-Flescher. Helen became a successful journalist, writing articles for a variety of magazines and papers before purchasing several weeklies in California, where she had moved with Lee to follow his dream of running an orchard.

Helen gave birth to two sons: Eric and Fred. Lee became a doctor after the horrendous delivery of their first child — a twelve-pounder whose arrival left Helen with severe lacerations and the possibility of permanent disability. Helen Gregory-Flescher was suddenly widowed in 1901 when Lee died of a blood infection. After his death she married a college sweetheart, lawyer James Henry MacGill, and they settled in Vancouver. The family soon included two girls: Helen and Elsie. A domineering husband who controlled the family finances, Jim worked in the wholesale grocery business, politics, and journalism, as well as a law practice. His many ventures brought little financial success to the struggling family and his speculations in real estate, using Helen's family money as well as his own funds, were disastrous. When Jim died in 1939 there was no estate to leave to his wife.

As her children were growing up in Vancouver Helen became very involved with many women's groups, fighting for suffrage and other rights. While suffrage was not the focus of her efforts, Helen was among those who played leading roles in obtaining the right to vote for women in B.C. in 1917. Helen MacGill also spearheaded the project to provide meeting space for local clubwomen, a venture that brought twenty women's organizations together in 1911 to establish the Vancouver Women's Building Ltd. — and open a new building in 1926. Helen became an active member of the University Women's Club of Vancouver soon after it was founded. It was through this organization that Helen undertook her first investigations of women and the law.

Shocked to learn that a married woman did not have custody of her children — the father being sole guardian — she began learning about the legal status of women and children and became a self-taught expert on the subject. Thanks to Helen's leadership, the provincial government repealed the dower law and made significant improvements to inheritance and guardianship laws. She also contributed to laws that guaranteed minimum wages for women.

Helen Gregory MacGill was appointed as the first female juvenile court judge in British Columbia in 1917 and gained international recognition as an expert in the field of juvenile delinquency. It was in this area that Judge MacGill made her most significant contribution. She attributed juvenile delinquency to family breakdowns and poverty, and worked for improvements in the social welfare system as a means of reducing crime. She believed that juvenile offenders should be put on probation whenever possible so they could receive the help they needed. Helen also campaigned to get more family involvement in the court, more probation officers, and more female police officers. She helped build B.C.'s family court system, and her proposals for legislation influenced the development of legal systems in both Canada and the United States.

Judge MacGill received many honours during her life and following her death. She was especially touched when the University of British Columbia awarded her an honorary L.L.D. in 1938. In response to Helen's worries that she did not have the $100 to pay for the required regalia, friends at the University Women's Club presented it to her as a gift. The *Vancouver Province* noted that UBC "has rewarded a lifetime of courage, devotion and self-sacrifice."[214] Helen's remarkable career no doubt inspired many young women, including her own daughters: Elsie MacGill became a notable aeronautical engineer (see Elizabeth MacGill, page 142), while Helen MacGill Hughes was a pioneer sociologist, editor, and writer.

"No single woman in Canada has made a greater contribution to the solution of social problems of children than Judge MacGill by her education of public opinion and her personal work in juvenile courts," reported the Quebec *Chronicle-Telegraph* after her death in 1947.[215] The Historic Sites and Monuments Board recognized Helen Gregory MacGill as a national historic person of Canada in 1998.

Quote:

"Most of us do not attempt to realize a fraction of our capabilities. Yet most of us could live not one but many different kinds of lives, each full, intense and complete."[216]

Mining Dynamo

Viola MacMillan
1903–1993

Viola MacMillan.

A self-made millionaire, she became a legend in the Canadian mining industry.

Viola was a hustler — in the finest sense of the word.

She was the thirteenth of fifteen children born in the family of Thomas Huggard, an illiterate farmer struggling to survive in the Muskoka Lakes resort area of Ontario.[217] Forced to quit school at the age of twelve to work on the farm, Viola Huggard spent long days doing chores and helping her mother scrub floors in nearby hotels. The young girl dreamed of returning to school and becoming a stenographer like some of the guests she saw. She eventually achieved her goal and landed a job in a law office in Windsor. In 1923 Viola married George MacMillan, a fellow from Northern Ontario who had begun working in a lumber camp when he was fourteen.

Viola soon decided to make her career in mining and prospecting, despite her success moonlighting in the real estate business. She was thrilled by her experience going underground in a mine at Cobalt (disguised as a man since it was considered bad luck for a woman to go down in the mines) and helping George do some assessment work on a mining claim for a relative. The MacMillans began spending their summers prospecting in the Ontario bush and Viola discovered they could finance their trips by creating syndicates. An energetic entrepreneur, Viola formed her first company in 1933 and began selling mining shares out of her office in Timmins.

The rest is herstory. Viola MacMillan was so effective at staking claims during staking bees that other prospectors dubbed her "the Queen Bee." She was a gambler who followed her hunches and eventually hit pay dirt. An expert locator and developer of mines, Viola was behind the discovery of the Hallnor and Canadian Arrow gold mines. She developed the Kam-Kotia base metal mine in Ontario, the Lake Cinch uranium mine in Saskatchewan, and the silver and lead deposits near Slocan Lake, British Columbia.

Viola MacMillan made important contributions to the mining industry in Canada, most notably in developing the Prospectors and Developers Association (PDA) from a group with only a handful of members to a dynamic organization with more than four thousand. Members in the male-dominated mining industry elected Viola as president of the PDA in 1944, a role she held for twenty years. Every year when she took the podium the members serenaded her with the tune "Let Me Call You Sweetheart."

Viola championed Canadian prospectors throughout her career and helped shape public policy. During World War II she convinced officials in the federal government to supply geologists to teach prospectors how to identify strategic minerals needed to support the war. She was active in the Wartime Metals Control Commission and after the armistice convinced the federal government to prevent catastrophe in the gold mining industry by adopting the Emergency Gold Mining Assistance Act. Outside of the mining world, Viola MacMillan also volunteered with the Women's College Hospital for several decades.

In the mid-1960s Viola MacMillan found herself in the midst of the Windfall Affair — a mining scandal that hit the front page of papers across Canada. Both Viola and George were charged with fraud but were acquitted. Viola was, however, convicted of insider trading violations in another case in 1967 and sentenced to nine months in reformatory. At the age of sixty-four the ailing Viola, who had previously suffered a heart attack, was put in prison. She served nine weeks before being paroled and eventually received a full pardon. While some critics still believe the mining giant was a scoundrel,[218] others feel Viola was a scapegoat at a time when the practice called "wash trading" was commonplace and no one else was charged for the tactic.

In 1978 the Canadian Institute of Mining and Metallurgy, an organization that once refused membership to Viola because she was a woman, designated her as a Life Member because of her service to the Institute and the mineral industry. In 1982 a nervous Viola MacMillan attended her first public function since the Windfall Affair — the fiftieth anniversary of the Prospectors & Developers Association of Canada (PDAC).[219] She wept as members gave her a standing ovation.

The mining giant provided $1.25 million to help buy one of the greatest mineral collections in the world for Canada, and the National Museum of Natural Sciences established the Viola MacMillan National Mineral Exhibition Gallery. Viola became the first woman inducted to the Canadian Mining Hall of Fame and received the Order of Canada on her ninetieth birthday. She died a few months later.

Each year the PDAC presents the Viola R. MacMillan Developers Award in her honour. In July 1998 *Maclean's* magazine identified Viola MacMillan as one of the hundred most important people in Canadian history.[220] She is regarded by many as a remarkable heroine of the mining industry.

Quote:

"...[going underground in a mine] was one of the most glorious experiences of my lifetime, and I was completely hooked on the glamour of mining."[221]

Viola MacMillan remembering her explorations in a silver mine at Cobalt, during the summer of 1922.

University of Toronto Archives A73-0026/293 (37)

Health Heroine
Helen MacMurchy
1862–1953

Helen MacMurchy.

She fought for mothers dying in childbirth, babies who didn't live to celebrate their first birthdays, and people who were called the "feebleminded."

Many a mother gained good advice thanks to Helen MacMurchy. Her popular publication *The Canadian Mothers' Book* could be obtained free of charge in the baby carriage departments of at least some Eaton's stores, or ordered when you registered the birth of your child.[222] In 1926 alone over seventy-two thousand copies were distributed to women across Canada. Dr. Helen MacMurchy was an exceptional woman who made a difference in the lives of many generations of Canadians because of the reforms she supported. She was an influential promoter of improvements in health care, whose work led to more federal involvement in public health and better services for women and children.[223]

Helen grew up in Toronto, the daughter of an authoritarian, anti-feminist father and a mother determined that her daughters would be as well-educated as any boys. She attended the Female Department of the Toronto Collegiate Institute (now Jarvis Collegiate), where her autocratic father, Archibald MacMurchy, served as principal. Helen spent the first twenty years of her working life as a school teacher, living with her parents as was deemed appropriate for an unmarried woman. Through her experiences as a teacher she witnessed first-hand the ridiculing of mentally handicapped children, the problems of poor students, and the rapid spread of infectious diseases in the classroom.

Helen MacMurchy decided to become a medical doctor, graduating at age thirty-nine from the University of Toronto with first-class honours in medicine and surgery. She is believed to be the first woman accepted to intern at Toronto General Hospital. Dr. MacMurchy continued her studies through postgraduate work at the prestigious Johns Hopkins Hospital in Baltimore and the Women's Medical College in Philadelphia.

Dr. MacMurchy began a private medical practice but became very involved in the public health movement. As a female physician she was able to play an important role in bringing the concerns of women's groups to the medical profession. In 1906 she was appointed as Ontario's first Inspector of the Feebleminded, a role she filled until 1919. From 1911-34 she also served as a special investigator on infant mortality in Ontario. When Dr. MacMurchy accepted a job as Chief of the Division of Child Welfare, in the federal Department of Health in 1920, she held the highest position of any woman in the Canadian civil service. Many important public health reforms were made during her fourteen years in the department.

Helen MacMurchy became a national figure, prominent because of her important research, lectures, writings, and lobbying on health issues. She was particularly well-known for her Blue Books (including *The Canadian Mother's Book*), a popular series of sixteen pamphlets which provided useful advice for Canadian mothers. In these publications the physician suggested such novel ideas as greater involvement of fathers in bringing up children, quality time with the family, and attention to the emotional needs of the young. She promoted many things that we take for granted today such as pasteurization of milk, prenatal checkups for pregnant women, vaccinations for children, health clinics for babies, and financial support for poor mothers.

Dr. MacMurchy was also active in many women's groups and served as first president of the Federation of Medical Women of Canada. From 1890 to 1920 she was one of the most notable leaders in the public health movement in Canada. As historian Dianne Dodd has noted, "No other individual brought as many aspects of the public health agenda to the attention of governments, the medical profession and the public, nor achieved the degree of prominence which she attained."[224]

In recognition of her important role in the field of medicine, Dr. Helen MacMurchy received a variety of honours during her lifetime. The University of Toronto granted her an honorary degree in 1923. She was named a Companion of the Order of the British Empire in 1934, a Life Fellow of the Academy of Medicine in 1939, and "one of the twelve leading women physicians in the western world" in the Elizabeth Blackwell citation in 1949. Considered a "widely known and much loved member of the medical fraternity of Canada,"[225] Dr. Helen MacMurchy was the guest of honour at a special evening hosted by the Federation of Medical Women of Canada in 1940; a new painting of her by artist Marion Long was then unveiled and presented to the Academy of Medicine.

Helen MacMurchy died in Toronto. The Historic Sites and Monuments Board of Canada recognized her as a national historic person in 1997 because of her role as a leading advocate of public health reforms.

Quote:

"Social service consists in looking ahead as well as in setting things right, and when so many immigrants are coming to our country there is no doubt but that they need you and me to look ahead for them."[226]

On the Hill
Agnes Macphail
1890–1954

She defined our image
of what a female
politician should be,
making a fine debut as the
first woman elected to the
House of Commons.

Agnes Macphail.

She was a country girl who grew up on a farm and taught school, but when Agnes Macphail began attending meetings of the United Farmers of Ontario, her impressive public speaking skills soon attracted admirers. After the 1919 act permitting women in Canada to run for office in federal elections, some constituents asked her to stand for office in the Grey-Bruce riding in Ontario. In December 1921, Agnes Macphail was elected as a Progressive to the House of Commons — where she served until defeated in 1940.

Agnes Macphail was born in a log house in the backwoods of Grey County, Ontario, in 1890 — the eldest daughter of a Scottish couple: Douglas Macphail, who became an auctioneer, and Henrietta Campbell Macphail. Agnes claimed she inherited her father's wit and her mother's tenacity, both of which helped her on Parliament Hill.

Agnes wanted to teach school, but it took her two years to convince her parents that she should be able to go to high school in Owen Sound, after which she managed to attend a Normal School. Though she was happy as a teacher, she got drawn into political issues involving tariffs in the 1911 election.

When she entered the House of Commons a decade later as an elected member, Agnes was thirty-one years old. She was a tall woman with thick wavy brown hair. She frequently wore her navy serge dress, as she considered it appropriate attire for the man's world she was going into. Agnes Macphail soon discovered that, as the first woman member, her every action was scrutinized and reported on — and frequently ridiculed, even by women reporters. Many criticized her clothes and she was even disparaged as a "sharp-tongued spinster." In writing about her first session in the House, Agnes wrote, "I was intensely unhappy. Some members resented my intrusion, others jeered at me, while a very few were genuinely glad to see a woman in the House. Most of the members made me painfully conscious of my sex."[227]

The critics were perhaps particularly harsh because Agnes Macphail became such a competent parliamentarian, effective in championing the causes she embraced. Opponents feared her verbal attacks. She fought for disarmament, penal reform, and social welfare, always trying to help farmers, women, workers, and the underprivileged. She delivered compelling speeches that brought significant results. She made her first major speech in the House in support of striking miners in Glace Bay, Nova Scotia, in 1925, and working people in the area never forgot her help. A folk song of the twenties paid her tribute in the opening lines: "God give us more women like Agnes Macphail; When the miners were hungry she never did fail."[228]

In 1929, Agnes Macphail became the first Canadian woman to attend a League of Nations conference and the first woman to sit as a member of the Disarmament Committee. Distressed at reports of the terrible conditions in prisons, she insisted on visiting Kingston penitentiary and then reporting back to parliament. Her efforts to bring improvements in prisons led to a royal commission and eventually brought major changes. Such was the impact of her involvement that inmates at Kingston marked her death with a special tribute in their newsletter: "Aggie is dead but lives on in the hearts of countless prison inmates who knew her and loved her..."[229]

Agnes Macphail lost her seat in the House of Commons in 1940 and never quite recovered from this defeat. She had recently turned fifty and was a fine parliamentarian and a popular speaker throughout North America. Stressed by an uncertain future and tight finances, she wrote a column for the *Globe and Mail* and also did some work for the Co-operative Commonwealth Federation (CCF). Then, in 1943, she moved to the provincial political scene, winning an election in Ontario to the provincial Assembly as a CCF candidate. She and another woman became the first two female members of the provincial parliament. Despite feeling she had come down in the world after leaving federal politics, Agnes continued fighting for the many causes she believed in. She lectured about reforms needed in education and farming, helped organize the Elizabeth Fry

Society to assist women prisoners, and played a key role in the passage of the 1951 pay equity legislation in Ontario.

Agnes was in poor health by the time she lost the provincial election in 1951. Still worried about poverty, she did not qualify for a newly initiated pension for federal MPs. Prime Minister St. Laurent had advised Agnes he would appoint her as a senator in the spring of 1954 but she died of a heart attack that year.

Politics had been her career and also her life. Biographer Doris French points out that to ensure history did not remember her as the frigid spinster created in the press, Agnes included love letters in the papers she donated to the National Archives.[230] Despite romances with and proposals from several men belonging to the Progressive group in Ottawa, such as Preston Elliott and Robert Gardiner, Agnes chose to remain unmarried. Explaining her fears of losing her independence, she wrote:

> One of the outstanding features of this age is the number of intelligent women who do not marry. I have talked to hundreds of these fine, alert and very capable women in business, the professions, and the arts, and their reason was the same as mine: the person could not be subjected.[231]

Agnes Macphail made an impressive entry for Canadian women on the national political stage. The Historic Sites and Monuments Board of Canada recognized her as a national historic person in 1985, and Canada Post issued a stamp in her honour in 1990 — the centennial of her birth. The Ontario New Democratic Party's Women's Committee marked this occasion by creating an annual award in her name. Agnes Macphail is also commemorated as the first woman member of the House of Commons by a bronze bust in its North Gallery.

Quote:

"The misery of being under observation and being unduly criticized is what I remember most vividly about those first months. Visitors in the Gallery couldn't help seeing one woman among so many men, but they made no effort to disguise the fact that I was a curiosity, and stared whenever I could be seen, in the House, the corridors or the dining room. Eating was the worst; it may be they thought I would eat peas with my knife or cool my tea in my saucer, but for whatever reason I was observed closely. So closely that I lost twelve pounds in the first month..."[232]

Agnes Macphail referring to early days in the House of Commons.

Jeanne Mance.

The Hospital ThatJeanne Built

Jeanne Mance
1606–1673

Jeanne helped found one of the greatest cities in North America: Montreal. She also built its first hospital and served as Canada's first lay nurse.

At the age of thirty-five, Jeanne Mance left the comforts of her home in France for an unknown future in the wilds of the New World. Her goal was to establish a hospital in New France.

Jeanne Mance was born in Langres, France, on November 12, 1606, to attorney Charles Mance and his wife, Catherine. The family was very spiritual, and by the age of six or seven Jeanne had made a personal vow to dedicate her life to God. She was probably educated by the Ursuline nuns in Langres.[233]

After her mother died at an early age, Jeanne assumed considerable responsibility in the household until the younger children grew up. Once relieved of these obligations, Jeanne decided that she wanted to have a life of action rather than one of religious contemplation in a convent. She gained some practical experience in nursing by volunteering at a local hospital established to care for those struck down by war and the plague.

On hearing tales of the missions to New France, Jeanne Mance decided to join in. The young woman visited Paris in search of spiritual and financial support and was asked by a wealthy philanthropist — Madame de Bullion — to establish a hospital in New France. The initiative was melded with plans of the Society of Nôtre Dame of Montreal, a group eager to create a colony on the Island of Montreal. They were led by Paul de Chomedy, Sieur de Maisonneuve. Jeanne Mance instigated the creation of a written document, Plans of the Montreal Associates, prepared with the goal of winning more members and thus financial supporters for the expedition.

Thanks to her efforts membership had increased from eight to thirty-nine by the end of 1642.

Jeanne set sail from La Rochelle, arriving in Quebec on August 8, 1641, after a relatively calm crossing. As Maissoneuve's ship was less fortunate and did not arrive until the end of September, Jeanne Mance supervised the construction of temporary lodgings and a storehouse. She made the first contact with the Quebec colony and its governor, Charles Huault de Montmagny. The party wintered in Quebec because of Maissoneuve's late arrival, setting out in early May the following spring.

Jeanne Mance and Maissoneuve consulted with each other frequently about the mission and were considered the two associates in charge. When the group arrived in Montreal in May 1642, a mass was celebrated to mark the event. The workers set up camp and began construction of a fort.

Jeanne Mance's role in the Society of Nôtre Dame led her to make three voyages to France in subsequent years. Her diplomatic efforts in securing funds and arranging alliances helped ensure the success of the Montreal colony. At one point she agreed to use some of the hospital funding to support the engagement of new recruits for the struggling colony. Thanks to this intervention, Maisonneuve was able to bring ninety-five new colonists in 1653. Jeanne had saved Montreal.

Aside from her involvement in founding the colony in Montreal, Jeanne Mance was of course devoted to establishing and operating a hospital. In her first year in what was called Ville-Marie, she had a small area inside the fort where she cared for ill colonists and Native people. The first real hospital was constructed in 1645: a structure of about sixty by twenty-four feet, with five rooms. A chapel and stable were built nearby. By this time Jeanne had three assistants to help care for the sick and wounded. With the 1651 problems with the Iroquois, the hospital staff had to retreat back to the fort.

Jeanne later rebuilt the hospital, which the St. Joseph Hospitallers took charge of operating in 1659. The new chapel became the parish church, and the social and religious life of the growing colony revolved around it and l'Hôtel Dieu. Madame Bullion in France continued to finance the hospital. She stipulated that Jeanne should continue in her role as hospital administrator throughout her life. In addition to administration duties, she had of course been the only nurse at the beginning — for about seventeen years — in very difficult conditions. Jeanne Mance is considered to be the first secular nurse in Canada and a remarkable pioneer in the history of Canada.

In 1998 the Historic Sites and Monuments Board of Canada recognized Jeanne Mance as a person of national historic significance. Her beloved creation, l'Hôtel Dieu, continues to serve the people of the city she helped found. A statue of Jeanne Mance stands at the entrance to the hospital, and Le Musée des Hospitalières de l'Hôtel-Dieu de Montréal includes information about this notable pioneer of New France.

Each year the Canadian Nurses Associations presents the Jeanne Mance Award for outstanding contribution to nursing; many consider it to be the highest award for nurses in Canada. Other tributes to Jeanne Mance include a street and a park in Montreal, which are named Mance, and designation as a national historic person of Canada. To mark the three-hundredth anniversary of her death Canada Post issued a commemorative postage stamp in her honour in 1973.

Quote:

"It occurred to me that I knew that about 22,000 livres were about to be paid by Mr. de Renty, which would provide a good way to take this sum to use it to find some men to save the settlement rather than abandon it without help."[234]

> Jeanne Mance writing of her reasons for borrowing money
> from the hospital foundation to help save Montreal.

Henri Julien/National Archives of Canada/C151431
Source: Mr. Laurent Allard, Laval, Quebec.

Jeanne Mance teaching natives.

Eccentric Genius Behind the Black Box

Hannah Matherly Maynard

1834–1918

Hannah Maynard.

She came, she saw,
she took pictures.

Hannah Maynard was an extraordinary artist who experimented with the latest photographic techniques to create unusual images — from montages with over twenty-two thousand children's faces to curious photos with multiple images of the same person in different poses. She established a photographic studio in the early 1860s in Victoria, British Columbia. During nearly fifty years as a professional photographer she claimed to have taken portraits of most residents of the town.

Hannah was born in Cornwall, England, and married an adventurous boot-maker who loved the sea. In 1852 the young couple set sail for Canada, where Richard Maynard set up a shop in Bowmanville (now in Ontario). Lured west by the 1858 gold rush, he prospected along the Fraser River and apparently struck it rich while Hannah was dutifully raising their children — and learning professional photography. Richard returned home to pick up the family. The Maynards headed for San Francisco, where they boarded the steamer *Sierra Nevada* bound for Victoria. Hannah discovered they'd landed in a town of "tents, gullies and swamps and the inhabitants mostly miners."[235]

The Maynards had found their home in America: they settled in Victoria and raised their five children there. Hannah set up her Photographic Gallery in about 1862, becoming a prominent and successful professional photographer. Biographer Claire Weissman Wilks notes that a photographic career for a woman at this time was considered "somewhat unusual," and the public boycotted her studio until they began to accept the oddity of a woman photographer.[236]

Hannah Maynard proved herself to be a talented artist, a photographer of fine portraits of middle-class citizens of Victoria, visitors, Navy officers and sailors, and Aboriginal people. Sometimes she used the uncommon technique of split lighting for a special effect in her portraits. She also photographed babies and children — thousands of them — many in remarkable photos with natural poses. In 1881 she started making the Gems: clever cards consisting of collages of children she had photographed.

Hannah would cut out sections of the photos, re-photograph them, glue them onto a background, and shape the hundreds or thousands of miniatures into a shape — such as a turtle shell, diamonds, a crown, a wreath, or a cross. On close examination one finds curious elements demonstrating her unusual vision of the world and perhaps her grief — there is a gravedigger and a crying child holding a dead bird. Sometimes the innovative photographer used thousands of faces to create the lettering. Hannah sent out these annual Gems as greeting cards to mothers that were her clients. She also mailed them to the *St. Louis and Canadian Photographer*, whose editors noted that "Mrs. Maynard is one of the most industrious and persevering ladies we have in our business. She stops at no impediment, in our art, but is a regular go-ahead, even beating our Yankee girls two to one in photography."[237]

Soon after setting up her photography business Hannah began experimenting with mirrors to show multiple perspectives. In later years she worked extensively with multiples, which often featured herself and members of her family. A bizarre portrait shows Hannah pouring tea into a cup, while a second Hannah in a framed picture pours tea onto the head of a third Hannah sitting at a table. One complicated scene shows five figures of Hannah in different poses, while another depicts an unusual image with two Hannahs, and her young grandson Maynard looking up at a photo sculpture of himself showing only his torso; the latter photo also includes the curious addition of three portraits of deceased women in Hannah's family. Much of her work was surreal, even macabre.[238]

Hannah seemed preoccupied with death after her lovely sixteen-year-old daughter Lillie succumbed to typhoid in 1883, her daughter Emma drowned in Seattle in 1888, and her daughter-in-law Adelaide died in 1892. Hannah had at least one meeting with spiritualists and attended a séance. The portraits of the beloved women she had lost often appeared in her photographs. Sometimes they were in framed portraits, but their images might appear on a pillow or a plate.

Hannah Maynard also photographed criminals. In 1897 Hannah was hired by the Victoria Police Department to be its official photographer — a position she held for five years. By using a special mirror that was supported on the shoulder of the prisoner, she could take both frontal and side shots on the same negative. She took mug shots of all the accused criminals in her studio — anyone from suspected murderers to scam artists, to arsonists and children arrested for theft.

Hannah Maynard taught her trade to her husband, and Richard Maynard became an accomplished landscape photographer. The couple took thousands of fascinating images, leaving irreplaceable records of their times. By the time Hannah retired in 1912 (at the age of seventy-eight) she had gained international recognition through her exposure in the *St. Louis & Canadian Photographer* magazine. An outstanding photographer with a unique perspective, she was British Columbia's first female photographer and "one of the foremost representatives of the profession in the country."[239]

Quote:

"We are now on top of a high rock taking a view of the indian camp whilst Maynard down to his tent, me on the top with the cameras, 3 indians came up with nothing on but a piece of old blanket, however they did not kill me. We took two negatives when the whistle blew for the starting, so it was pack up and off for the steamer."[240]

Hannah Maynard speaking of an 1879 excursion she and her husband took around Vancouver Island.

A unique self-portrait by Hannah Maynard.

Nellie McClung.

Sowing Seeds of Reform

Nellie McClung
1873–1951

As "vivid as a tiger lily at a funeral,"[241] she created a buzz wherever she went.

Nellie McClung continues to be one of the most widely recognized heroines in Canadian history[242] and an inspiring role model to many women. The daughter of immigrants struggling to farm a poor piece of land near Owen Sound, Ontario, Nellie and her sisters grew up with a mother who believed in the "old-world reverence for men." Mrs. Mooney decreed that the girls must defer to men, go out only with their father or brothers accompanying them, and refrain from playing "shinny" (hockey) lest their red bloomers droop.[243]

After the Mooney family homesteaded in Manitoba, Nellie was able to start school at the age of ten and later taught in Manitou. Young Nell decided she must escape farm life and help other women "to do for the people around me what Dickens had done for his people."[244] When she met the dynamic Annie E. McClung, wife of the Methodist minister, Nell found "the only woman I have ever seen whom I should like to have for a mother-in-law." Nell later met and married a son, pharmacist Robert Wesley McClung, in 1896. He shared his mother's progressive attitudes and encouraged his wife to pursue her ambitions. The couple began raising a family and Nellie McClung joined the Women's Christian Temperance Union (WCTU).

It was Nellie's mother-in-law who gave the young mother a break from household chores and urged her to enter a writing contest. While the aspiring author didn't win, she expanded her story into a novel that was published as *Sowing Seeds in Danny*. The publication sold more than one hundred thousand copies and launched her successful career as a writer and lecturer. Nellie McClung eventually published sixteen books as well as many articles that conveyed her social messages. And she soon proved to be a formidable public speaker.

In 1911 the McClungs settled in Winnipeg, where Nellie gave birth to their fifth child. The busy mother became active in the reform movement there, playing a leading role in the battle to obtain the vote for women. She was active in Winnipeg's Political Equality League, as well as the WCTU, Women's Press Club, and Canadian Authors' Association. Nell's most famous stunt was her hilarious impersonation of Manitoba's chauvinist Premier Sir Rodmand Roblin in a play called *The Women's Parliament*. The production ridiculed his stance against granting the vote to women and brought public support for the suffragists. Such tactics resulted in critics over the years caricaturing Nell as a pesky mosquito and a hatchet-wielding mad woman.[245]

Nellie continued her activism when the McClungs moved to Alberta. She became a prominent leader in the fights for prohibition, female suffrage, dower rights for women, rural health care, improvements in factory safety, equal opportunities for women in education, and many other causes. In 1921 Nellie McClung was elected to the provincial legislature, where she served one term. She joined Emily Murphy in the Persons Case, which eventually saw women proclaimed as "persons" eligible to sit in the Canadian Senate.

A popular speaker, Nell gave readings of her work and lectures about suffrage and temperance. She toured extensively in Canada as well as the United States, England, and Scotland. In 1936 she became the first woman member of the board of governors of the Canadian Broadcasting Corporation. Nellie McClung served as a Canadian delegate to the League of Nations in 1938.

One of Canada's greatest social activists, Nellie McClung was a remarkable feminist, politician, prohibitionist, lecturer, and writer. She has been honoured in a variety of group commemorations for her involvement in the Persons Case (See Emily Murphy, page 192). Nell's significant contributions have been recognized in many ways, including the designation as a national historic person of Canada by the Historic Sites and Monuments Board of Canada and the issuing of a stamp by Canada Post.

Quote:

"Never retract, never explain, never apologize — get the thing done and let them howl."[246]

Louise McKinney.

A First in the British Empire

Louise Crummy McKinney
1868–1931

She devoted much of her life to battling what she considered to be public enemy number one: booze.

Louise McKinney was somewhat surprised to find she'd won a seat in the 1917 provincial election in Alberta. It was the first time women there had been allowed to vote or run for office, and she and Roberta MacAdams were the first two women elected to the Alberta Legislative Assembly. Louise was sworn in first — becoming the first female legislator in the British Empire.

Born in Frankville, Ontario, Louise Crummy grew up in a large family of Irish descent. Despite dreams of being a doctor she had to settle for teaching. A devout Methodist, she became an organizer for the Women's Christian Temperance Union (WCTU) while working in North Dakota. She married James McKinney and they settled in Claresholm, Alberta, in 1903. They named their son Williard after the founder of the WCTU: Frances E. Williard.

A firm believer in the merits of a Christian lifestyle, Louise McKinney directed most of her considerable energy to the WCTU. She founded a local chapter in Claresholm, and then served as President of the Alberta WCTU and Vice-President of the Dominion WCTU from 1908-30. She became Acting President and hosted the World Convention in Toronto in 1931, where she was elected World Vice-President for the WCTU. Throughout her decades of hard work for the organization Louise McKinney supported social reforms such as the vote for women, but she focused her efforts on fighting alcohol — and its destructive effects on families and society. Louise played an important role in pushing Alberta to accept prohibition in 1915, and under her leadership the WCTU had a significant impact on the political and social development of Alberta.

Louise's involvement in the WCTU led her to politics and the provincial legislature. Eager to promote social change, she decided to run as a candidate for the Non-Partisan League since she distrusted the established parties that accepted funding from liquor companies. Soon recognized as an impressive debater, Louise McKinney pushed for stricter liquor control laws, aid for the disabled, and assistance for immigrants and widows. She worked with Henrietta Muir Edwards on the successful passage of the Dower Act. Louise served just one term as an MLA but played another significant role on accepting Emily Murphy's offer to become a petitioner in the Persons Case. The conclusion of the landmark dispute was the ruling that Canadian women were deemed persons eligible to sit in the Senate.

Louise McKinney remained active in the WCTU at the local, national, and international levels. She attended many conventions in America and Europe, but died shortly after being elected World Vice-President. She was praised for "making her influence felt in the cause of peace, purity, and prohibition."[247]

Now considered one of the Famous Five women involved in the Persons Case, Louise McKinney is included in a variety of group commemorations (See Emily Murphy, page 192). A pioneer prohibitionist, educator, legislator, and social activist, she was recognized by the Historic Sites and Monuments Board of Canada as a national historic person of Canada in 1939. Canada Post issued a stamp in her honour, the City of Edmonton named a park after her, and the Government of Alberta established a scholarship in her memory.

Quote:

"The purpose of woman's life is just the same as the purpose of man's life — that she may make the best possible contribution to the generation in which she is living."[248]

Violet McNaughton.

Champion of Farm Women
Violet Clara McNaughton
1879–1968

Fearful of scaring away supporters of the farm movement, she was reluctant to admit her true colours in public: feminist.[249]

Violet made a difference. Heartbroken that problems with a tumour left her unable to have children, Violet McNaughton eventually resolved that this personal tragedy would give her the time to help other children and their families. She became actively involved in a variety of social causes, becoming "one of Canada's most influential farm women in the first half of the twentieth century."[250]

Violet had a tough start. Born in a village in England, she couldn't walk until she was three because she had rickets. After her mother passed away and her fiancé died of tuberculosis, the young woman immigrated to Saskatchewan to try homesteading with her father and brother.

Violet soon married farmer John McNaughton and they settled south-west of Saskatoon in a leaky sod shack: "...much of the time it leaked in thirteen places, and we started with apple boxes for chairs and home-made beds and not much else. We not only started, but we stayed that way a long time."[251] The McNaughtons became grain farmers but also had some cows and chickens. They hauled their drinking water from a neighbour's place two miles away. In 1924 the couple moved to a small house they built on their property, though they still lacked conveniences such as electricity.

The McNaughtons felt that Canadian farm families were being exploited by what John called a "vicious system" — and both were ready to do something about it. John had grown up in New Zealand, where a new group of activist farmers was so assertive they were labelled "the cow cockies." Violet considered herself a "rebel against the established order." Raised in county Kent with tales of rebellions and reformers, her father's experiences as a child labourer, and an ancestor's creation of an early co-operative in England, she believed that common folks should unite and take action.

Determined to improve the living conditions of prairie farmers, Violet and John McNaughton became leaders of the Hillview Local of the Saskatchewan Grain Grower's Association. Violet created a local chapter of the Women Grain Growers (WGG) and launched campaigns for "medical aid within the reach of all" and women's suffrage. In 1915 she managed to bring together three very different groups that shared the goal of gaining the vote for women: the WGG, the Woman's Christian Temperance Union, and the Political Equality League. With Violet McNaughton as "the moving force behind the organization,"[252] they created the Provincial Equal Franchise Board. This group led the suffrage movement until Saskatchewan finally granted the vote to women in 1916.

Violet McNaughton also worked with the WGG to fight for government support to provide doctors, nurses, midwives, and hospitals. In 1911 one in four women in Saskatchewan gave birth — and Violet knew the young families weren't getting the medical services they needed, particularly in rural areas. "A new baby is an asset of $1000 to the country," she wrote. "If the country paid $50 to ensure a healthy start in life for each of its coming citizens, it would not be too much."[253]

Effectively putting medical care on the political agenda, Violet built alliances of key organizations and gained endorsements of support for improvements to the system. Faced with such strong support for change, the provincial government of Saskatchewan passed important legislation in 1916 that enabled municipalities to provide medical services and facilities. Plus the province gave grants for hospitals. The efforts of Violet McNaughton and the WGG led to the development of a health care system, which was an important step in the eventual creation of medicare in Canada.

Through her activism in the suffrage movement and the struggle for good medical care Violet McNaughton became known across Canada as a champion of farm families. Building on her reputation as a leader, she worked for many years to build national farm and women's movement groups that could change the country. She gave up in 1923, concluding that the only way for westerners to make improvements in their lives was to mould their own institutions in Western Canada.

Violet supported the formation of the prairie Wheat Pools and helped establish the important farm paper the *Western Producer*. She became a full-time agrarian journalist for the newspaper in 1926, where she worked until 1960. Through her writing Violet McNaughton continued to try to improve the lives of farm families by influencing public opinion and encouraging women to voice their views. She is credited with pushing the government to increase old age pensions, helping to establish the School for the Deaf in Saskatoon, and supporting maternity grants.

For her many contributions to Canadian agriculture and to farm people, Violet McNaughton received the Order of the British Empire in 1934 and an honorary doctorate from the University of Saskatchewan in 1951. The Historic Sites and Monuments Board recognized her as a national historic person in 1997.

Quote:

"Go Slow! Aim High!"[254]

Photo LH2157 courtesy of the Saskatoon Public Library - Local History Room.

The McNaughtons' sod house.

Rediscovering an Impressionist

Helen McNicoll
1879–1915

National Library of Canada-4370

Known as the "painter of sunshine," she lived in a silent world.

Portrait of Helen McNicoll by Robert Harris, 1910.

If you've never heard of Helen McNicoll you're not alone. Thanks to the investigations of researchers like Natalie Luckyj, the works of art of this talented Canadian impressionist painter have recently been rediscovered.[255]

Helen Galloway McNicoll was born in Toronto but soon moved to Montreal, where her father, David, was transferred in his successful career with the Canadian Pacific Railway. He later became first vice-president, and the family enjoyed an affluent lifestyle in their Westmount home. The eldest of eight children, Helen became deaf at age two after a bout with scarlet fever. The young girl received her early education at home from a tutor. She learned to lip-read, play the piano, and paint. Both parents sketched and encouraged their artistic daughter to develop her talents.

With no concerns about financial security, Helen was fortunate in being able to devote herself to artistic pursuits. She began her art training with William Brymner, a proponent of outdoor painting and the Impressionist style, at the Art Association in Montreal. Helen then studied for two years at the Slade School of Art, University of London, where female students had the same opportunities as males to develop their skills. Helen spent an inspiring three-months studying in Paris but in 1905 decided to continue her formal studies at St. Ives, Cornwall. Her style developed with the guidance of English painter Algernon Talmage, another enthusiast of painting in nature. Helen's luminous paintings captured women and children at work and play, often in the outdoors.

Helen McNicoll faced the challenge of establishing herself as a professional artist in of time when the world of art was dominated by men.

Through persistence and talent the aspiring artist gradually gained some recognition. Beginning in 1906, when she was twenty-seven, Helen McNicoll contributed some of her work for exhibitions of the Art Association of Montreal (AAM). In 1908 the AAM awarded her the Jessie Dow Prize for Painting, and in 1913 the Royal Society of British Artists elected the painter to their prestigious group despite the opposition of older members who objected to her modern style. The artist continued to work out of a studio in London, but each year exhibited paintings with the Royal Canadian Academy — which elected her an associate in 1914, since women were denied full membership. The following year, at the age of thirty-five, Helen died suddenly from diabetes.

Despite being marginalized by both her sex and her deafness, Helen McNicoll created some exceptional drawings and paintings during her short life and made a notable contribution to Canadian impressionist painting. Following her death, an article in *Saturday Night* hailed her as "one of the most profoundly original and technically accomplished of Canadian artists."[256] A decade later the Montreal Museum of Fine Arts exhibited 141 of her paintings and drawings, which were held primarily by family members since Helen had had no financial need to sell her art.

Familiarity with Helen McNicoll's work faded with the years, until some of her paintings were offered for sale in the 1970s. In 1999 the Art Gallery of Ontario launched a major Helen McNicoll exhibition, curated by Natalie Luckyj, which created new awareness of a largely forgotten figure in Canadian art history. She is now being recognized as one of Canada's most accomplished women painters.

Quote:

"The older members [of the Royal Society of British Artists] ... didn't like my things."[257]

Picking Flowers by Helen McNicoll, ca. 1912.

National Library of Canada-4371

Preaching the Gospel

Aimee Semple McPherson
1890–1944

A spiritual giant, she led a religious revival that touched millions.

Sister Aimee preaching, ca. 1927.

One of the most famous evangelists in the world, Aimee Semple McPherson, loved to preach the sermon that she called "The Story of My Life: From Milk Pail to God's Pulpit." She always claimed to be a farm girl. A farm girl from Canada.

Aimee was born and raised on a diary farm in southern Ontario, near Ingersoll. Her religious mother, Minnie Kennedy, who had prayed for the birth of a daughter who would become a preacher, first took her baby to the Salvation Army Citadel when she was three weeks old. The energetic child became a fervent believer, an outspoken girl who took elocution lessons and won prizes in speaking contests sponsored by the Women's Christian Temperance Union.

At the age of seventeen the auburn-haired beauty fell in love with a handsome thirty-year-old stranger in town: a Pentecostal evangelist called Robert Semple. Within six months they had wed, and the two sailed to China to do missionary work. They stopped in London en route, where the young woman gave her first sermon in Victoria and Albert Hall. Before the couple could establish themselves in China, Robert died of malaria. A couple of months later Aimee gave birth to a daughter, Roberta. A nineteen-year-old widow stranded in a foreign country, Aimee managed to get enough money to get back to America. A few years later she married an accountant called Harold McPherson and gave birth to their son, Rolf — but a housewife she was not. After a near-death experience Aimee fled her home to follow her religious calling.

She began saving souls in Mount Forest, Ontario, in the summer of 1915, even though the idea of a woman preacher was a horrifying thing to most people.[258] Within a week the passionate Canadian preacher was attracting crowds of five hundred farmers a night. For years Sister Aimee wandered across North America as a travelling preacher, praying and speaking in tongues, singing and playing her tambourine, spreading her message in more than a hundred towns and cities. Aimee and various members of her family lived like gypsies, without plans or money. She preached in a tattered tent, concert halls, boxing rings, and the back seat of her Gospel Car — and was the first evangelist to address mixed audiences of Blacks and Whites. Thousands of people flocked to hear the Canadian revivalist.

While Sister Aimee preferred to focus on spreading the gospel, word of her miraculous healing powers quickly spread. She and her followers would pray for the invalids who lined up to see her, and Aimee would anoint them with sacred oil. Even the most skeptical journalists were astounded at what they witnessed: "The blind saw again; the deaf heard. Cripples left their crutches and hung them on the rafters."[259]

Aimee Semple McPherson arrived in Los Angeles, California, with just "ten dollars and a tambourine" — plus her domineering mother and Aimee's two small children. Here she would build the popular Angelus Temple, which she opened in 1923 with ministers from across the country, representing many denominations. Funded completely by donations by the time it was built, the new $1.25 million facility was "Dedicated to the cause of inter-denominational and worldwide evangelism."[260]

The 5,300-seat auditorium was filled to capacity when Aimee delivered her sermons, twenty times per week. Most popular were her illustrated sermons, the elaborate Sunday presentations she staged to interpret stories of the Bible. Audiences sat enthralled as one of the most captivating speakers on the planet spread the word of God, with costumes that rivalled any Hollywood movie, professional props and scenery, and a full orchestra playing contemporary music — even jazz. A camel appeared the night that Sister Aimee preached about it being "easier for a camel to go through the eye of a needle, than for a rich man to enter into kingdom of God."[261]

Charlie Chaplin was not a believer but was reputed to give advice on sets. A choir of a hundred might sing and a brass band would play. A poor Mexican boy who became the famous actor Anthony Quinn played the saxophone and would sometimes translate her sermons into Spanish. Years later, after watching the craft of the best actresses in Hollywood, Quinn would write, "As magnificent as I would find Anna Magnami, Ingrid Begman, Laurette Taylor, Katherine Hepburn, Greta Garbo, and Ethel Barrymore, they all fell short of that first electric shock Aimee Semple McPherson produced in me."[262] He also credited Sister Aimee with keeping most of the local Mexican community alive for years, thanks to the supplies of food from the Angelus Temple.

The new facility was a hubbub of activity, with a "prayer tower" of volunteers praying twenty-four hours per day, sewing circles for the poor, a team of ministers that responded to calls from those in despair, and much more. Sister Aimee founded the first religious radio station in the world and within months was reaching hundreds of thousands of listeners each day. The first woman to use what was called "the wireless telephone" to deliver sermons to mass audiences, she became a famous radio preacher. Aimee created the popular LIFE Bible College, which by 1929 had a thousand students and dozens of instructors. During the Depression she organized soup kitchens that distributed food to the needy in Los Angeles, a venture that became the largest private charity in the city — feeding eighty thousand people in the first month alone.

Aimee Semple McPherson's temple in Los Angeles became the centre of the International Church of the Foursquare Gospel, with churches and members across America and around the globe. With the growing complexity of the operation and an incredible cash flow came a major management challenge. Aimee focused on preaching and teaching and hoped that her mother, and then a series of trusted accountants, lawyers, and publicists, would handle the business of running the Angelus Temple and associated operations. The press went wild as they gleefully reported successive mistakes in judgement, fights for money and power, scandals, and lawsuits.

Yet Aimee Semple never faltered in her faith. She dedicated her life to God, sacrificing her personal life and her own health to tirelessly preach the gospel. After suffering for years from a variety of ailments, Aimee Semple McPherson died suddenly at the age of fifty-three in 1944, from an accidental overdose of sleeping pills. Her estate consisted of just $10,000, which was left to her two children. Sister Aimee's son, Rolf, assumed leadership of the Foursquare Church, whose assets at the time were valued at about $2.8 million.

Newsweek proclaimed that "with her radio ministry and her theatrical sermons, Sister Aimee ushered in the modern religious age."[263] An extraordinary woman, she served throughout her life as an evangelist and faith healer. She brought her message of reconciliation and love to millions during her lifetime, and today the International Church of Foursquare Gospel has more than 3.5 million supporters in 123 countries.

How has Canada remembered Aimee Semple McPherson? The Ontario Heritage Foundation has installed a commemorative plaque near her birthplace in Ingersoll, and a short entry in the Canadian Encyclopedia notes that she was "the most publicized revivalist in the world."

Quote:

"What is my task? To get the gospel around the world in the shortest possible time to every man and woman and boy and girl!"[264]

From a sermon by Sister Aimee at Angelus Temple.

Used by Permission of the Heritage Department of the International Church of the Foursquare Gospel.

Sister Aimee, ca. 1940.

The Brilliance of a Biochemist

Maud Menten
1879–1960

She was one of the first Canadians to make her mark in chemistry, but no universities here would hire her.

Maud Menten.

If you're a biochemist you're familiar with the famous Michael-Menten equation. Canadians can be proud that Menten was a gifted scientist from Port Lambton, Ontario. Along with colleague Leonor Michaelis at the University of Berlin, she developed this important equation, which provided a mathematical method for measuring the rate of a biological reaction catalyzed by enzymes. An understanding of this process is necessary for the production of most modern drugs. The equation is internationally recognized, though the identity of our Maud is not.

Little is known of Maud's background. A graduate of the University of Toronto, she received her Bachelor of Arts in 1904, and a Masters in biology in 1906. After conducting research at the Rockefeller Institute on the effects of radium on tumors, Maud came back to Toronto to earn her M.D. in 1911. Following her work in Germany, Dr. Menten obtained a Ph.D. in biochemistry at the University of Chicago in 1916. Unable to secure an academic position in Canada, she accepted an offer of employment from the medical school at the University of Pittsburgh.[265]

Dr. Menten was an innovative and versatile scientist who managed to conduct research, teach medical students, and do clinical work by working eighteen-hour days. She worked as the head of pathology at the Children's Hospital of Pittsburgh, where patients loved her soft eyes and pediatricians sought her advice on every puzzling case. An active researcher, Dr. Menten wrote or co-wrote about one hundred research papers.[266] She made important contributions to scientific knowledge with work such as the first study of human hemoglobins using electrophoresis (predating studies by Linus Pauling, though he is usually credited for this) and the discovery of the azo-dye coupling reaction. Dr. Menten also detected the hyperglycemic effects of salmonella toxins and the value of immunization in treating animals with infectious diseases. Promoted to associate professor in the medical school in 1925, she became a highly respected and inspiring teacher.

In addition to her passion for science Maud loved mountain climbing, Arctic expeditions, homemade scones, Paris hats, and Buster Brown shoes. She was particularly fond of her Model T Ford, which she drove in the streets of Pittsburgh from 1918-50. A fan of astronomy, playing her clarinet, and studying languages, she could speak German, Italian, French, Russian, and at least one Native-American language. Maud was also a talented artist whose paintings were exhibited in galleries in Pittsburgh.

Despite her academic accomplishments Dr. Menten was not granted a full professorship until 1949 — when she was seventy years old and a year from retirement. Following her departure from Pittsburgh, Dr. Menten returned home to Canada to conduct research at the Medical Institute of British Columbia. Illness finally stopped the incredible Maud, who colleagues noted "...did not waste away. She used herself up."[267] Dr. Menten died in Ontario in 1960.

Maud Lenora Menten was inducted into the Canadian Medical Hall of Fame in 1998 in recognition of her role as a pioneering woman doctor and brilliant scientist who laid the foundation for biochemistry and modern drug therapy. The Ontario Heritage Foundation erected a commemorative plaque in her memory at the University of Toronto. Dr. Menten is remembered at the University of Pittsburgh with an annual pathology lecture and a chair in her honour: the Maud L. Menten Professor of Experimental Pathology. A full-length portrait of the outstanding doctor hangs in the main auditorium at Pitt.

The legacy of Maud Menten seems not well known in Canada, where mention of her name as a heroine of science would likely bring the response of "Maud who?" Pity.

Quote:

"I've stirred them up, so now I can go."[268]

> Dr. Menten's frequent exclamation as she scurried out of a laboratory, having directed the scientists to work harder or try a new approach in their research.

Kidnapped
Mikak
ca. 1740–1795

Mikak, 1769.

An Inuk leader who helped Moravians bring the gospel to Labrador, she refused to be controlled by them.

Mikak belonged to the "people of the whale." A daughter of Inuk chief Nerkingoak, she grew up along the coast of Labrador — where the Inuit lived mainly from the sea — hunting whales, walrus, and seals. Mikak married the son of an Inuk chief about 1762.

A few years later the young woman enjoyed an encounter with Moravian missionaries on an exploratory trip, but her next meeting with Europeans was a violent confrontation that resulted in the murder of her husband. A detachment from Fort York at Chateau Bay attacked an Inuit band in retaliation for the killing of some men and theft of boats at a fishing station in November 1767. The forces killed more than twenty Inuit men and kidnapped their families. Mikak and the other women and children spent the winter as prisoners in a blockhouse at Chateau Bay, where her keen mind and beauty attracted the attention of the raid's leader: naval officer Francis Lucas.

Lucas began teaching Mikak English, and the following spring transported his prisoners to St. John's, Newfoundland. Governor Hugh Palliser was also impressed by Mikak and decided she could help him achieve his goal of "establishing communication and trade with the Esquimaux savages."[269] In the autumn of 1768 Palliser ordered that Mikak, along with her son Tutauk and an orphan boy called Karpik, be sent to England — where she gained an appreciation of the great nation and returned to her people as a messenger of British interest in developing trade.

Mikak was apparently well treated by her paternalistic hosts and impressed the many people she met. Augusta, Dowager Princess of Wales and mother of King George III, became fond of her, and Mikak had an active social life. The Duke of Gloucester gave her a fine bracelet and King George III provided a coronation medal. Society painter John Russell did a portrait of Mikak, which was exhibited in the Royal Academy of Arts.

Mikak also became reacquainted with missionary Jens Haven and played an important role in helping the Moravians receive their grant to establish a mission in Labrador. As Haven noted, "Her repeated applications were of great use in putting forward the business of the projected Mission, for she was noticed by many persons of rank and influence, and her request attended to."[270] Mikak hoped that the missionaries could improve the relationship between her people and the growing number of Europeans frequenting her homeland.

Mikak's captivity finally ended in the summer of 1769 when she and her son were shipped home by warship. She urged the Inuit to be friendly towards the Moravians who were planning to settle. Considered a wealthy and prestigious woman, Mikak soon remarried a Native religious leader (angakok) called Tuglavina. In 1771 the pair guided the Moravians along the coast of Labrador to select a mission site at Nain. When the missionaries arrived there were about seven hundred Inuit there, and Mikak provided her large tent for the first gospel meeting. She played an important role in land negotiations for the mission. Mikak also conveyed the message that the "great Lord in London" promised that no more Inuit would be killed if they decided to trade in an orderly manner with the English.

Mikak served an important role in helping the Moravians settle in Labrador and promoting peaceful relationships between the Inuit and Europeans. She remained a staunchly independent woman who resisted the Moravians' entreaties to live at the mission in Nain, to be baptized, to stay away from European traders in southern Labrador, and to forsake the traditional healing methods of the shamans. As noted by historian William H. Whiteley, "She seems to have remained her own woman, receptive to the Moravians' teachings but not without a degree of reserve, enjoying European society but conscious of her influence and place in the Inuit community."[271]

Quote:

"Oh, you miserable person! You know God and you live worse than the Inuit. I do not believe that you know God."[272]

Mikak to naval officer Francis Lucas.

Her Beloved Anne of Green Gables

Lucy Maud Montgomery
1874–1942

Maud was a lonely child who followed her dreams to become an internationally renowned novelist, author of the best-selling books featuring the spunky Anne of Green Gables.

Lucy Maud Montgomery, 1894.

She was a little girl who grew up on a beautiful island and fashioned her memories of childhood in a thousand different ways in her writings. Her most memorable creation was Anne of Green Gables, a spirited red-haired heroine who captured the hearts of millions of readers around the world.

People called her Maud. Lucy Maud Montgomery was born in a village on Prince Edward Island on November 30, 1874.[273] When she was just twenty-one months old her young mother died, and her father Hugh Montgomery headed west, settling in Prince Albert, Saskatchewan. Her mother's parents took the baby girl — raising her at their Cavendish home on the Island.[274]

Aside from a short period when she lived with her father and his new family, Maud grew up on the Island. Her grandparent's household was strictly Presbyterian, but the lively child found happiness in a solitary world of imaginary playmates and characters from the books she read. She frolicked in the fields and farms, the orchards and the secret paths in the woods. Rambled along the red-sand beaches of the sea.

The lonely little girl also wrote. At the age of eleven she submitted her first manuscript to an American magazine. It rejected her submission, but the determined child continued to write and send off stories and poems. Maud persisted, until about four years later the *Charlottetown*

Patriot printed one of her poems about Island history on the front page of the newspaper.

In 1893 Maud moved to Charlottetown to attend Prince of Wales College. She obtained a teacher's licence and began teaching, but still managed to crank out manuscripts to send off. Encouraged by her increasing success at getting her writing published, the aspiring author went to Halifax in 1895 to get more training by attending Dalhousie College. That year she finally began earning money for her publications.

Maud continued teaching back on P.E.I., but resigned her job in 1898 when her grandfather died. At the age of twenty-two she promised her grandmother she would look after her — and began her struggle to survive from writing. Maud moved to Halifax for a year to accept a job as proof-reader at the Halifax *Daily Echo*, where she also wrote a weekly gossip column, edited society letters, and prepared copy for ads. She settled back on the Island in 1902.

While continuing to work hard on her various writing projects, Maud began a relationship with Reverend Ewan Macdonald, a Presbyterian minister. But the young woman rarely left her grandmother and spent most of her time caring for the household and writing. Exciting news arrived with word that her manuscript, *Anne of Green Gables*, had been accepted by a Boston publishing house. In 1908 the first novel of L.M. Montgomery was published and quickly became a best-seller. Maud received a flood of letters, including a welcome congratulatory note from author Mark Twain that praised her for having created "the dearest, and most lovable child in fiction since the immortal Alice."[275]

Unfortunately, the terms of the publishing contract were not very favourable for the young author, and in later years she launched a lawsuit against the company. The case dragged on for about nine years, frustrating Maud and bringing her to the attention of fellow authors; literary societies frequently asked her to speak.

Pressed by her publishers and public demand, Maud worked on sequels to *Anne of Green Gables* and also penned other novels. During her lifetime the famous Island writer would pen twenty-two books of fiction, a volume of poetry, a serial about her life, plus about five hundred short stories and 450 poems. She also left over five thousand pages of unpublished writings from her diaries.

Maud's life changed dramatically in 1911 with the death of her grandmother. On July 1 of that year she married her faithful suitor, Ewan Macdonald, and the pair moved to his posting at a church in Leaskdale, Ontario. Maud soon became immersed in a new life at the manse and duties with the choir, Sunday school, and women's groups. Then motherhood: son Chester born in 1912, Hugh, who did not survive, in 1914, and Ewan in 1915. Maud also faced the challenge of her husband's unstable mental health — and his frequent bouts of severe clinical depression.

Despite the demands of her family life, Maud somehow managed to continue her writing. The list of her publications grew, as did her popularity. In 1935 the family moved to Toronto after Rev. Macdonald retired, and Maud became involved with the Women's Press Club, the Canadian Author's Association, and other groups. She read voraciously and enjoyed the official public recognition that she began to receive in 1935. She became an officer in the Order of the British Empire and a Fellow of the Royal Society of Arts and Letters. The Institute des Lettres et des Arts (France) granted membership to her and later gave Maud a silver medal.

In the last years of her life Maud was in poor spirits, distressed at her husband's health and resentful about the long ago contractual relationship with a publisher that prevented her from sharing fully in the amazing success of her *Anne of Green Gables* — the new editions that brought her little, the movies and plays that brought her nothing. Maud's health was poor, and she knew she would never write the classic novel she had hoped to.

When she died on April 24, 1942, L.M. Montgomery passed away with the knowledge that her books were a popular success. Her wonderful imaginary characters, in particular Anne of Green Gables, live on in the hearts of millions of readers throughout the world. Many make special trips to visit the places in Prince Edward Island that inspired her stories.

The Historic Sites and Monuments Board of Canada recognized L.M. Montgomery a national historic person in 1943, and in 1975 Canada Post issued a stamp depicting Anne of Green Gables in honour of the author.

Quote:

"I never expect to be famous. I merely want to have a recognized place among good workers in my chosen profession."[276]

The Lens of a Lady
Geraldine Moodie
1854–1945

The first woman photographer in the Eastern Arctic, she was also the first female to establish a photo studio on the Canadian prairies.

Geraldine Moodie.

Geraldine Moodie's impressive contribution to the photographic record of Canada was nearly forgotten until researcher Donny White discovered some of her work in the late 1970s. He spent several decades piecing together her story and compiling two books that provide a fascinating glimpse of a Canadian woman who left a precious legacy.[277]

Born in Toronto, Geraldine Fitzgibbon was the daughter of illustrator Agnes Dunbar Moodie and lawyer Charles Thomas Fitzgibbon. Geraldine was just eleven when her father died, leaving Agnes with six children to raise. The young widow's famous mother, Susanna Moodie, and her aunt Catharine Parr Trail tried to assist Agnes, who earned some money by illustrating Catharine's book *Canadian Wild Flowers*. Geraldine helped paint the pictures for this and future publications, developing a useful skill as well as a lifelong commitment to documenting plant life.

In 1870 Geraldine's mother married Lieutenant-Colonel Brown Chamberlin, a member of Parliament. Geraldine joined them in their Ottawa home, where Grandma Susanna was pleased to see that she now "moved in the best of society." It was on a trip to England seven years later that Geraldine met and married John Douglas Moodie (J.D.) — a distant cousin.

The Moodies eventually settled north of Brandon, Manitoba, and Geraldine sketched and painted watercolours of prairie wildflowers in her spare time. After their brief experiment in farming failed, J.D. secured a commission with the North-West Mounted Police in 1885 and worked for the force until retirement in 1917. During the intervening thirty-two years the Moodies were stationed throughout Western Canada and the Hudson's Bay district of the Eastern Arctic. J.D. was first posted to Calgary and then Medicine Hat, where Geraldine's sixth and last child was born. The cross-country postings brought Geraldine more travel and adventure than most women of the time could imagine and also launched her photographic career.

She apparently began her serious involvement in photography after the family moved to Battleford in 1891, and she had a bit more time as the children were growing up. In 1895 Geraldine had a photographic studio built in Battleford, where she would take portraits. She also photographed the North-West Mounted Police and Native people of the area. Among her notable photos were those of their Sun Dance ceremonies, which showed the participation of women.

Geraldine Moodie received important recognition of her work when she was awarded a government commission in 1895 to photograph historic sites and other areas visited by Prime Minister Mackenzie Bowell and a party of government officials who were touring in the west. In 1897 Geraldine, who the local paper noted was "an artist of the first rank," established a studio in her new hometown of Maple Creek as well as a branch operation sixty miles away in Medicine Hat. Hiring a housekeeper to help at home, Geraldine would periodically spend a couple of weeks away taking pictures — then return home to develop the negatives. She kept busy taking portraits as well as travelling around the country by carriage to photograph cowboys, the NWMP, and prairie plant life. She also did hand-coloured photos of wildflowers.

In September 1904 Geraldine and her son Alex headed for the Arctic by steamer to join J.D. on his latest assignment. They lived for a year in a small post at Fullerton, near Southampton Island. While an official photographer had already been assigned to the mission, Geraldine was the first woman to take professional photos of the Inuit. She took many photos of the women and children and was particularly interested in the workmanship in their clothing. Geraldine also photographed extensively during the three years she lived at Fort Churchill, where she often accompanied the police patrols on both land and sea.

When Geraldine left Hudson Bay she was fifty-five. Settling temporarily at their ranch in Cyprus Hills, the Moodies were anxious to be posted in the north again — "as far away as possible from civilization..."[278] The couple were no doubt disappointed to be posted to Regina in 1910, but managed to get another northern posting in June 1912 to Dawson, Yukon. Geraldine again photographed her new home on the frontier.

Geraldine Moodie died in 1945 at Midnapore, Alberta, ending a lifetime of adventure and travel in some of the most remote areas of Canada. The accomplished pioneer photographer took some remarkable photos that captured rare images of lands and peoples that were rapidly changing as settlements sprung up in western and northern areas of the country.

Quote:

"It is very fascinating work and I can make enough to pay expenses and something over when I fill the orders I have."[279]

> Geraldine Moodie describing her involvement in photography
> to Catharine Parr Traill, her great-aunt.

Geraldine Moodie/National Archives of Canada/C-001815.

A photo of Inuit women and children taken by Geraldine, ca. 1904.

Upon a Mountaintop

Phyllis James Munday
1894–1990

North Vancouver Museum & Archives #9782

She made her mark in mountaineering — and encouraged other women to roam alpine meadows, glaciers, and grand peaks.

Phyllis Munday on Franklin Glacier.

The summit was hers. On July 29, 1924, Phyllis Munday became the first woman to reach the top of Mt. Robson — the highest mountain in the Canadian Rockies. After a tough thirteen-hour climb from high camp with the famous Austrian guide Conrad Kain, she scrambled onto the snow cornice and gazed down at Berg Lake. The gutsy pioneer mountaineer climbed about one hundred mountains, with one-third being first ascents.[280]

Phyllis James was born in Ceylon, where her father managed Lipton's tea estates. The family moved to British Columbia, where Phyllis thrived on the outdoor life. When they lived in the Kootenays she ran wild in the bush, rode bareback on an old horse, and hunted grouse with a rifle. After the family moved to Vancouver "Phyl" began a lifetime involvement with Girl Guides and mountaineering.

Phyllis James was fifteen when she convinced a Scoutmaster to permit the creation of a Girl Scout troop and volunteered to be the Patrol Leader. On learning that a separate movement had been created for girls, they switched to Girl Guides. In 1912 the fearless Phyl led her group to the top of Grouse Mountain. She began the Girl Guide movement in

British Columbia, created the Lone Guides for girls in remote areas, and rose to the position of Division Commissioner. Through her devotion to Guiding and her remarkable achievements in mountaineering, Phyllis inspired countless young women to explore the outdoors, appreciate the natural world, and undertake their own wilderness adventures.

Phyl joined the B.C. Mountaineering Club as soon as she became eligible at age twenty-one. Bound for her climbing expeditions in a respectable skirt, she would cache it in the woods once she left the city and proceed in bloomers — only in later years would she dare wear knickerbockers or trousers. While working as a stenographer at a hospital she met patient Don Munday, a wounded soldier (and writer) who had served at Vimy. The pair soon discovered their mutual passion for mountaineering and were married in 1920. They became inseparable climbing partners, spending years scaling some of B.C.'s highest peaks and even bringing along their baby daughter on some climbs. A courageous adventurer, Phyl once saved Don from a charging grizzly bear by threatening it with an ice axe.

The Mundays were recognized as outstanding climbers who were the first to explore many spectacular mountain areas, most notably the Coast Mountains and a "Mystery Mountain" they spotted.[281] For more than a decade Don and Phyl spent every climbing season exploring this rugged area of mountains and glaciers, meticulously documenting their findings. They mapped, photographed, and named features of the region and got to within eighteen metres of the summit of the unknown peak that was eventually named Mt. Waddington — the highest mountain in British Columbia. In 1928 the Geographic Board of Canada named Mt. Munday to honour the important work of these pioneer mountaineers. When famed Everest climber Sir Edmund Hilary took an airplane tour of the Coast Mountains in 1955 it was Phyl Munday who accompanied him.

As the renowned geologist and climber A.P. Coleman remarked, "By their courage and determination the Mundays have disclosed to the climbing world one of the most splendid regions of high mountains and vast glaciers in America."[282] On their many climbs Phyl demonstrated her prowess in the primarily male-dominated field of mountaineering. She was a strong and skilful climber despite being plagued by arthritis in her knees since her mid-twenties. The Mundays were active members of the Alpine Club of Canada and Phyl was named Honorary President and was also the recipient of the Silver Rope Award for Leadership. The Appalachian Mountain Club, the American Alpine Club, and the Alpine Club in England gave her honorary memberships.

During her lifetime Phyllis Munday received many awards and honours for her accomplishments in mountaineering as well as her volunteer work with the Girl Guides and the St. John Ambulance Brigade — including the Order of Canada and an honorary doctorate in law from the University of Victoria. She was indeed thrilled to be flown back to Mt. Waddington in 1982, where the crew of the television show *Thrill of a Lifetime* recorded her walking on the Homaathko Icefield as she had nearly half a century before. The feisty heroine of mountaineering died in 1990 at the age of ninety-five and has since been commemorated with a stamp issued by Canada Post in their Legendary Canadians series.

Quote:

"My spirit belongs to all of the mountains — for this to me is heaven."[283]

Courtesy Linda Ohama

Secrets of a Picture Bride

Asayo Murakami
1898–2002

Only after her hundredth birthday would she reveal the mystery of her past life.

Asayo Murakami playing her violin as a young woman in Japan, pre 1923.

The young Japanese woman arrived in Vancouver in 1923 with only a few possessions, including her treasured violin and a few family photographs. After a long journey from her native Hiroshima, Asayo scanned the docks to find the husband she had seen only in a photograph. She was a "picture bride" — one of about six thousand women who came to Canada between 1908 and 1924 through arranged marriages. After an exchange of photos by mail the couple was married by proxy in Japan. The men, eager for wives from their homeland, paid for the passages of their brides.

"I knew he was not my type. I didn't like him at all..."[284] remembered Asayo of her meeting on the docks in Steveston. Despite being alone in a foreign country where she didn't speak the language, she broke off her marriage contract on the spot. The frightened immigrant spent the next three years working in the nearby strawberry fields and salmon canneries to pay back the $250 she owed for her fare. Then she was free, and eventually married Otokichi Murakami, a widower with two children.

For eighteen years the couple lived in Steveston, where Otokichi built boats and fished. In their home next to the boatyards the Murakamis raised eight more children and Asayo planted a natural flower garden full of poppies and climbing roses. Their happy life on the coast ended abruptly in

1942, when the Murakamis and other Japanese Canadians were forced from their homes on the Lower Mainland during World War II. Asayo and her family quickly packed what they could, boarded up their house, and were moved to Manitoba.

Asayo laboured in the sugar beet fields there, then worked on a potato farm in Alberta where the family moved after the war. She spent her final years with relatives in Calgary. As Asayo Murakami's hundredth birthday approached, filmmaker Linda Ohama decided to document the life of her strong and independent grandmother. As Obaachan (grandmother) reluctantly began to share the story of her life, the family was astounded to learn the painful secret she had been ashamed to share. Asayo revealed that she was once married to a man from a prominent Japanese family. The couple was deeply in love and Asayo gave birth to a son, who soon died, and two daughters. Considered a failure because she hadn't produced an heir, Asayo's in-laws broke up the family and her husband took the girls. A heartbroken Asayo went to Canada.

As depicted in the moving film *Obaachan's Garden*, Asayo eventually showed her second family two cherished photos of the long-lost daughters who were always in her heart and her dreams. Fumiko was six and Chieko was four when their mother had to leave them; they were later given up for adoption. When Asayo was 101, granddaughter Linda arranged an amazing reunion in Obaachan's former home in Steveston, B.C. Chieko was still alive and travelled from Japan to meet her mother. The moving reunion took place in the flower garden Asayo had lovingly tended half a century before, where four generations of Murakamis had gathered recently to replant it. Her spirit replenished, Obaachan lived until a few months before her 105th birthday.

Murakami House, where Asayo and her family lived in Steveston, was reconstructed as part of the development of the Britannia Heritage Shipyard and this historic site is open to visitors. The restoration of the home and the creation of the powerful documentary *Obaachan's Garden* will help ensure that a "picture bride" with incredible determination and endurance is not forgotten.

Quote:

"As a Buddhist I have always believed that we will all come together one day ... and life would come full circle, bringing everything into a harmony."[285]

Janey Canuck

Emily Ferguson Murphy
1868–1933

Emily Murphy, ca. 1910–1920.

She led a fight for equality, winning an important victory for Canadian women.

"To hell with Women Magistrates, this country is going to the dogs because of them," charged a furious attorney who disagreed with a ruling by Judge Murphy.[286] Never one to back away from challenges, Emily Murphy soon advised the lawyer in writing that until she received his apology she would be obliged to refuse him admittance to her court. A self-taught legal expert who became the first woman magistrate in the British Empire, Judge Murphy had been appointed as police magistrate for the city of Edmonton in 1916.

Born in Cookstown, Ontario, Emily Ferguson grew up in a prominent family involved in politics and the law. At the age of nineteen she married Anglican minister Arthur Murphy and began raising a family. During the early years of their marriage the family moved frequently, as Rev. Murphy did missionary work in Ontario and England. By the time they moved to Edmonton Emily Murphy was a popular and well-known writer — often using the pen name Janey Canuck. In a takeoff from the nationalist cartoon character Jack Canuck, the author wrote a series of books depicting the adventures of Janey Canuck. Emily also worked as an editor and book reviewer and served for seven years as President of the Canadian Women's Press Club.

Concerned by the inequalities faced by women, Emily became actively involved in promoting women's rights. Horrified that a farmer could sell his homestead and give nothing to his wife, Emily Murphy successfully campaigned with Nellie McClung for the passage of the Dower Act in Alberta; this ensured that a woman had the right to one-third of her husband's property. Emily became a familiar figure in the courts: a vocal political and legal reformer who belonged to more than twenty professional and volunteer groups. She and Nellie McClung helped gain the vote for women in Alberta.

After pleading for the appointment of a female magistrate, Emily Murphy was surprised to be offered the job. Judge Murphy strived to rehabilitate offenders rather than punish them and to remedy the social problems that led to crime. She also began waging a battle against the use of narcotics, and her writings about the drug trade resulted in new regulatory laws. Emily Murphy earned a reputation as a stern judge who was compassionate and caring.

Judge Murphy was accused of having no right to preside in a court-room since she was not a person in the eyes of British law — because she was a woman. Emily Murphy led a ten-year fight to gain legal recognition of women as "persons" — persons who were eligible for appointments to bodies such as to the Senate. Emily plotted to challenge the Supreme Court of Canada about the constitutionality of appointing women. On August 27, 1927, she convinced four other notable Albertans to join her in the battle: Louise McKinney, Henrietta Edwards, Nellie McClung, and Irene Parlby.

The group that became know as the Famous Five signed a petition to the Supreme Court of Canada. When the court ruled against them the women appealed to the Privy Council in England. On October 18, 1929, it ruled that the term "person" in the BNA Act included women and hence they could serve in the Canadian Senate. This legal victory was but one of the many achievements of the remarkable Emily Murphy — a feisty social activist and author who championed the disadvantaged throughout her life. She died at the age of sixty-five in 1933.

In 1938 Prime Minister William Lyon Mackenzie King unveiled a plaque in the Senate Lobby in honour of the Famous Five, and the following year portraits of each of the women were installed in the Alberta Legislature. On the fiftieth anniversary of the Persons Case the National Action Committee on the Status of Women issued a commemorative medallion, the Province of Alberta created the Persons Case Scholarship, and the Government of Canada established the Governor General's Awards in Commemoration of the Persons Case. Thanks to the lobbying of Frances Wright and The Famous Five Foundation, bronze monuments of the five Alberta women were installed in Calgary in 1999 and on Parliament Hill in 2000.

The Historic Sites and Monuments Board of Canada recognized Emily Murphy as a national historic person, and Canada Post issued a commemorative stamp in her honour in 1985. The City of Edmonton named a city park after the famous feminist, helping to ensure that Judge Murphy and her achievements will not be forgotten.

Quote:

"It is good to live in these first days when the foundations of things are being laid, to be able, now and then, to place a stone or carry the mortar to set it good and true."[287]

The 1938 unveiling of a plaque commemorating the Famous Five. (Front row, left to right): Mrs. Muir Edwards, daughter-in-law of Henrietta Muir Edwards; Mrs. J.C. Kenwood, daughter of Judge Emily Murphy; Hon. Mackenzie King; Mrs. Nellie McClung. (Rear row, left to right): Senators Iva Campbell Fallis and Cairine Wilson.

Off to See the Queen

Nahnebahwequay (Catherine Bunch Sonego Sutton)
1824–1865

County of Grey-Owen Sound Museum

A pioneer in the fight for Native rights, she refused to accept the theft of her land.

Nahnebahwequay.

Nahnebahwequay fought valiantly for the right of Native people to be treated fairly by Europeans. She was one of the few Native women in her day to have learned enough of the ways of the white men to understand how to battle for justice in their world.[288]

Nahnebahwequay (also known as Catherine Bunch Sonego) was born on the Credit River Flats of Ontario to Tyatiquob of the Eagle totem and Myarwikishigoqua of the Otter clan. They were Ojibwas: the Mississauga people. After her parents adopted Christianity the family joined a Methodist settlement and Nahnebahwequay attended a mission school. She spent a year in Great Britain with an English aunt, where they were joined by her uncle Kahkewaquonaby (also known as Peter Jones), who successfully appealed to Queen Victoria to grant land title deeds to the Credit band. Jones, who had become the young girl's adoptive father, was a notable Methodist minister, farmer, author, and translator who served as a powerful role model.

Nahnebahwequay attended a British school and after her return home fell in love with an English immigrant named William Sutton, who was about twice her age. The young Native woman was about fifteen years old when Rev. Jones married the happy couple. They eventually settled at Owen Sound, where they obtained two hundred acres of land from the Newash band. Returning to this land in 1857, after doing missionary work in Michigan for a few years, the Suttons discovered it had been surveyed and was being sold by the government. The Superintendent of Indian Affairs claimed their land title was worthless because the chiefs had not had the power to dispose of lands belonging to the tribe. He also refused to grant Nahnebahwequay her share of the band annuities because she had married a white man and had been out of the country.

Nahnebahwequay managed to buy some of her land back during a public auction, but the Indian Agent would not accept her purchase because she was by birth an Indian. Now a busy mother of five children, the outraged young woman joined with two Mississauga men who had land complaints to petition the provincial parliament in 1858. After the failure of this legal action, Nahnebahwequay was elected by the Indian council of her band to present the land claims of her people in Britain. But she needed money to get there and connections to arrange an audience with Queen Victoria.

The courageous woman headed to New York in search of funds. She gave a series of moving presentations that were reported in the press. As one observer noted, "She spoke in a touching strain for nearly an hour, giving a narration of the wrongs done to her tribe..."[289] Thanks to the support of some sympathetic Quakers, Nahnebahwequay was able to sail to England with a letter of introduction to a couple who were eventually able to arrange her presentation to Queen Victoria in 1860. The Native ambassador made a considerable impression on the Brits she met and one article reported, "Probably no Indian ever visited this country who excited more general interest than Mrs. Sutton."[290]

Nahnebahwequay gave birth to her sixth child in England before returning home. Through actions taken by the British government she eventually got permission to buy back her land, though the other Indians received no support. Catherine Sutton continued to speak out for the rights of her people in dealing with white settlers. She died in Canada West in 1865 at the age of forty-one.

As historian Donald Smith described Nahnebahwequay: "She is a giant; there are few women in the 19th century who were more courageous."[291] Her heroism seems largely forgotten today, but a display in the Grey County Museum commemorates the story of this remarkable woman.

Quote:

"I am an Indian; the blood of my forefathers runs in my veins, and I am not ashamed to own it; for my people were a noble race before the pale-faces came to possess their lands and home."[292]

Battle of the Rust

Margaret Newton
1887–1971

Prairie farmers were losing 30 million bushels of grain a year to rust. Until Margaret came to the rescue.

Margaret Newton.

Why did the Russian government offer this woman a fleet of camels for travel in the desert? Plus a staff of fifty scientists and an impressive salary of $10,000 per year? Because Margaret Newton was a brilliant scientist — an internationally renowned researcher who could help save Russian crops from the ravages of rust. Dr. Newton declined the offer in order to continue her research in Canada.

Margaret Newton was born in Montreal but spent much of her childhood on a family farm in western Quebec. Her father, John Newton, was very interested in the idea of scientific farming — and all five of his children studied agricultural science, graduating with doctorates. Margaret started out as a school teacher, using her savings to finance studies at university. She specialized in pathology and began investigating plant rust diseases. She became the first Canadian woman to earn a Ph.D. in agricultural science on graduation from the University of Minnesota in 1922.[293]

Due to severe economic losses from the destruction of crops attacked by rust, the federal government established the Dominion Rust Research Laboratory in Winnipeg and invited Dr. Newton to manage it. During a twenty-year period she and her team made important contributions to knowledge of cereal rusts, providing information that led to the development of rust-resistant grains. Wheat-producing countries around the world benefited from her findings. The scientist shared the results of her research in more than forty published papers, representing Canada at international conferences and lecturing in universities abroad.

When the renowned plant pathologist retired in 1945, because of health problems related to inhaling mould and rust spores, there were few Canadian crop losses from rust. Dr. Newton was granted a full pension only after farmers petitioned the government on her behalf, declaring, "This woman has saved the country millions of dollars."

Dr. Newton managed to support herself in a very successful career in science, gaining recognition in Canada and other countries. Historian Marsha Hay Snyder points out that Margaret Newton's distinguished career in science was a rarity for a woman in North America.[294] Most struggled just to get paid employment in their field, but Margaret had exceptional abilities, was incredibly persistent, and chose a botanic field that few men at the time were interested in. She was also fortunate in having the support of some influential male scientists who recognized her incredible talents at an early stage in her career. Margaret's success as a scientist was no doubt linked to the fact that she worked to the point of exhaustion, her only major breaks being canoe trips and foreign travel. She never married and devoted herself entirely to conquering stem rust.

Margaret Newton made an outstanding contribution to research in this area, helping the western economy and preventing a national disaster. She received many honours in recognition of her important scientific achievements, including election as a Fellow of the Royal Society of Canada in 1942; she was the second woman fellow, after the geologist Dr. Alice Wilson. In 1948 Dr. Newton was awarded the Society's prestigious Flavelle Medal. The Historic Sites and Monuments Board of Canada recognized Margaret Newton as a national historic person of Canada in 1996. She was also added to the Canadian Science and Engineering Hall of Fame, and the University of Victoria named one of its residences Margaret Newton Hall.

Quote:

"During my whole stay in Leningrad Dr. Vavilov and his staff went to infinite trouble to allow me to see as much as possible of each of the different phase of plant research now being carried on in Russia through the Lenin Academy of Agricultural Sciences ... As most of the magnificent palaces of Russia were vacant at the close of the revolution, a large number of these now house the (agricultural) institutes."[295]

Dr. Newton reporting on her research trip to Russia in 1933.

Farm Women Unite!

Mary Irene Marryat
Parlby
1868–1965

Irene Parlby.

> A reluctant politician,
> she became an eloquent
> champion of farm
> families and women.

She would have preferred to be gardening. Bored and disillusioned by the procedures needed to make new laws, Irene Parlby often joked that when her days in the Alberta provincial legislature were over she would love to dump her political papers in a bonfire — and joyfully dance round it. Bound by duty, she suffered the tedium for many years, working with colleague Nellie McClung and others to make remarkable improvements in the lives of women and children.[296]

Born in England in 1868, Irene Marryat was the oldest child of a British Army colonel. She was a privileged girl who spent part of her childhood in Punjab, India, and attended exclusive schools in Switzerland and Germany. On a visit to Western Canada the elegant young lady fell in love with Walter Parlby — an Oxford scholar who had become an Alberta farmer. After their marriage the happy newlyweds settled into a comfortable home on their farm near Alix, where they raised son Humphrey. Many of their English relatives joined them in Western Canada.

Irene quickly discovered the challenges of pioneer life, particularly those faced by prairie farmers. The Parlbys became involved in organizing farmers and joined the United Farmers of Alberta (UFA). Irene reluctantly agreed to serve as President of the United Farm Women of Alberta because she wanted to ensure that farm families had access to municipal hospitals, public health nurses, travelling medical clinics, and good education for their children. A few years later Irene was asked to run as a UFA candidate in the provincial election and was elected as the party swept into power. A member of the Alberta legislature for fourteen years, the Honourable Irene Parlby became the first woman in Alberta to hold a cabinet post in government, and the second in the British Empire.

While Irene Parlby was not one of the most vocal members of the legislature, her speeches made a big impact. As one reporter for the *Edmonton Journal* noted, "If all orators spoke with the culture and sincerity of Hon. Irene Parlby the world of public affairs would be better off. She is in every way a rare treat to listen to."[297] Despite her reserved nature Irene proved to be extremely effective in criticizing her political opponents. It was noted on one particular occasion that "Her words tinkled like hailstones on a metal roof. She opened a broadside which for intense brevity and point has seldom been equalled."[298]

During the UFA government's years in office eighteen acts were passed relating to the welfare of women and children, many of which were due to the efforts of Irene Parlby. She encouraged measures to provide more opportunities for higher education to students, some of which were influenced by her 1928 study of educational systems in Sweden and Denmark.

On the invitation of Prime Minister R.B. Bennett, Irene Parlby represented Canada at the 1930 meeting of the League of Nations in Geneva. She was a tireless advocate for peace among nations. Irene Parlby was one of the Famous Five who succeeded in gaining legal recognition of women as persons, eligible for appointment to the Senate of Canada, in October 1929 (See Emily Muphy, page 192.) Irene was concerned about the recognition of women as persons in a broad sense, considering it a major step in the advancement of the status of Canadian women. In 1935 she became the first woman to be awarded an honorary doctorate by the University of Alberta. On presenting her with the degree of Honorary Doctor of Laws, President Wallace noted: "In shaping the policies of one of the great social movements among women in our country, Mary Irene Parlby has played a leading part."[299]

Irene Parlby welcomed the end of her political career in 1935. She returned to gardening, cooking, family, and the farm. But she continued to make her views known through publications, speeches, and radio broadcasts, including some early coast-to-coast broadcasts undertaken by the

Canadian Broadcasting Corporation. She participated in one notable panel on "The Position of Women in Canada" along with Quebec suffragist Thérèse Casgrain and *Saturday Night* editor B.K. Sandwell.

Irene Parlby died in Red Deer, Alberta, at the age of ninety-seven. This notable pioneer made significant contributions to Canadian society — helping to make important improvements that continue to benefit women and children in particular. In addition to her inclusion in commemorations for the Famous Five, Irene Parlby has been recognized by the Historic Sites and Monuments Board of Canada as a national historic person. The City of Edmonton created Irene Parlby Park as a tribute.

Quote:
"The mind is not a vessel to be filled, but a hearth to be lighted."[300]

Mona Parsons.

Escaping the Nazis
Mona Parsons
1901–1976

After fleeing from a Nazi prison in World War II she survived a perilous walk — much of it in bare feet — across Germany, before reaching Allied troops in Holland.

She was filthy and scrawny, just eighty-seven pounds, when she spied the soldier in Holland. Mona Parsons advised the incredulous young man that she had just walked across Germany, having escaped a Nazi prison during Allied bombing. By amazing coincidence he belonged to a regiment from her home province in Canada: the North Nova Scotia Highlanders.

Mona Parsons was born in Middleton, Nova Scotia, but grew up in Wolfville, where she attended the Acadia Ladies Seminary and the Conservatory of Music and Fine Arts.[301] After studies in Boston and Arkansas the striking brunette headed to New York City, where she landed a spot in the Ziegfeld Follies. After working for years as an actress and chorus girl, she trained to be a nurse and worked in a medical office on Park Avenue.

Mona's life suddenly changed when her brother introduced her to Willem Leonhardt, a millionaire businessman who was visiting America. The two were wed on September 1, 1937, in Holland, where Mona settled with her new husband in a beautiful home in Laren. It was in her beloved Ingleside that the couple hid Allied airmen trying to escape to England after the outbreak of World War I. In September 1941 officers in the Gestapo arrested her and Willem was captured three months later.

Both survived the war, but Mona spent four harrowing years in Nazi prisons. In March 1945 a forty-something Mona and a young baroness escaped during bombing of Vechta, Germany. After an incredible three-week walk across the country the pair reached the safety of Holland. Mona was hospitalized until the end of the war and returned to Ingleside, where her husband joined her following his liberation from a concentration camp. For her efforts to help the resistance efforts during World War II, Mona Parsons received citations from the governments of Great Britain and the United States.

Mona's welcome return to her home was disrupted by the 1956 death of Willem and the news that non-Dutch residents could not inherit property — Mona was still a Canadian citizen. Apparently ignored by Willem's family, Mona was evicted from her home of nineteen years. In December of 1957 she set sail for Canada, settling in Halifax.

In June 1959 Mona Parsons married a retired military man — Major General Harry Foster. After he died in 1964 she settled again in Wolfville, Nova Scotia.

When Mona became seriously ill in 1976 the nightmares of Nazi prisons haunted her. The courageous Canadian is buried in the Wolfville cemetery, where the engraving notes only that she was the "wife of Major General H.W. Foster."

Quote:

"I had steeled myself for this moment. I knew that all eyes were on me, expecting me to burst into tears. I determined not to humble myself before any of them. As I left the courtroom, I put my heels together and bowed toward the judge, the prosecutor and my German counsel, who were standing together in a group. 'Guten morgen, meine herren [Good morning, gentlemen],' I said."[302]

> Mona Parsons' memories of the moment she received
> news of her death sentence in a Nazi courtroom.

A signed photo of Mary Pickford for the
Honourable Mackenzie King.

Gladys Goes to Hollywood
Mary Pickford
1892–1979

To adoring audiences around the globe she was the first Hollywood superstar. She transformed herself from the sickly Gladys Louise Smith of Toronto to the first female movie mogul in America.

Mary Pickford was Hollywood's first superstar, a great power as well as an actress. She was the most famous woman of her era — and also the best paid.[303] Dubbed "America's Sweetheart" by an adoring public, Mary became a successful actress and married Hollywood's most famous male star: Douglas Fairbanks. The couple were key players in the founding and operation of United Artists (the major movie distribution company). Mary wrote and produced films. The diminutive blonde, who stood just five feet tall, paved the way for other women to become successful directors and producers.

Mary was born in Toronto on April 8, 1893, as Gladys Louise Smith. Both sets of grandparents had settled in Toronto, Ontario, about the middle of the nineteenth century. Gladys's father, John Charles Smith, was the son of English Methodists, while her mother, Charlotte Hennessey, was born to Catholics who hailed from County Kerry in Ireland. John and Charlotte lived in a tiny house at 175 University Avenue.

Gladys adored her gentle father despite his alcoholism and problems in supporting the poor family. John Smith died at the age of thirty, perhaps in an alcohol-related accident, leaving his twenty-four-year-old wife with three small children: Gladys, nearly six, Lottie, and baby Jack. For a while the three were cared for in other homes, as the widowed Charlotte tried to face the challenges of her predicament. At one point a wealthy doctor and his wife offered to adopt little Gladys, but the child refused to leave her family.

During her childhood Gladys lived through diphtheria, pneumonia, tuberculosis, and nervous conditions. She missed a lot of school, until Charlotte withdrew the children after an angry teacher scolded them for being late, threatening that the devil would take them away from their mother if they were tardy again. Gladys spent only a few months in the formal education system.

Charlotte tried to support her children as a seamstress, until a man who worked as a stage manager suggested she try to put the three on the stage. The desperate widow, horrified at the idea of exposing her darlings to what most people assumed went on in the world of theatre, was pleasantly relieved when she dared to visit. So in September 19, 1898, Gladys Smith appeared on stage at the Princess Theatre in Toronto in the play *The Silver King*. For six evening performances and two matinees the six-year-old girl earned eight dollars.

Soon the entire Smith family was getting small parts, and eventually they toured across the United States. They didn't make a lot of money and the travelling was tough, but much of the time they were together. Sometimes they spent their breaks in Toronto. They were surviving, often eating poorly and crashing in sleazy hotels. A stressed Charlotte began to drink heavily.

By the age of fifteen Gladys was fed up and decided she wanted to work for the esteemed David Belasco, a noted theatrical producer. Gladys managed to audition for the great one and sent home a triumphant letter to her mother in Toronto: she was engaged to appear on Broadway, with the stage name of Mary Pickford. She premiered on December 3, 1907.

Despite working with David Belasco, Mary Pickford still had a tough life and wasn't making much money. After considerable urging from her mother, Mary decided to try her luck with something new: films. Serious actors considered such productions shameful and unimportant compared to Broadway. But given that one could earn five dollars a day, Mary agreed to approach Biograph, the leading film company in New York. Filmmaker D.W. Griffith hired Mary Pickford, and she played forty-five roles for him in 1909.

Life finally became easier for Mary and her family. She married a Biograph actor, Owen Moore. It is possible that in the early years of their marriage Mary Pickford became pregnant and had an abortion that made her unable to have other children.

By the time Mary Pickford performed in her fifth film for the studio Famous Players, she'd become a star. By early 1915 she was receiving five hundred letters from fans each day and earning $4,000 per week. The press reported she was the highest paid woman in the world. Mary later signed a contract with Famous Players, where she was guaranteed to receive $10,000 weekly. At the age of twenty-three, Mary Pickford was at the financial peak of her profession; in addition to being the highest paid movie star in history, she was also the most powerful.[304]

In 1918 Mary Pickford and her mother created Mary Pickford Company. Mary would select her own stories and hire her own directors and casts. As an independent producer, Mary signed a contract for distribution of her films with First National; her basic salary rose to $675,000 per year. In 1919, when there was talk in Hollywood that the big studios were going to take tighter control of the movie stars, Mary helped create the corporation United Artists, along with Douglas Fairbanks, Charlie Chaplin, and D.W. Griffith; the goal was to make their own movies and be independent. Mary's first production, *Pollyanna*, was a smashing success.

After divorcing Owen Moore, Mary married the famous actor Douglas Fairbanks in 1920. Throughout their European honeymoon the pair was swarmed by crowds of fans, who welcomed them in Southampton with roses dropped from airplanes. The celebrated newlyweds lived in a Hollywood home called Pickfair, where the pair was apparently very happy for many years. Famous people from around the world visited, everyone from the King and Queen of Siam, the Crown Prince of Japan, and Babe Ruth, to Einstein, Marconi, and Lindbergh.

In 1927 the couple were among the Hollywood greats who created the Academy of Motion Picture Arts and Sciences. Sound was coming to motion pictures and a nervous Mary Pickford decided to try the "talkies." She bought rights to a Broadway play and played the leading role in the film adaptation of *Coquette*, released in April 1929. She received the Academy of Motion Picture Arts and Sciences Best Actress Award that year, but her subsequent films didn't do well. In 1932 Mary Pickford decided to retire from acting while she was still a star. Reflecting on the success she'd had playing young girls in the movies (even as an adult), Mary wrote:

> The little girl made me. I wasn't waiting for the little girl to kill me. I'd already been pigeonholed. I know I'm an artist and that's not being arrogant, because talent comes from God. I could have done more dramatic perform-ances than the ones I gave in *Coquette* and *Secrets* but I was already typed.[305]

Mary's relationship with Douglas Fairbanks soured and she filed for divorce in 1935. On June 26, 1937, Mary Pickford married a band leader and former actor called Buddy Rogers. In 1943, when Mary was fifty-one and Buddy forty, the couple adopted two children: Mary and Ronnie.

In 1976 Mary Pickford was awarded an honorary Oscar at the Academy Awards. Too ill to attend, weighing less than ninety pounds, she posed for pictures from home to accept the award. Mary Pickford died May 25, 1979, at the age of eighty-seven, with her beloved husband Buddy at her side. In October of that year the Academy of Motion Picture Arts and Sciences held a tribute for one of their own.

Throughout the years Mary Pickford retained her ties with Canada, refusing to give up her citizenship even when threatened by U.S. authorities that she would have to do so. During the First World War she had put thousands into the Canadian War Loan and had her mother bring the money to Toronto in person. In January 1948 she premiered her movie *Sleep My Love* in Ottawa, dining with Prime Minister William Lyon Mackenzie King prior to the show.

Mary would have liked to have received the Order of Canada, but was advised that she could not be considered because she left the country at an early age and only visited in subsequent years.[306]

Quote:

"I've worked and fought my way through since I was twelve, and I know business."[307]

Wartime Adventures in Nursing
Georgina Pope
1862–1938

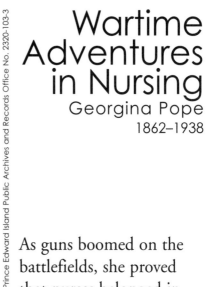

As guns boomed on the battlefields, she proved that nurses belonged in the military.

Georgina Pope.

During the Boer War in South Africa Georgina Pope often slept in a tent "in terror of scorpions and snakes as bed-fellows."[308] Georgina was among the first civilian nurses who volunteered to assist the British Staff Medical Corps and led Canada's first contingent of four nurses in 1899. As they cared for the wounded the nursing sisters faced everything from heavy rains and blowing sand during the Cape southeaster, to temperatures so cold that medicine would freeze in the glasses carried to patients.

Born in Charlottetown, Prince Edward Island, Georgina Fane Pope belonged to a prominent family. Her father, William Henry Pope, was a judge and politician who had served as colonial secretary of P.E.I. and was a Father of Confederation. After training at the School of Nursing, Bellevue Hospital, in New York City (America's first nursing school inspired by the teachings of Florence Nightingale), Georgina began a career as a nurse in the United States. She managed three Civil Hospitals.

Following the outbreak of war in South Africa in 1899 she volunteered to serve overseas, and was appointed superintendent of Canada's military nurses. They wore khaki uniforms consisting of a bicycle skirt, a Russian blouse and brown leather boots. These Canadian nurses had the rank, pay, and benefits of lieutenant. At this time no other nurses in the world had official military status in an army.[309] During their first year of service Georgina and her companions worked at various hospitals, many of which were huts or tents. While posted to Kroonstadt, Lieutenant Pope and her team looked after thirty officers and two hundred men, most of whom had enteric fever.

When hostilities in South Africa seemed to peter out at the end of 1890, the sisters returned to Canada and were put on reserve status. By August 1, 1901, the Canadian Nursing Service in the Army Medical Corps was official, with Georgina Pope among the seven members. After it became evident that the fighting had not ended, she returned for another stint of duty in South Africa in 1902. Georgina Pope became the first Canadian to receive the Royal Red Cross — for her service as a military nurse in the Boer War.

With the creation of a permanent Army Medical Corps in Canada in 1906 Georgina was appointed as Canada's first Nursing Matron and was stationed primarily in Halifax at a military hospital. She had responsibility for all its military nurses, which included about five permanent staff and up to eighty reservists in 1914. As a result of Georgina's recommendations their khaki uniforms were replaced by blue ones, which during the Great War earned the Canadian Nursing Sisters the nickname of "Bluebirds." Eager to serve overseas during World War I despite a variety of health problems, Matron Pope worked at a number of military hospitals in Europe before being admitted herself in February 1918 — suffering from shell shock and nervous debility, among other things. She retired the following year due to disability acquired during service.

At this time Matron-in-Chief Margaret Macdonald paid tribute to her esteemed colleague, noting, "Whilst her individual work has always commanded the highest praise and admiration, it must also be remembered that to her is largely due the success that has ever attended the C.A.M.C., Nursing Service — a success that might never have been attained but for the lofty ideals set and maintained by Matron Pope from the inception of the Corps."[310]

When Georgina Pope died at the age of seventy-six her death was determined to be related to service, so she received a full military funeral attended by many war veterans. The Historic Sites and Monuments Board of Canada recognized Georgina Pope, one of Canada's pioneer Nursing Sisters, as a national historic person of Canada in 1983.

Quote:

"Here under canvas in June, like our Sisters at Springfontein we suffered acutely from cold. Each morning the hoar frost was thick, both inside and out of our single bell tents. We were very short of water, and lived on rations which an orderly cooked for us on a fire on the veldt."[311]

Georgina Pope's memories of service in South Africa.

National Archives of Canada/PA-136938
Isabella Preston with lilies, ca. 1956.

For the Love of Lilies

Isabella Preston

1881–1964

She was a blooming success, creating everything from "Stenographer Lilies" to lilacs named after Shakespearean heroines.

Isabella Preston came to Canada to see if she liked the life here — and she did. She was a talented and determined woman who became a world-renowned horticulturalist, famous for developing hybrids of flowers and other garden plants.[312] She created nearly two hundred hybrids during her long career and became the federal government's leading authority on ornamental horticulture. One plant breeder wrote, "You are one of my heroes, not only because you have been successful in a line which I should like to be successful in, but because of your long record of helpfulness and human sympathy."[313]

Isabella grew up in a middle-class family in Lancaster, England. A keen gardener, she took a short course at Swanley Horticultural College when she was twenty-five. After the death of her parents she accepted the invitation of her adventurous sister Margaret to accompany her to Canada. The pair settled in Guelph, Ontario, where Isabella got a job picking peaches and plums on a fruit farm. Eager to make her interest in horticulture more than a hobby, Isabella enrolled at the Ontario Agricultural College.

While working as a greenhouse labourer she began learning about plant breeding and experimenting with lilies. In 1916 she made an important cross that led to the development of the Creelman lily and many other hybrids — and Isabella Preston became a notable plant hybridist in North America. In 1920 Isabella managed to get a job as day labourer at Ottawa's Central Experimental Farm, where there was a lot of research and breeding of ornamental plants. Through her work she gained the knowledge that made her a professional: a specialist in ornamental horticulture.

Because of Isabella's work in developing hybrid lilacs in the 1920s, Canada gained international recognition in this field. Fifty of the crosses she developed were named after heroines from Shakespeare — Adriana, Portia, etc. Isabella Preston also developed many hybrid roses and created some prize-winning irises that she named after Canadian rivers. The Ottawa, for example, received an international prize. Isabella also developed thirty-three hybrids of crab apples, named after Canadian lakes.

And of course there were more lilies. She made hundreds of crosses of different lilies in her plant breeding program, producing such notable hybrids as the "Stenographer Lilies" — named after seven stenographers from the Horticulture Division at the Central Experimental Farm. These lilies became popular with lily growers around the world.

Isabella Preston was also a prolific writer, corresponding with amateur growers and professionals round the world, writing books and articles. Though a shy person, she led garden tours and gave radio talks. Among the many tributes to her enduring contribution to horticulture was the creation of the Isabella Preston Trophy by the North American Lily Society in 1956. Preston Street in Ottawa is named for this notable scientist, and many beautiful species of flowers blooming in gardens throughout the world are a testimony to her achievements.

Quote:

"Dr. Macoun was looking for someone to do breeding work with ornamental plants so I applied for the position. I wanted to discontinue working with vegetables which I had to do during the war. Dr. Macoun gave me a list of plants and told me to see what I could do with them."[314]

Isabella Preston explaining how she began working as a hybridist.

Susie Carson Rijnhart in Tibetan costume.

Tragedy in Tibet

Susanna Carson Rijnhart
1868–1908

Risking her life to bring the gospel to Tibetans, she paid a terrible price.

Susanna Carson (commonly referred to as Susie) dreamed of being a foreign missionary at an early age. Born in Chatham, Ontario in 1868, she received a liberal classical education thanks to the progressive views of her father, J.S. Carson — a school principal. She joined the Methodist Church at the age of sixteen, becoming an ardent Christian active in the Epworth League (the Methodist youth organization) and Christian Endeavor.[315] Susie entered Woman's Medical College in Toronto and graduated with an M.D. in 1888. She practised medicine in London and Strathroy.

Susie discovered a kindred spirit when she met Petrus Rijnhart. A charismatic Dutchman who worked in a Toronto factory and gave presentations appealing for missions to Tibet, he had already served in Lanzhou with the China Inland Mission (CIM). Susie may not have known that the poorly educated man had been dismissed by the CIM for being an imposter, but she married Petrus in 1894 and the couple sailed for the Orient a few weeks later. The Rijnharts planned to spend their lives working in Tibet as independent missionaries.

The pair faced an incredible challenge in even reaching the mountainous land, which few Europeans had managed to visit and where no one had established a permanent mission. Eager to avoid the closely guarded borders that would not admit foreigners, the Rijnharts undertook an incredible 3,200-kilometre trip across China to enter Tibet.[316] After a six-month journey they settled on the border of Outer Tibet at Lusar near a major Buddhist monastery. Many Tibetans welcomed Dr. Rijnhart's medical skills and she heeded their pleas to treat the wounded on the battlefields during a terrible Muslim rebellion that killed one hundred thousand.

Because of their sincerity and respect for local customs and religious practices, the Rijnharts seem to have been accepted by the Tibetans in Lusar and were befriended by the head abbot. But the couple made no converts and yearned to do missionary work in the interior of Tibet. They moved on to the trading town of Tankar, but were anxious to reach their ultimate goal: the forbidden capital of Lhasa (the city which the Rijnharts believed to be the only one in the world absolutely inaccessible to Westerners). The zealous missionaries set out in the spring of 1898 with the conviction that "if ever the gospel were proclaimed in Lhasa, someone would have to be the first to undertake the journey, to meet the difficulties, to preach the first sermon and perhaps never return to tell the tale..."[317]

Now travelling with their infant son, Charlie, the Rijnharts began their journey well-equipped with guides, horses, tents, clothing and bedding, food supplies for a year, drugs, trading goods, and five hundred New Testaments. The guides soon deserted them and the baby suddenly became ill and died. The grieving parents buried their son in the Dang La Mountains, after placing a bunch of blue poppies and wild asters in his tiny coffin. Several days later mountain robbers attacked the caravan, forcing the couple to continue with one horse and a few supplies. Petrus spotted a camp of nomads across a river and planned to swim across to seek help. He never returned and it was later determined that he had been murdered.

After anxious days of waiting for her husband, Dr. Susie Rijnhart realized she was lost and alone. She survived a hazardous two-month journey before reaching the safety of a missionary settlement at Tachienlu in Sichuan province. Her hair turned white by her horrendous ordeal, Susie returned home to Chatham in 1900 and lectured about her experiences. The medical missionary was hailed as "a Canadian heroine"[318] and persuaded to write a book about her four years in Tibet.

Despite the tragic conclusion of her travels, Dr. Rijnhart returned to Tachienlu in 1902 to establish a mission in Tibet. She married missionary James Moyes in 1905 and they returned to Canada several years later because of Susie's ill health. Dr. Rijnhart died at the age of forty, leaving behind her two-month-old baby. Today the remarkable doctor and pioneer missionary is remembered primarily because of the moving book she wrote about her adventures in Tibet.

Quote:

"...The cold earth of Tibet, the great forbidden land, closed over the body of the first Christian child committed to its bosom — little Charles Carson Rijnhart, aged one year, one month and twenty-two days."[319]

Dr. Rijnhart's painful recollection of burying her baby boy.

The Jewish Public Library Archives, Montreal

Militant on the March
Léa Roback
1903–2000

Léa Roback.

Raised to believe that every injustice requires action, she never backed down from a fight.

"Knitting isn't my passion — social causes are," said the spunky activist Léa Roback.[320] She became a fearless union organizer.

Born in Montreal, Léa Roback was the daughter of Jewish immigrants from Poland. She spent her childhood in Beauport, where her parents operated a general store and raised a family of nine children. Léa quickly became fluent in English and French as well as Yiddish — and had her first experience with racism when a young customer called Mr. Roback a "dirty Jew."

At fifteen Léa began working in Montreal. Encouraged by her mother to explore the world, she saved enough money to go to Europe when she was twenty-two. The young adventurer studied literature in Grenoble and earned a Bachelor of Arts. After a stint working in New York she joined her brother in Berlin, where she studied and taught English until 1933. During these years of political unrest in Germany the young woman witnessed the rise of Hitler. She joined the Communist Party and participated in protests against Nazism, learning useful techniques for militant socialism. Léa returned to Canada to escape the growing anti-Semitism.

Back in Montreal Léa Roback began her lifelong work as a social activist and reformer. Along with Norman Bethune she began organizing to help the unemployed. In 1934 she spent three months in the midst of the Russian revolution in the Soviet Union, joining a lover there; Léa apparently married in Europe at some point but the union was annulled.[321] On her return home she began working in the suffrage movement with Thérèse Casgrain, established the first Marxist bookstore in Montreal, and organized a Marxist study group. Léa also campaigned for Communist

Party candidate Fred Rose, who in 1943 became the first Communist member in the House of Commons. She survived RCMP harassment for her leftist connections and police raids on her store, but eventually became disillusioned with the Communist Party and dropped out in 1958.

In 1936 Léa got a job with the International Ladies' Garment Workers' Union. Shocked by the sixty-hour workweek, meager wages, and appalling working conditions, she was determined to help the unskilled workers in the garment industry — most of whom were women. She managed to unite the immigrant workers and the many French-Canadian women who were reluctant to challenge authority figures such as the factory owners. It was an incredible feat when Léa Roback led five thousand garment industry workers on a massive strike in 1937. In one of the first organized labour battles involving women in Quebec, they pounded the pavement for twenty-five days before winning some significant improvements.

The zealous union organizer then tackled RCA Victor, where she was hired to work on an assembly-line at a munitions plant. In 1941 Léa organized a union in St. Henri to help improve working conditions for the more than four thousand employees. She worked as a grievance officer until the company fired all union members in 1952.

A long-time activist in the feminist group the Voice of Women, Léa was throughout her life involved in causes to support women and children, and any other groups she felt needed support. Léa was always marching — fighting for women's rights, world peace, wage equity, free education, the right to therapeutic abortions, and just treatment for the Mohawks of Kanehsatake. Protesting against the war in Vietnam, nuclear armament, apartheid in South Africa, pornography, toys that encourage violence, and many other issues.

Léa received the Order of Quebec and an honorary membership from The Canadian Research Institute for the Advancement of Women. On her ninetieth birthday about 250 people gathered to show their affection and respect for an exceptional woman, and to form the Léa Roback Foundation to promote the advancement of women through education. Never at a loss for colourful commentary on the issues of the day, Léa Roback was still giving interviews (to Radio-Canada) until the day before she died at the age of ninety-seven. Today she is widely celebrated as a heroine who courageously fought for her ideals and inspired others to do the same.[322]

Quote:

"There is nothing that I like better than to be standing on a street corner, passing out Leaflets, because it is how you come to understand what people are about."[323]

Detail of National Archives of Canada/PA-151007

World's Greatest Woman Athlete
Fanny "Bobbie" Rosenfeld
1903–1969

She was an extraordinary athlete, stealing the hearts of Olympic fans with her incredible speed and sportsmanship.

Fanny Rosenfeld, right, at the 1928 Summer Olympic Games, Amsterdam.

In her day she was thought to be the world's greatest woman athlete.[324] She was the obvious choice when named Canadian woman athlete of the half-century in 1949. Only the early onset of severe arthritis was able to stop the amazing Bobbie.

Fanny Rosenfeld was born in Russia, and immigrated to Canada with her family shortly after. They settled in Ontario, where she soon began participating in a variety of sports and became known as an outstanding athlete. Friends nicknamed her "Bobbie" because she preferred to wear her hair bobbed, in a short haircut convenient for sporting activities.

While working as a stenographer at a chocolate factory in Toronto, Fanny competed in her favourite sports: basketball, softball, hockey, and track and field. A natural athlete, she never had a coach. She excelled in all but swimming — though her passion was hockey. Fellow athlete Constance Hennessey remembered, "She was a fine hockey player ... She checked hard and she had a shot like a bullet."[325]

In the 1920s she played on several championship basketball teams. In 1924 she won the Toronto grass court tennis championship. But it was at the 1928 Amsterdam Olympics, where for the first time women were permitted to compete in track and field, that Bobbie Rosenfeld shone. She had already set three national records in track and field that year, records that would not be broken until the 1950s. She won a silver medal in the hundred-metre race and a gold in the four-hundred-metre relay. Bobbie gained more points for Canada than any other athlete at the Games.

Bobbie also ran in the eight-hundred-metre race to encourage fellow Canadian Jean Thompson, who'd injured her leg during training. Bobbie ran along with Jean, coaxing her to go on and refusing to pass her. Jean came fourth, with Bobbie following at fifth, though many observers felt that Bobbie could have pushed ahead and won a medal. But it was not her style. As her team manager Alexandrine Gibb said later, "Bobbie Rosenfeld's sportsmanship in this event was one of the high spots of the games ... In the annals of women's athletics, there is no finer deed than this."[326]

In less than a year Bobbie was in bed with severe arthritis, then spent a year on crutches. She managed to return to compete in some sports, becoming the best home run hitter in a major softball league in 1931, and the outstanding player in Ontario women's hockey in 1931–32. Arthritis finally forced her from athletic competition in 1933.

Bobbie Rosenfeld spent about twenty years as a sports columnist for the Toronto *Globe & Mail*, becoming a prominent advocate for greater participation of women in sports. She celebrated female pioneers and encouraged more physical education programs for girls in school.

Bobbie retired from sports writing in 1966 due to illness. She died three years later, with one newspaper reporting, "The golden girl who had won fame with the speed of her legs and the skill of her arms had become an ailing and lonely figure."[327] Perhaps she wondered what might have been if she had been able to compete longer.

Bobbie Rosenfeld is remembered as a superb athlete and a strong advocate for women in sports, as well as for her impressive sportsmanship. In 1949 she was inducted into Canada's Sports Hall of Fame, and in 1976 the Historic Sites and Monuments Board recognized her as a national historic person. Bobbie's accomplishments have also been celebrated by the 1991 creation of Bobbie Rosenfeld Park in Toronto and the issuing of a commemorative stamp by Canada Post in 1996. Every year the Canadian Press awards the Bobbie Rosenfeld trophy to Canada's Female Athlete of the Year.

Quote:

"Athletic maids to arms! ... We are taking up the sword, and high time it is in defense of our so-called athletic bodies to give the lie to those pen flourishers who depict us not as paragons of feminine physique, beauty and health, but rather as Amazons and ugly ducklings all because we have become sports-minded."[328]

Gabrielle Roy.

Literary Legend
Gabrielle Roy
1909–1983

She was one of the few French-Canadian authors to reach people across the country.[329]

A child of the prairies, Gabrielle Roy grew up lamenting "the misfortune of being French-Canadian." She was the youngest of eleven children born to Léon and Mélina Roy in the French Catholic community of St. Boniface, Manitoba. Her father, a Quebecker who left his home province in search of greater opportunities, enjoyed working as a federal employee who helped immigrants settle in Western Canada. Disaster struck the family when Léon was laid off in 1913 for political reasons, just six months before the elderly Léon was to retire and receive a pension. The family was left destitute.

During Gabrielle's childhood the Roys struggled to cope with their sudden poverty and Mélina was forced to take in boarders. Gabrielle discovered that Franco-Manitobans were treated as second-class citizens, that her French-speaking mother was scorned for asking to be served in her own language in Winnipeg stores. The francophone child began attending the Académie Saint-Joseph at the time the nuns faced the challenge of complying with Manitoba's new policy that decreed that English was to be the primary language of teaching. Gabrielle, determined to please her mother and be a "dazzling success,"[330] eventually became a model student proficient in both English and French. Proving herself to be brilliant as well as hardworking, she brought home countless medals and prizes.

A cash prize funded her first year at the Winnipeg Normal Institute, with the stipulation that she become a teacher. Gabrielle received her Teacher's Certificate in 1929. She managed to secure a permanent position in St. Boniface despite the Depression and also became a member of a drama troupe. She took a composition course, selling her first story (in English) to the *Free Press* in 1934. Gabrielle had a good job and an active social life but became increasingly anxious to flee from the confines of St. Boniface. As she would later write, "Can I deny finding in my heart that perhaps I'd always wanted to break the chain, escape from my poor dispossessed people?"[331]

Gabrielle left for Europe in August 1937, bound for London and Paris to study drama. Encouraged by her success in having some articles published in a French publication, she returned to Canada several years later determined to gamble on a writing career. With only her trunk, a typewriter, and about fifteen dollars left to her name, Gabrielle decided not to go back to her secure teaching job in Manitoba. She rented a room in Montreal and earned money as a journalist while beginning her first novel, *Bonhour d'occasion*, about the poor in the grimy tenements of the Saint-Henri district. Published in 1945, the book became a best-seller that sold more than 1 million copies and earned her the Prix Fémina. The English translation, *The Tin Flute*, earned the acclaimed author a Governor General's award.

In 1947 Gabrielle Roy wed physician Dr. Marcel Carbotte. The marriage lasted until her death but brought considerable anguish as the two lived in different worlds, and Marcel was a homosexual who had a secret lover for twenty years.[332] Gabrielle began writing another novel during the three years the newlyweds spent in France. They later settled in Quebec City and she spent every summer writing at a nearby cottage in Charlevoix.

Gabrielle Roy was a prolific writer who penned many fine novels, all with Canadian settings, which gained popularity with both Francophones and Anglophones. She depicted immigrants, the poor, and underprivileged — characters inspired by her native Manitoba. The first female member of the Royal Society of Canada, the reclusive author won the Prix Duvernay, the Prix David, and the Molson Prize. Considered to be one of the foremost French-Canadian novelists,[333] Gabrielle gained international renown, and for many Franco-Manitobans, "Her many books have been our voice."[334]

Quote:

"Saint-Boniface breathed, prayed, hoped, sang and suffered in French, but it earned its living in English, in the offices, stores and factories of Winnipeg. The irremediable and existential difficulty of being French-Canadian in Manitoba or elsewhere!"[335]

Gabrielle Roy looking back on her childhood in Manitoba.

Idola Saint-Jean, ca. 1940-1945.

Are Women People?
Idola Saint-Jean
1880–1945

Once called the suffrage saber,[336] she took on the Quebec establishment with her "shock feminism."

Charm was not her strong point. Idola Saint-Jean preferred the direct approach in demanding equal rights for women. The fiery feminist was outraged that while most Canadian women had won the vote in 1918, the women of Quebec were still denied this right. To remedy the situation she was prepared to confront the government and the Catholic clergy.

Idola Saint-Jean was an influential activist, journalist, and teacher who used her many talents to help women in Quebec finally win the right to vote in 1940. She courageously withstood hostile personal attacks for decades as she fought to obtain basic rights for women in Quebec: to vote and run in provincial elections, to pursue their chosen professions, and to have legal rights within marriage. Critics seemed particularly vindictive towards Idola because she was an assertive unmarried career woman — one Quebec MLA even offered her his trousers, while shouting insults as she participated in a suffragist delegation to Quebec City.[337]

Born in Montreal, she was the well-educated daughter of prominent lawyer Edmond Saint-Jean and his wife, Emma Lemoine. After studying theatre in Paris with teachers from the Comédie-française, Idola supported herself by teaching French and diction in Montreal schools and French literature at McGill University. She also worked as a journalist, whose credits included a bilingual weekly radio program in the 1930s and a guest editorship at the *Montreal Herald* — which promoted her as a "vigorous, virile, but distinctly feminine woman."[338]

As leader of one of the two major suffrage groups in Quebec, Idola played a major role in securing basic rights for women in that province. A one-time prominent member of a suffrage association formed in Montreal in 1922, she founded another group in 1927 (Alliance canadienne pour le vote des femmes du Québec) with plans for more aggressive activity and promotion of the needs of working-class women. Until 1940 the activist joined the yearly delegations of women who headed to Quebec City in support of a female suffrage bill. She sought support from federal politicians, the Supreme Court, and even King George V — to whom she sent a petition with ten thousand signatures. For decades Idola lobbied through her powerful speeches, radio programs, and articles in newspapers and magazines.

In addition to her key role in the struggle for suffrage in Quebec, Idola championed many other social causes. During the 1918–19 Spanish influenza epidemic she created a charitable group that helped the poor in Montreal and adopted a Black girl whose parents had died; the child only lived a few years. In November 1929, in one of Idola's efforts to ridicule Quebec's discriminatory Civil Code, which treated married women as subordinates of their spouses, she put together twelve cartoons and texts that appeared in a series called "Are Women People?" Idola worked for better conditions for female rural teachers and labourers in industry, access of women to the professions and federal civil service jobs, pensions for mothers and the elderly, and reforms relating to juvenile offenders. She also supported the international peace movement and chaired the Peace Committee of the Royal Empire Society in the 1930s.

Courageously taking on the many opponents of the social changes she supported, Idola Saint-Jean played a leading role in the fight for women's rights and social justice. She contributed to many significant improvements in the status of women in Quebec as well as across Canada. In 1997 the Historic Sites and Monuments Board of Canada recognized Idola Saint-Jean as a national historic person of Canada. Canada Post issued a special stamp to commemorate her important contribution to Canadian history, and the City of Montreal named a park in her honour. Each year the Quebec Federation of Women awards the Idola St-Jean Prize in remembrance of this feminist pioneer.

Quote:

"Feminism is based on social justice, for it claims but the equality of rights and possibility between men and women."[339]

A Daughter of Iceland

Laura Goodman Salverson
1890–1970

She became the voice
of Icelandic immigrants
in search of their place
in Canada.

Laura Salverson at age fourteen.

Laura Goodman was the child of Icelandic immigrants who settled in the West in 1887. Born in Winnipeg in 1890, she grew up in poverty. Her father's wanderlust took the struggling family from the prairies to a sheep ranch in Dakota to Duluth, Minnesota, and the Deep South — and back to Manitoba. Frequently ill, Laura survived diphtheria, whooping cough, malaria, pleurisy, anemia, and a weak heart. Until the age of ten Laura spoke only Icelandic and had little formal education. She began learning English when the Goodmans settled in Duluth. The eager student discovered the public library and dreamed of being a writer.

Despite Laura's enthusiasm for finishing school, the frequent moves and economic necessity soon pushed her into the workforce. After doing housekeeping and sewing tents and awnings the young woman moved back to Winnipeg, where in 1913 she married George Salverson, a man of Norwegian ancestry. Laura continued to live an itinerant lifestyle as her railway-man husband was frequently transferred and also tried homesteading in Saskatchewan. Laura gave birth to a son, George, but felt she had no life of her own, no inner satisfaction. "Nothing but endless work."[340]

Laura decided to use some of their limited funds to take an English course by correspondence. She wrote a few poems that were published in country papers. A man called Austin Bothwell heard one of her verses at a meeting of the University Women's Club in Regina and encouraged Laura to do more serious writing. She was thrilled to later have Lady Byng award her the Canadian Club prize for her first short story, "Hidden Fire." It was clear to the aspiring author that "she wanted to write a story which would define the price any foreign group must pay for its place in the national life of the country of its adoption."[341]

Laura Salverson's writings grew out of this passionate need to present her people and the challenges they faced in America. Her childhood was filled with stories of her Icelandic heritage, the sagas and legends of illustrious ancestors like Gunnar Hamundson, who was the last of the Norse nobles to live as a Viking. This heritage was an important part of her identity. She ached to tell of the deception that lured many Icelanders to America and the broken dreams of a proud race trying to find their place in the New World.

Despite continuing health problems Laura persevered. She fictionalized the stories of Scandinavian settlers in her novels *The Viking Heart* (1923), *When Sparrows Fall* (1925), *Johann Lind* (1928), and *The Dark Weaver* (1937). The latter earned a Governor General's Award, as did Laura Salverson's autobiography, *Confessions of an Immigrant's Daughter* (1939). She published some other novels, as well as about 150 magazine stories. Laura Salverson was a leader in the creation of the *Icelandic Canadian* magazine in 1942 as a means of preserving Icelandic heritage in North America, and was its first editor. The Paris Institute of Arts and Sciences awarded her a gold medal for literature.

Laura Salverson became a popular writer — almost as famous as her contemporary Nellie McClung.[342] A pioneer author of immigrant literature in Canada, she was the first novelist to depict the experiences of immigrants in the West.[343] She played a significant role in preserving Icelandic cultural identity and merits greater recognition than she has been given.

Quote:

"Having suffered ostracism and condescension because of their foreignness, it seemed as though all the national energy of the people had been expanded to acquire a blameless Canadian skin, Canadian habits, and Canadian houses."[344]

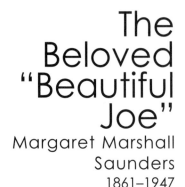

The Beloved "Beautiful Joe"
Margaret Marshall Saunders
1861–1947

Margaret Marshall Saunders, ca. 1920s.

Her phenomenally successful novel sounded the alarm about inhumane treatment of animals.

Margaret Marshall Saunders wrote the first Canadian best-seller — the autobiography of a cruelly treated dog. The novel *Beautiful Joe,* published in 1894, became the first Canadian book to sell more than a million copies.[345] The saga was translated into seventeen different languages and sold more than 7 million copies by 1939.[346]

Born in the Annapolis Valley in Nova Scotia, Margaret grew up in a family of seven children strongly influenced by their father, Edward Manning Saunders — a Baptist clergyman and author. Saunders held progressive ideas about the role of women in society and ensured that Margaret received a good classical education in Halifax and then overseas. Margaret attended a boarding school in Scotland before continuing her education in France. After teaching school for a short time she began pursuing a writing career, with the full support and encouragement of her father.[347]

Margaret was twenty-eight when her first novel, a romance, was published in 1889. While visiting Meaford, Ontario, she heard about a dog rescued by a local miller after a brutal master cut off the animal's ears and tail. She wrote the manuscript *Beautiful Joe: The Autobiography of a Dog* for some competitions, using the pen name Marshall Saunders on the assumption that a male author would be more readily accepted than a woman. Marshall won the contest to find a sequel to the story *Black Beauty* and the American Humane Society award. The book *Beautiful Joe* soon earned her an international reputation. It also created widespread awareness of the often inhumane treatment of animals.

A prolific author, Margaret Saunders wrote some twenty-five books featuring places she visited in her extensive travels through Canada, the United States, and Europe. Her tales about animals were most appealing, making her Canada's most popular writer of children's stories for decades. None of Margaret's works attained the popularity of *Beautiful Joe*. Critics suggest her moralistic writings were most noteworthy for their advocacy of kindness to animals, protection of children, and living in the countryside.[348] A passionate woman with a social conscience, Margaret belonged to many organizations fighting for change — including the Child Labour Committee.

Margaret also gave public lectures about humane treatment of animals and cared for a menagerie of creatures. She named her friends after the places she found them, hence her family included a pigeon called "38 Front Street" and a dog known as "Billy Sunday" whom she found after attending a presentation by the famous evangelist.[349] In 1914 Margaret settled in Toronto with her sister and widowed father. King George V awarded her the Commander of the British Empire in 1934 because of her contribution to the establishment of standards for the humane treatment of animals. The acclaimed author and humanitarian died in Toronto in 1947.

The Historic Sites and Monuments Board of Canada designated Margaret Marshall Saunders as a national historic person of Canada. The Ontario Heritage Foundation erected a commemorative plaque in her honour in Beautiful Joe Park in Meaford, Ontario. The Beautiful Joe Heritage Society, established in 1994 to celebrate the life of Beautiful Joe and the achievements of Margaret Marshall Saunders, created the park and is developing a museum in the home where Joe was welcomed by the Moore family.

Quote:

"It was absolutely necessary that I should be on the scene where my story was laid."[350]

Loyalist Laura —And Not a Chocolate in Sight!
Laura Secord
1775–1868

J.R. Skelton illustration/A Picture History of Canada, 1933.

Laura Secord and a U.S. sentry, 1813.

Perhaps the most celebrated heroine in Canadian history, she risked her life to convey a message about a surprise attack by American forces.

What do you think of when someone mentions Laura Secord? Chocolates, the War of 1812, or perhaps a pioneer woman milking a cow to conceal her secret mission in the woods? Yes to the war but forget the cow: Laura never mentioned one. A creative historian seems to have added the beast to her story. And the chocolates? More about them later.

Laura was a British patriot at a time when Americans were making inroads in what is now Canada. Born in Great Barrington, Massachusetts, in 1775, Laura Ingersoll emigrated to Upper Canada with her family at the age of twenty. She married merchant James Secord and the couple soon settled in Queenston.

When American soldiers attacked the village on October 13, 1812, Laura Secord quickly fled to a farmhouse in the countryside with her five small children. Listening to the booming of the guns, the fearful brood knew that their father was fighting in the battle — as a sergeant in the 1st Lincoln militia. Laura rushed to the battlefield at the end of the day, discovering that the Americans had surrendered. The anguished young woman searched frantically among the wounded and dying. She found James alive but bleeding profusely from a serious shoulder wound — and suffering intense pain from a bullet in his knee. With the help of an offi-cer Laura managed to carry James Secord to their nearby home, which had been looted by American soldiers.

The following summer British and American troops were still fighting for control of the Niagara Peninsula. Canadian settlers often encountered American soldiers, and it seems that Laura Secord somehow learned of a secret American plot to surprise the British outpost at Beaver Dams, commanded by Lieutenant James Fitzgibbon. As James Secord was still an invalid and could not make the trip to warn Fitzgibbon, Laura planned to leave early the next morning to carry the message. A woman considered to be of "slender frame and delicate appearance," Laura Secord courageously set out despite her fears of meeting American sentries or being taken prisoner by Indians. She dressed as if undertaking a casual trip to visit relatives — wearing a long brown dress with small orange flowers, and house slippers. Laura took an indirect route of about twenty miles in hopes of avoiding confrontation.

As the June day grew hotter and more humid, the exhausted mes-senger trudged along muddy roads and through swamps and forest. After dark she was terrified at finding herself suddenly surrounded by Indians, but convinced them that she had important news for Fitzgibbon. The chief agreed to accompany the determined housewife to her destination, where she conveyed her message to the amazed com-mander. Thanks to Laura's courage, the American forces en route to Beaver Dams were ambushed two days later by Indians and surrendered to FitzGibbon.[351] Laura Secord helped the British win an important battle in the War of 1812.

Nearly half a century later, after years of poverty and petitions for a pension, Laura Secord was publicly recognized for her heroic walk by the Prince of Wales. He learned about her contribution during the war thanks to Laura's insistence on having her name included in the list of veterans and submitting a memorial that described her service. In early 1861 the future Edward VII sent Laura Secord, now an elderly lady of eighty-five, a gift of one hundred pounds in gold in appreciation of her heroism during the War of 1812. Newspaper coverage of the honour and subsequent books gradually brought recognition of Laura Secord as a great Canadian heroine.

Laura's fame continued to mushroom following her death in 1868. Monuments to her memory were erected in Lundy's Lane (1901) and Queenston Heights (1910), and the Government of Ontario exhibited her portrait in the provincial parliament buildings. In Laura's hometown, the Laura Secord School built a memorial hall featuring paintings about her life. In 1913 Toronto businessman Frank O'Connor named his new brand of chocolates after the heroine, and the ongoing success of the chain probably accounts for the fact that public opinion polls show Laura Secord is Canada's "best-known war hero" and the top "woman hero."[352] In 1971 the chocolate company now called Laura Secord Inc. reconstructed the Secord Homestead in Queenston, which is now operated by the Niagara Parks Commission.

Canada Post released a commemorative stamp for Laura Secord in 1992, and in 2003 she was designated as a national historic person of Canada.

Quote:

"I request that your Royal Highness will be pleased to convey to your Royal Parent Her Majesty the Queen the name of one who in the hour of trial and danger ... stood ever ready and willing to defend this Country against every invasion come what might."[353]

Meeting between Laura Secord and Lieut. Fitzgibbon, June 1813.

National Archives of Canada/C-11053.

Did Kate Strike Gold?
Shaaw Tlaa (Kate Carmack)
ca. 1862–1920

Many men were racing to find gold — but Shaaw Tlaa may have beaten them.

Kate Carmack in California, 1898.

Shaaw Tlaa was the first woman to be part of the Klondike gold rush — probably one of the group that made the 1896 discovery of gold on Rabbit Creek, which was renamed Bonanza after the strike. But the official discoverers were her husband, George Carmack, her brother Keish (Skookum Jim), and her nephew Kaa Goox (Dawson Charlie).

She was born near Bennett Lake, the daughter of the head of the coastal Tlingit crow clan and a woman of the Tagish wolf clan from the inland. Shaaw Tlaa married a Tlingit man, but both her husband and baby daughter died of influenza in the 1880s.[354] Returning home to her village of Caribou Crossing near the present town of Carcross, Shaaw Tlaa was encouraged to form an association with her deceased sister's husband — an American called George Washington Carmack. A one-time marine become packer, the man nicknamed "Lyin' George" hunted and prospected with her brother and nephew until the strike of gold launched the Klondike gold rush.

Shaaw Tlaa married George Carmack in 1887 and six years later gave birth to their daughter, Graphie Grace Carmack. In the summer of 1896 the Carmack family was living at a salmon fishing camp when Skookum Jim and Dawson Charlie joined them. There are many different stories of how one or more in the party discovered gold on Rabbit Creek in mid August. Maybe all of the group were present, maybe only the men, or per-haps Kate Carmack discovered the gold herself. One version of events, related by a Nevill Armstrong who knew George Carmack, insists she was doing some panning while the men napped in camp.[355] Another account explains that "...while Carmack was resting, his wife in wandering around, found a bit of bedrock exposed and, taking a pan of dirt, washed it and found that she had some four dollars in coarse gold."[356]

George Carmack rushed to register the two discovery claims, apparently because he was the lone white man in the party. He also registered claims for his Native partners Skookum Jim and Dawson Charlie. During the long winter before the family claims brought in more than a million dollars worth of gold, Kate (as she was called by her husband) supported the group by doing laundry and selling bread, moccasins, and mittens. The sudden wealth in the family thrust Kate into a new world, with trips to big cities in the south and stays with unwelcoming Carmack relatives in California. Culture shock and unfamiliar pressures in the new lifestyle pushed Kate to alcohol, and George Carmack abandoned her to marry a Dawson woman called Marguerite Laimee in 1900. Kate tried to file for divorce but was unable to prove she had been legally married for twelve years.[357]

A destitute Kate returned home to her Tagish family, settling in Carcross in a cabin built for her by Skookum Jim. Her daughter left her for a life in Seattle. Kate earned a small income from selling needlework until she died of influenza in 1920. Shaaw Tláa had courageously struggled to adapt to the flood of gold seekers in her native Yukon and the sudden wealth that shattered her life.

George Carmack and the other men involved with the Bonanza Creek strike, heralded as the discoverers of placer gold that initiated one of the world's greatest gold rushes, became rich and received widespread recognition. The Canadian Mining Hall of Fame, for example, inducted George Carmack, Skookum Jim, Tagish Charlie, and miner Robert Henderson, noting that these four men sparked the stampede that brought over a hundred thousand gold seekers.

Yet the Native woman who was the "true queen of the Klondike"[358] — who was likely present at the discovery and may even have found the gold — is largely unrecognized for her role in the historic event that yielded more than $500 million dollars worth of gold and transformed the Yukon. Kate Carmack "has largely been erased from Yukon history and the story of the Klondike" because of her race and gender[359] — and because George Carmack's second wife, Marguerite, removed all references to Kate from his diaries and papers.[360]

Quote:

"Yellow hair she come to town. Tagish Kate she no good after that."[361]

Shaaw Tláa referring to being abandoned by George Carmack after the arrival of Marguerite Laimee.

Let Them Be Free

Mary Ann Shadd (Cary)
1823–1893

National Archives of Canada/C-029977

She was the first woman to found, publish, and edit a newspaper in Canada. Not to mention being a civil rights activist, feminist, teacher, and abolitionist.

Mary Ann Shadd Cary, ca. 1845–1855.

In the middle of the nineteenth century, Mary Ann Shadd was one of the most accomplished women in British North America.[362] Despite living in Canada only twelve years, she played a significant role here as an important leader of the Black fugitive movement and editor of the newspaper *Provincial Freeman.*

Born in Wilmington, Delaware, on October 9, 1823, Mary Ann was the first of thirteen children in the family of Abraham Doras Shadd and Harriet Parnell. They were free Blacks, active in the struggle to abolish slavery. Their home was a "station" on the Underground Railway, where slaves would hide along their journey north to freedom.

For six years Mary Ann attended a Quaker school in West Chester, Pennsylvania, where the Shadds had moved because Blacks were not allowed in Delaware's public education system. In 1839, at the age of sixteen, Mary Ann began teaching school. But after the 1850 passage of the Fugitive Slave Act in the United States, the young woman moved to Windsor in British North America. Thousands of fugitives also fled to avoid the provisions of the new act, which made it easier for slave owners to capture escaped slaves.

Mary Ann Shadd founded, published, and edited the *Provincial Freeman* newspaper. Through her writings and lectures she encouraged the abolishment of slavery, the immigration of slaves to Canada West, and the importance of independence as a means for Blacks to adjust to their new lives. She promoted integrated education, thrift, and hard work for the refugees in order to became part of their new communities — and vehemently opposed the creation of Black communal settlements. Mary Ann also wrote about the need for women to become more active in politics and public affairs.

On January 3, 1856, Mary Ann married Black businessman Thomas Cary in St. Catharines, Upper Canada. When he died in the fall of 1860, she had two young children to raise as well as her career to pursue.

Mary Ann became a naturalized British subject, but stayed in America after the Civil War to help her people adjust to the new opportunities available. She continued to work on behalf of the rights of Blacks and women, becoming a notable writer and public speaker. After obtaining an American teaching certificate, she eventually settled in Washington, D.C., and became principal of a public school. In 1883, at the age of sixty, she began a career as a lawyer on becoming the first Black woman to graduate in law from Howard University. Mary Ann Shadd was one of the few women of the nineteenth century to have a career in this field. She died on June 5, 1893, in Washington.

In 1994 the Historic Sites and Monuments Board of Canada recognized Mary Ann Shadd as a national historic person of Canada, and the following year the Ontario Heritage Foundation honoured her by installing a commemorative plaque in Chatham. While in British North America she played a significant role as a pioneer female journalist, advocate of the emancipation of women, and leader of the anti-slavery movement.

Quote:

"To colored Women we have a word — we have broken the 'Editorial Ice' whether willingly or not for your class in America, so go to editing as many of you are willing and able and as soon as you may, if you think you are ready."[363]

A Canadian Tragedy
Shanawdithit
ca. 1801–1829

She was a courageous woman who helped document the history of her dying race, until she too died — the last of the Beothuks.

Portrait believed to be of Shanawdithit.

She watched them die one by one: hunted down and shot by white settlers, furriers, and fishermen. Starving, dying of the new diseases they could not resist. Until she was alone — the last of her people. The Beothuks, the Aboriginal people of the island of Newfoundland, extinct.

Shanawdithit was born about 1801 along the shore of a large lake in Newfoundland.[364] Her birth was no doubt welcomed by the small band of Beothuk, whose numbers were dwindling with each passing year. Her people were hunters and gatherers who once lived all around the island, eating sea birds, shellfish, seals, salmon, and caribou in fall hunts. Their traditional way of life had begun to suffer as whites established year-round settlements on Newfoundland in the seventeenth century. As English settlements grew in the eighteenth century the Beothuk were losing access to their food sources from the sea, then furriers or trappers moved into the interior.

By the time of Shanawdithit's birth the small population of Beothuks lived along the Exploits River system, trying to survive on the limited resources available to them in the interior. When the Beothuks did try to reach the sea they were regarded as thieves by the new inhabitants of the coast. Furriers, enraged by the Beothuks taking their traps, were among the leaders of the ferocious attacks against the Aboriginal people.

As a child Shanawdithit was the victim of an unprovoked attack, shot at by a trapper as she was washing some venison along a river. She was lucky that the bullets left her just wounded, not dead. Many trappers and fisher-men boasted of how many Indians they had killed. A fellow called Rogers claimed to have killed sixty, while Noel Boss had murdered ninety-nine and expressed frustration that he couldn't make it an even one hundred.

While some government leaders eventually showed concern about the "various acts of violence and inhuman cruelties,"[365] their efforts were often inappropriate and brought no improvements. When Shanawdithit was about six, Governor John Holloway offered a £50 reward for capturing a live Beothuk, and in 1810 Governor Sir Thomas Duckworth doubled the reward. Greedy trappers and fishermen anxious to line their pockets didn't worry about killing Beothuks in their pursuit of live ones. In 1809 Governor Holloway had tried to establish friendly relations with the Beothuks by hiring William Cull and some other men to travel to the interior with gifts; it would seem that the Governor did not realize that the entire party had been murdering the Aboriginal people for years so the expedition was of course a failure.

By the time Shanawdithit was ten years old, in 1811, there were only about seventy-five Beothuks left. Much of the time they lived in fear of surprise attacks, trying to stay in hiding while they searched for enough food to survive. In 1812 another twenty-two starved to death. When she was fifteen years old, the young girl witnessed the killing of one of the remaining women by a man called John Peyton Sr., who was the father of Magistrate John Peyton Jr.

A couple of years later Shanawdithit watched another tragedy, with her dear uncle — Chief Nonosbawsut — murdered and her aunt Demasduit captured on March 5, 1819, by Judge John Peyton Jr. and his father. Accounts of the events differ, with Peyton Jr.'s story that he had undertak-en an expedition to recover stolen property. But there was speculation that he wanted reward money for capture of a live Beothuk. One of the party, Mr. E. Slade, later wrote a letter outlining what both he and Shanawdithit's people had watched — a husband killed as he was trying to rescue his wife, and the murderer saying "it was only an Indian, and he wished he had shot a hundred instead of one."[366] The baby of Demasduit died several days after its mother was taken. The mother, whom the white people called Mary March, was eventually returned to her people. In a coffin.

By the winter of 1822–23, there were only twelve people remaining from Shanawdithit's village. Among them were her mother and father, sister, an uncle, and a cousin. The uncle and cousin decided to travel to the coast in search of food but were both shot by fishermen Curnew and Adams, even though the uncle arrived begging for food, and the cousin bared her breasts in the custom of her people — to show she was a woman and beg for mercy. Shanawdithit, her mother, and sister later discovered the frozen bodies. The father had gone to hunt deer and had not returned.

The starving women wandered along the coast at Badger Bay, where they were found by furrier William Cull, who apparently spared their lives in hopes of collecting reward money. But shots rang out and Shanawdithit's father appeared, with trappers pursuing him and William Cull's musket pointing at him. He ran for the thin ice of the river and disappeared from sight.

The three captive women were taken to St. John's, Newfoundland, where Judge Peyton arranged the reward money for Cull. The three were later taken back to the Bay of Exploits, supposedly for a reunion with their people which, of course, never came.

They had no shelter and little food. They waited for help, but the sister had tuberculosis and they soon buried her. A week later the mother died. Shanawdithit paddled across the bay to Burnt Island, where she was taken into the household of John Peyton Jr. as a servant. She stayed there about five years.

In 1828 Shanawdithit was taken to live in the home of W.E. Cormack in St. John's, where he studied her in his capacity as president of the Beothuk Institution and recorded a lot of information about the culture of the Beothuks. Shanawdithit drew many sketches to show the way of life of her people, and also diagrams of the various attacks and murders she witnessed. A friend of Cormack's, John McGregor, later described the young woman as follows:

> Her person, in height above the middle stature, possessed classical regularity of form. Her face bore striking similarity to that of Napoleon, and the olive cast of her complexion added to the resemblance. Her hair was jet black; her finely penciled brows — her long, darting lashes — her dark, vigilant, and piercing eyes, were all remarkable striking and beautiful. Her teeth were white, even, and perfectly sound. Her hands and feet, small and well formed. She never laughed.[367]

Shanawdithit became ill with tuberculosis. Cormack travelled off to England and the dying woman was placed in the home of attorney general James Simms. She was then transferred to hospital, where she died on June 6, 1829, at the age of twenty-eight. Shanawdithit was buried in the Church of England cemetery at St. John's, and when this was dismantled a small monument was erected.

In her short and painful life the young woman showed amazing courage and helped bring greater understanding of the Beothuk. The Historic Sites and Monuments Board of Canada recognized Shanawdithit as a national historic person in the year 2000.[368]

Quote:

"She is fearful that her race has died from want of food."[369]

From Bishop John Inglis' interview with Shanawdithit.

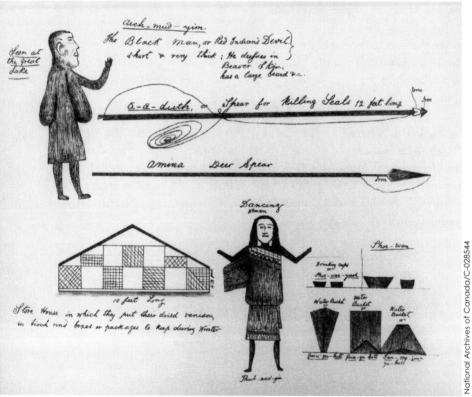

Beothuk drawings by Shanawdithit.

National Archives of Canada/C-028544

Fighting for Justice

Hide Hyodo Shimizu
1908–1999

She could never erase the painful memories of racial persecution after the Japanese attacked Pearl Harbour in World War II.

Hide Shimizu.

"It was a great shock,"[370] remembered Hide Shimizu years after the event. During World War II the young Japanese Canadian woman suddenly became an enemy alien in her homeland.

Born in Vancouver in 1908, Hide Hyodo was the eldest of eight children born to Hideichi and Toshiko Hyodo. The hard-working couple was Issei (first-generation Japanese) who had emigrated from Uwajima. Hide attended the University of British Columbia and then teacher training, becoming one of the first Nisei (second generation) to earn a teacher's certificate when she graduated in 1926. She began teaching a Japanese-Canadian grade one class at Lord Byng School in Steveston, B.C., where she taught until 1942.[371]

Recognizing Hide as an important organizer in the community, the Japanese Canadian Citizens League (JCCL) invited her to join a delegation of four that visited Ottawa in 1936. The group appeared before the Elections and Franchise Acts Committee of the House of Commons, which was considering extending the right to vote to "Orientals." Hide and her companions each gave fifteen-minute presentations, then responded to questions. Unable to convince committee members to end the franchise ban, the delegation returned home to Vancouver to announce the disappointing news to a crowd of three hundred at a public meeting.[372]

When World War II began Hide was one of more than twenty-three thousand persons of Japanese origin in Canada, of which 75.5 percent were

Canadian citizens. In 1941 she and all other Japanese Canadians over sixteen had to register with the Royal Canadian Mounted Police. When their belongings were confiscated, Hide's parents lost the ten-lot parcel of land they'd sacrificed so much to buy. After most of the Japanese were forced to relocate in detention camps in the interior of B.C. or enforced labour camps, Hide worked with the JCCL to develop a school system for the detainees. She did so under the strict supervision of the British Columbia Securities Commission, established to oversee the evacuation of the Japanese from coastal areas.

Hide Hyodo established a remarkable system to ensure that Japanese children would continue to receive an education.[373] She recruited, trained, and supervised a group of 120 inexperienced Japanese teachers, primarily high-school graduates or students, who taught in the many settlements. She was advised by the BCSC that the schools had to operate exclusively in English. Hide continued to teach at Lord Byng School, and every other day commuted to Vancouver to prepare assignments for the children in internment camps. She had to make sure she was home by nine o'clock each night to comply with curfew requirements. Hide made monthly visits to each of the camps, where about three thousand children were taught.

Hide Hyodo moved to Toronto after the war and married Rev. Kosaburo Shimizu, a widowed United Church minister with four children. Hide was active in many community organizations and lobbied for compensation to Japanese Canadians for the seizure of property and forced migration during the Second World War. In 1982 Governor General Edward Schreyer presented Hide Shimizu with the Order of Canada for her outstanding achievements in overseeing the education of children of Japanese ancestry during their internment. In 1997 school officials dedicated a traditional Japanese rock garden in her honour at Lord Byng Elementary School, "where her legacy of hope will remain."[374]

When she died at the age of ninety-one Hide Shimizu was remembered fondly as a leader in the Japanese-Canadian community — a dedicated educator and passionate activist.

Quote:

"We weren't the enemy. Neither were we alien. But we lost everything."[375]

The Florence Nightingale of Newfound- land

Mary Meager
Southcott
1862–1943

She made a shocking
career choice — nursing!

Mary Southcott.

Mary Southcott helped make nursing respectable, following her dream of becoming a nurse in spite of family protests that it was not a suitable occupation for a lady. She became the most prominent nursing leader in pre-Confederation Newfoundland. Mary founded, on the model of the Nightingale System, its first (and for many years only) nurse training school: the St. John's General Hospital School of Nursing.[376]

Her Victorian middle-class parents were strongly opposed to their daughter becoming a nurse, considering that such work was usually done by poorly paid domestic servants in dingy and unsanitary facilities infested by rats. So Mary waited until both Mr. and Mrs. Southcott died to begin her training. At the age of thirty-seven she began studying nursing at the London Hospital in England. Graduating in March 1901 with two awards, Mary then completed a four-week course in midwifery. She gained some practical experience working in London before returning home to St. John's.

In 1903 Mary Southcott was appointed as Superintendent of Nurses at St. John's General Hospital, a government hospital that provided care for all residents of the colony of Newfoundland. Following what was known as the Nightingale System of nursing, she worked to professional-ize nursing. On her arrival at the hospital there were twelve untrained nurses — only two of whom could read and write. Mary Southcott strived to raise the standard of nursing, developing a three-year educational program. Trained midwives taught the young women about maternity care, an aspect of their education that was superior to that of other nursing schools in North America. Mary also led the battle to improve working conditions and pay for Newfoundland nurses, and helped organize their first professional association.

Mary Southcott was a strong leader of Newfoundland nurses, commanding respect as well as admiration. The Local Council of Women noted:

> In her position as matron of General Hospital, Miss Southcott was noted for her fairness in dealing with people. A good teacher and administrator, she was very forthright in manner. Very decisive looking and forceful in appearance, her blue penetrating eyes took in every detail as she carried out uniform inspection every evening for nurses on night duty and made her daily round of the hospital wards.[377]

Anxious for the nurses to have respectable living quarters outside the hospital, Mary Southcott supported construction of a separate residence for them at St. John's Hospital. The King Edward VII Home for Nurses opened in 1911–12, with a study room, kitchen, dining room, scullery, and larder, as well as bedrooms. Eager to encourage a family atmosphere, Mary invited the women for afternoon tea in her apartment every Sunday.

In her zealous efforts to protect the professional autonomy of nurses, Mary Southcott challenged the authority of Medical Superintendent Dr. Lawrence Keegan. Though the Colonial Secretary had given Mary control of all nursing appointments, Keegan refused to accept this. A 1914 Royal Commission of Inquiry was launched to settle their dispute — and sided with Keegan. Nurse Southcott was forced to take an "honourable resignation," though a subsequent Royal Commission in 1929 recommended that it should indeed be the Superintendent of Nurses who had full responsibility for nursing staff.

Mary Southcott continued to be active in the nursing community, creating a private hospital in 1916. At the request of the government of Newfoundland, that same year she also accepted responsibility for a temporary facility dealing with an epidemic of measles. Mary continued to help educate local midwives, designing a training course for Newfoundland's second nurse training school, established by the Salvation Army's Grace Maternity Hospital. She also supported the suffrage cause and was involved in a campaign to improve the health of mothers and babies; she served as vice-president and president of the Child Welfare Association.

At a time when folk medicine prevailed in pre-Confederation Newfoundland, Mary Southcott courageously introduced the Nightingale Nursing System and helped improve health care services. In recognition of her important contribution to nursing the Historic Sites and Monuments Board of Canada has recognized her as a national historic person. In 1954 the newly built nurse's residence at St. John's General Hospital School was named Southcott Hall in her honour.

Quote:

"It seemed to me a strange anomaly that women banded together for the relief of suffering should cause so much suffering to each other."[378]

Mary Southcott remembering the conflicts among
nurses where she trained in London.

Nightingale of the North
Georgina Ann Stirling
1867–1935

Georgina Stirling.

She enchanted audiences across Europe and the United States — until tragedy struck the prima donna from the outports of Newfoundland.

Georgina Ann Stirling was a girl with a golden voice who grew up in Twillingate, Newfoundland.[379] Born to Anne Peyton and medical doctor William Stirling, she was the youngest child of a large family that enjoyed music. Dr. Stirling encouraged the musical education of his daughters, and Georgie demonstrated unusual musical talent from a young age. Tutored by an accomplished local musician, Georgie sang in community concerts and played the organ at church services.

When Georgie was just sixteen her mother died. The following year Dr. Stirling arranged for his gifted daughter to study music and liberal arts at the Toronto Ladies' College. She returned home after several years but in 1888 headed to France with the dream of becoming an opera singer. A talented Mezzo Soprano, Georgina Stirling trained in Paris with the renowned teacher Mathilde Marchesi before joining an opera company in Milan in 1890. Author Edward B. Moogk reported that Miss Stirling debuted at the famed La Scala opera house — with the Royal Family of Italy watching her performance.

While in Milan in 1891 the opera singer was devastated to receive news of her father's death. Once her singing contract expired Georgie continued her studies at the prestigious École Marchesi. In 1893 she made her Paris grand opera debut. Having completed her training with Madame Marchesi, the promising singer launched her operatic career with a new stage name. Using the original French name for her home in Twillingate, she became Marie Toulinguet — Newfoundland's first opera singer.

Newfoundlanders proudly noted the progress of her operatic career. The local press frequently reported on her successes overseas as well as her visits home. In 1892 the *Twillingate Sun* wrote: "She is ranking amongst the world's most famous singers and from time to time is very highly complimented in the leading newspapers of Paris as well as in Italy..."[380] The citizens of Newfoundland raved about their "native star," her enchanting voice and electrifying performances. They praised her generous participation in many fundraising concerts and other efforts to help others, and in 1895 the grateful residents of St. John's presented her with a jewelled bracelet, a letter of appreciation, and a testimonial to a woman they hailed as the "thrice gifted daughter of the ice-bound coast."[381]

Georgina performed on tours throughout Europe and the United States as a member of the New York–based New Imperial Opera Company in 1896 and the Scalchi Company in 1897. Toulinguet earned impressive reviews in cities such as New York, Philadelphia, and Boston. She was heralded as a prima donna with an astonishing voice — a voice that one hears only once in a lifetime.

At the peak of her operatic success, the singer returned to Italy in the summer of 1898. The widespread praise for her riveting performances included a comment from a Venice newspaper, which reported, "The favourite of the public is without doubt the prima donna Marie Toulinguet."[382] Chioggia, a cathedral city in Italy, begged her to perform in the leading role of a new Mass and then organized a special night in her honour — an evening of incredible applause, a testimonial of praise, and the presentation of bouquets of flowers from which live canaries and doves flew into the air.

Marie Toulinguet's brilliant career continued through to 1901 in Italy. A gifted dramatic soprano, she was an international opera star. At the age of thirty-four Georgina seriously damaged her vocal cords and her singing career suddenly ended. Crushed by this tragic turn of events, the depressed singer turned to alcohol. She spent time at a treatment centre in England over a period of several decades, and eventually returned home to Twillingate.

Georgina Stirling died of cancer at the age of sixty-eight and was buried in an unmarked grave for nearly thirty years — seemingly forgotten. It was only after a fundraising campaign in the 1960s that an impressive head-stone was finally erected to the memory of Georgina Stirling, Prima Donna. It reads: "The Nightingale of the North sang fairer than the larks of Italy. She entertained royalty by the sweetness of her voice, and the poor by the kindness of her heart. Erected by an admiring public 1964."

Only a few scratchy recordings of the famous opera singer's voice remain. And who remembers her now — the internationally acclaimed Canadian songstress?

Quote:

"[Mathilde Marchesi] said 'My dear young lady, yours is a voice that the world is waiting for & you will be a great great woman' ... fancy Jan such praise from her, the greatest teacher in the world."[383]

> Georgina Stirling writing to her sister Janet about her audition with the acclaimed teacher Mathilde Marchesi.

Georgina in Milan.

Twillingate Museum Association

244

Emily for Equality

Emily Howard Jennings Stowe
1831–1903

National Archives of Canada/C-9480

She defiantly broke the law — becoming the first Canadian woman to work as a physician in this country.

Emily Stowe.

Supported by Quaker beliefs in equality, education, and integrity, the independent Emily pursued her goals in spite of the many barriers she faced. A determined lady, Emily Stowe achieved many firsts: first woman to apply to be a student at a Canadian university (refused), first woman to apply to a Canadian medical school (refused), first woman principal of a public school, and first Canadian woman to practise medicine in Canada.[384] She also became one of the most influential leaders in the women's rights movement in Canada.

Emily Jennings was born in Norwich, Ontario, to American Quakers who became Methodists. At the age of fifteen she began teaching school, and later accepted a post as principal of the public school in Brantford. In 1856 she married carriage maker John Stowe. When her husband became ill with tuberculosis, the young wife and mother decided to become a doctor. She returned to teaching, so while John was in a sanatorium she could support the family and save money to pay for medical training and their expenses during her studies. Teaching jobs weren't normally open to married women, but Emily was presumably able to obtain this job because the school principal was a close family friend.

Refused admittance to medical school in Canada because of her sex, Emily had no choice but to head south. Her sister cared for Emily's three children. The young mother studied at the New York Medical College for Women, where she learned about the homeopathic methods supported by its founder Dr. Clemence Lozier — and also worked with the women's movement. Dr. Emily Stowe triumphantly returned home as Canada's first female physician in 1867.

Emily set up her own medical practice in Toronto, advertising in *The Globe* that Mrs. E.H. Stowe, M.D., was now seeing patients daily between 9:00 a.m. and 3:00 p.m. Though many folks in mid-Victorian Canada still believed that respectable women should be tending the home fires, patients duly arrived on her doorstep. But Emily still had another obstacle to face: she did not have a licence to practise medicine in Ontario. As a graduate from the United States she was required to pass a matriculation exam and attend a session of lectures at an Ontario medical school. Just one problem: the Canadian medical schools still wouldn't accept women. So Dr. Emily Stowe continued to practise medicine without a licence.[385]

In the early 1870s Emily Stowe and an aspiring physician called Jennie Trout were finally permitted to attend a session at the Toronto School of Medicine. The two ladies survived ridicule, rude jokes, crude drawings on the classroom walls, objectionable stories during lectures, and much more. But survive they did, though it was not until 1880 that Dr. Stowe received her licence to practise medicine; Dr. Trout attained her licence first, thus becoming the first licensed female physician in Canada. At the age of forty-nine Dr. Emily Stowe finally received all the necessary papers to be a licensed doctor in her own country. Once her husband had regained his health she supported his training as a dentist. Following his graduation in 1875 the egalitarian couple worked in a joint practice at 111 Church Street in Toronto.

During her studies in the U.S. Emily Stowe became acquainted with the notable American suffragists Elizabeth Cady Stanton and Susan Brownwell Anthony, and was inspired by their example. Having grown up with the belief that she had an equal right to be educated and play a meaningful role in society, Emily was not about to sit back and accept unfair treatment for herself or other women. The obstacles she faced in trying to gain an education and train as a doctor led Emily to become a prominent crusader for women's rights on her return to Canada. She focused her efforts on winning the vote and getting admission to higher education.

In 1876 Dr. Stowe created Canada's first suffrage group, named the Toronto Women's Literary Club to disguise its true purpose. Members lobbied to improve conditions for women working in factories and stores and petitioned the provincial government for the right to vote. As the group became more political Emily Stowe transformed it into a national organization, the Dominion Women's Enfranchisement Association, for which she served as president until her death in 1903. The issue of suffrage for women gained considerable public attention because of Dr. Stowe's efforts, including inviting the famous Susan B. Anthony to be a guest speaker for the association in 1889; the presentation was covered extensively by the press.

One of her most notable publicity stunts was the Mock Parliament, which Emily and other suffragists staged in Toronto in 1896 to draw attention to the foolishness of not allowing women to vote. Dr. Stowe played the role of the Attorney General, who was approached by men begging for the vote. Newspapers covered the witty farce, but Emily Stowe did not live to see the historic day in 1918 when Canadian women finally won the right to vote in federal elections. She was, however, heralded as one of the country's greatest suffragists.

Dr. Stowe also battled to gain more opportunities for Canadian women to gain a university education. She led the fight to have the University of Toronto accept them and to create a separate medical college for women. Thanks to Emily Stowe and her supporters, the Woman's Medical College in Toronto opened in 1883.

Dr. Emily Stowe was a courageous Canadian who helped open many doors to the women who would follow her — including her daughter, Augusta Stowe-Gullen, who became the first woman to obtain a medical degree in Canada and the first female professor of medicine. A Canadian heroine who is now recognized as much for her outstanding contributions to the women's movement as for her achievements as a pioneer in field of medicine,[386] Dr. Stowe was recognized by the Historic Sites and Monuments Board of Canada as a national historic person in 1995. Canada Post issued a stamp in her honour in 1981, in a series to commemorate Canadian feminists. Other tributes in memory of this notable Canadian include the Emily Stowe Shelter for Women in Ontario and the Dr. Emily Stowe Award, which is presented each year to a promising young woman at Norman Bethune College.

Quote:

"The day will come when these doors will swing wide open to every female who chooses to apply."[387]

Dr. Emily Stowe replying to the University of Toronto
after being refused admission.
The response: "Never in my day Madam."

Tookoolito, C.F. Hall, and Ebierbing.

Guiding the Kabloonas
Taqulittuq (Tookoolito)
ca. 1838–1876

Probably the most well-travelled Inuit woman of her time, she served as a devoted guide and interpreter to explorers who would transform her Arctic homeland.

Born near Cumberland Sound on Baffin Island, Tookoolito was nine years old when the Franklin expedition disappeared in 1847 while looking for the Northwest Passage. As the Inuit girl was growing up in the traditional ways of her people, she came into contact with white travellers looking for whales, or traces of Franklin. In the peak of the whaling activity there were as many as one hundred vessels at a time in the Davis Strait area near her home.

In 1852 Tookoolito (also known as Hannah or Taqulittuq or Tackritow) started learning English from William Barron, a crewman on a British whaling ship.[388] By the age of about fifteen she was married to a skillful Inuit hunter called Ebierbing (also known as Joe Ebierbing or Ipirvik) and the couple sailed to England with whaling captain John Bowling. During their twenty-month stay Tookoolito improved her English, learned about Christianity, and adopted such skills as knitting and making a fine cup of tea. Tookoolito was presented to Queen Victoria, and dined with the monarch and Prince Albert.[389]

After their return home to Baffin Island, Tookoolito and Ebierbing served as guides for whalers and a number of expeditions led by non-Inuit "kabloonas." The remarkable couple earned an impressive reputation for their expertise and loyal service, which was essential to many successful voyages. In many cases the kabloonas survived the challenges of the Arctic only because of these devoted Inuit guides. Tookoolito and Ebierbing worked most extensively with American adventurer Charles Francis Hall, who became a strong admirer and close friend.

Hall worked as a blacksmith, engraver, and journalist before deciding to pursue his dream of finding the remains of Franklin's expedition. When the enthusiastic explorer landed in Frobisher Bay in the summer of 1860, alone with a whaleboat and some supplies, he was anxious to meet the Inuit couple and arrange for their assistance in his first expedition. Hall was amazed when Tookoolito — attired in faded finery including crinoline, heavy flounces, a toga, and bonnet — greeted him in English:

> She was the Tookoolito I had so much desired to see, and directly I conversed with her she showed herself to be quite an accomplished person. She spoke my own language fluently ... Simple and gentle in her way, there was a degree of calm intellectual power about her that more and more astonished me.[390]

For the next couple of years Hall engaged the Inuit couple to assist him in learning about their language and culture, Arctic survival skills, and the oral history related to exploration. Ebierbing worked primarily as pilot, guide, dog-sled driver, and hunter, while Tookoolito was an excellent interpreter, trusted advisor, cook, and provider of clothing. Hall proved to be an attentive student, becoming a competent dog-sledder and speaker of the Inuit language. He wrote detailed notes about Inuit culture and learned that to survive in the Arctic one must travel lightly and live from the land. After his expeditions with Tookoolito and Ebierbing, Hall probably knew more about living in the Arctic than any other kabloona.[391] Hall's published accounts of his travels benefited explorers who followed him — such as Robert Peary and Vilhjalmur Stefannson.

When Hall returned home in 1862 after his first Arctic expedition, he had found some relics of Frobisher's expedition and was eager to return North. His Inuit guides, with their infant son Tukeliketa, accepted Hall's invitation to go to the United States with him and help get funding for a second expedition. Attired in their finest Arctic clothing, Tookoolito and Ebierbing appeared at the American Geographical and Statistical Society, speaking engagements, and Barnum's Museum in New York. Tookoolito and Tukeliketa became ill, and the baby died of pneumonia. The bereaved family headed to the home of whaling master Sideny Budington in Groton, Connecticut, where Tukeliketa was buried.

In the summer of 1864 Tookoolito and Ebierbing returned north with Hall on a five-year expedition, the culmination of which was reaching King William Island. Hall discovered a body from the Franklin expedition and recovered some artifacts. Tookoolito gave birth to another son, Little King William, in 1865 and the baby accompanied his parents on the journeys with Hall. Despite Tookoolito's desperate attempts to save his life using modern medicine provided by Hall and the traditional methods of the Inuit shaman, the infant died of pneumonia in May of 1866. A couple of years later Tookoolito and her husband adopted a young Inuit girl called Punny, and the trio returned to the United States with Hall in 1869.

Charles Francis Hall was now an experienced Arctic adventurer — a celebrity. The U.S. Congress approved funding for his planned voyage to the North Pole. When Hall returned North in the summer of 1871 on the steamer *Polaris*, he was accompanied by his trusted Inuit assistants as well as a motley crew (primarily Germans). In Greenland they picked up Inuit guide Hans Hendrick, his wife, and four children.

The ship managed to reach the highest latitude ever reached by Europeans: the northern mouth of Robeson Strait. Tragedy struck after the group anchored for the winter. Hall suddenly became ill and died; when Hall's body was exhumed more than a hundred years later it was proven to have significant amounts of arsenic — and speculations remain that the expedition leader was murdered. In October 1872 the *Polaris* was caught in a severe storm and seemed to be sinking. The drunk Captain Budington quickly ordered his crew to throw supplies overboard to safety on the ice. The *Polaris* suddenly broke loose.

Tookoolito watched in amazement as their ship disappeared in the Arctic night, leaving her and eighteen companions drifting away on an ice floe.[392] The group included the two Inuit families, nine crew members, and George Tyson, who struggled to take charge. The castaways began a horrific six-month journey on an ice pack, during which they drifted about 2,080 kilometres south. They faced bitter quarrelling and pilfering of provisions, starvation, loss of supplies, breaking up of the ice floe, and heavy gales that soaked them to the skin. Ebierbing later noted that he could have tried to reach shore with his family, but didn't out of loyalty to the expedition and Tyson.

Miraculously, thanks primarily to the survival skills of the Inuit, all survived the incredible journey. From the shores of Ellesmere Island, down Baffin Bay past Greenland to the Labrador coast — where a Newfoundland sealer rescued the group on April 30, 1873.

While Ebierbing continued to spend much of his time in the North, Tookoolito and Punny settled in their small house in Groton,

Connecticut. The young girl died in 1875 and Tookoolito succumbed to tuberculosis the following year — at the age of thirty-eight. In 1981 the Historic Sites and Monuments Board of Canada designated Taqulittuq (Tookoolito) and Ipirvik (Ebierbing) as national historic persons of Canada in a joint commemoration of the couple. The pair played important roles in decades of Arctic exploration that would forever change the lives of their people and lead to declarations of Canadian sovereignty in the North.[393]

Quote:

"I visited her [Queen Victoria], and liked the appearance of her majesty, and every thing about the palace. Fine place, I assure you, sir."[394]

National Archives of Canada/C-3313

Lily of the Mohawks
Kateri Tekakwitha
1656–1680

Kateri Tekakwitha.

Persecuted for her religious beliefs, Kateri fled her home after being threatened with death.

Kateri Tekakwitha is the first Aboriginal person in America to be declared venerable[395] (the first step to sainthood) by the Catholic Church. She adopted the Christian faith in spite of strong opposition from some of her people.

Kateri was born in Ossernenon near Auriesville, New York, in 1656. She was the daughter of a pagan Mohawk warrior of the Turtle clan and a Christian Algonkin woman, who had been captured by the Mohawks in about 1653. Kateri's mother had acquired her religious beliefs at Trois-Rivières, Quebec, where she grew up with French settlers.

Smallpox ravaged Kateri's people and she became an orphan at age four. She survived, but her face was permanently disfigured by pockmarks and her eyesight impaired. The chieftain of the village, Kateri's anti-Christian uncle, adopted the child. When she was ten the Mohawk settlement was burned to the ground by an expedition from Quebec. The villagers rebuilt in a place they called Gandaouagué, and sought a more peaceful life. Little Kateri learned about Christianity from some visiting Jesuit missionaries.

At the age of twenty the young woman asked to be baptized, and the ceremony was performed by Father Jacques de Lamberville on Easter Day 1676. The following year she fled her village because of the resulting persecution she suffered and went to the Saint-François-Xavier mission at Caughnawaga, on the St. Lawrence River near Montreal. Kateri devoted herself to prayer and caring for the sick and elderly.

She was eager to create a community of Aboriginal nuns but was dissuaded by Father Lamberville. Kateri herself took a vow of chastity and was criticized because she chose not to marry.

Kateri Tekakwitha died of tuberculosis on April 17, 1680, at the age of twenty-four. Father Cholenec reported that her disfigured face suddenly became beautiful. Many of her people began to show their devotion to her memory and pilgrims visited her grave in Caughnawaga; in 1884 Rev. Clarence Walworth erected a monument there in her honour.

On June 22, 1980, Kateri Tekakwitha was beatified by Pope John Paul II. Her feast day is celebrated on July 14. People throughout Canada, the United States, and other areas of the world are devoted to Blessed Kateri Tekakwitha, and more than fifty biographies have been written about her in at least ten languages.[396] She continues to serve as a spiritual inspiration, particularly to Native Catholics who admire her "heroic survival."[397]

Quote:

"I have given myself entirely to Jesus Christ; and it is not possible for me to change masters. The poverty with which I am threatened gives me no uneasiness."[398]

A Priceless Prize of War

Thanadelthur
?–1717

Once considered as nothing but a prize of war, she rose
to a position of power and influence in the fur trade —
paving the way for other Aboriginal women to play
important roles.

Thanadelthur was an enterprising Chipewyan Dene woman who held a
position of power and influence in fur trade society.[399]

In the spring of 1713 Thanadelthur and another woman had been
captured as prizes of war by the Crees in a raid upon the Chipewyans.
More than a year later the captives saw a chance to escape. They were
camped along the Nelson River, which flows into Hudson Bay, in an area
that is now part of Manitoba. The pair hoped they would have a chance
to reach their own people before winter but only Thanadelthur survived.
On Ten Shilling Creek she discovered goose hunters who worked for the
Hudson's Bay Company.

The men took Thanadelthur back to York Factory on Hudson Bay,
where Governor James Knight had taken command in 1714. Knight was
pleased to meet the new arrival — who he would call "Slave Woman"
because she'd been held captive by the Cree. He thought she could help
him bring peace between the Chipewyans and the Crees, who were using
their newly acquired firearms to prevent northern Indians from coming to
bayside posts with furs. Eager to improve trade in the area and establish a
new trading post at Churchill, Knight was encouraged by Thanadelthur's
talk about the rich fur resources of her people.

In June 1715, Knight arranged to have a peace mission of about 150
people set out to meet the Chipewyan. The group included Home Guard
Cree and Upland Cree, along with employee William Stuart and
Thanadelthur as interpreter. Knight provided the young woman with
presents to give to her people. With sickness and lack of food on a tough
trek across the Barren Grounds, many turned back and the group dwin-
dled. Thanadelthur used all her persuasive powers to convince the small
remaining group of Cree to wait in camp for ten days while she tried to
find her people.

On locating a large band of Chipewyans, Thanadelthur again had a tough task in trying to convince her people that the Cree sincerely wanted peace. After considerable arguing and scolding, she finally engineered peaceful discussions. Stuart admired Thanadelthur's negotiating skills: "Indeed She has a Devillish Spirit and I believe that if thare were but 50 of her Country Men of the same Carriage and Resolution they would drive all the (Southern) Indians in America out of there Country."[400]

When Stuart and his party returned to York Factory on May 7, 1716, he credited the success of the mission to Thanadelthur, "the Chief promoter and Acter." Knight permitted her and three others to winter in the fort at York Factory, and the rest of the Chipewyans stayed with the Home Guard Cree.

During that winter Governor Knight learned a lot from Thanadelthur, who told him about deposits of copper and possibly gold. He valued her "Extraordinary Vivacity of Apprehension" and the advice she gave him about plans to build a new fort at Churchill the following summer. They agreed that Thanadelthur would accompany the expedition in the spring. Unfortunately she fell ill and died on February 5, 1717. Knight, who had grown fond of the woman, wrote, "I am almost ready to break my heart ... She was one of a Very high Spirit and of the Firmest Resolution that ever I see any Body in my Days and of great Courage & forecast."[401]

Thanadelthur had played an important role in developing a peace accord, which helped to consolidate the English fur trade on western Hudson Bay and permit expansion to the new Churchill River Post in 1717. An adept negotiator, she could speak Cree and English as well as her own Athapaskan language. Her story is recorded in the oral history of the Dene as well as the written records of the Hudson's Bay Company — the latter being rare for an Aboriginal woman.[402]

Thanadelthur held a position of genuine power, and because of the respect accorded her by the white fur traders she was able to dictate to Native men in a way that customarily would not have been accepted. The important role played by Thanadelthur set a precedent, paving the way for other Chipewyan women who followed her to have influential positions in trade relations.[403]

The Historic Sites and Monuments Board of Canada recognized Thanadelthur as a national historic person of Canada in the year 2000, thanks to a nomination by the Churchill Ladies Club.

Quote:

An account of how Thanadelthur arrived at York Factory:

The factor saw her through the glass, opened the door and called her in. She entered and he asked, "Who are you?" She answered in Cree. He inquired if her people were numerous, and she said they were many.

"Are they good-looking people?"

"You see me. Do I look bad?"

"No, you look better than these people."

"Well, that is how my people look."[404]

Thanadelthur as depicted in the comic book *Tales from the Bay—Thanadelthur*.

What a Viking!

Gudridur Thorbjarnardottir
Pre-1000 –?

Photo by Glen Purdy

An amazing Icelandic explorer, she visited North America before Columbus.

Statue of Gudridur and son Snorri.

Perhaps it was a cold day, thick with fog. Somewhere on the eastern coast, probably in what is now Atlantic Canada, a beautiful young woman gave birth to a baby boy called Snorri — the first European child born in North America. The mother was Gudridur Thorbjarnardottir, a Viking who made at least two voyages to North America about a thousand years ago.

About five centuries before Christopher Columbus landed in America, Vikings had reached the continent via Iceland and Greenland. The Norsemen were farmers, fishermen, and hunters looking for new homes. Among them was Gudridur, the central character in the ancient Vinland Sagas that tell the story of this incredible Viking and the discovery of America.[405] The sagas describe Gudridur as "a very exceptional woman" who was attractive as well as knowledgeable. "A woman of striking appearance and wise as well, who knew how to behave among strangers."[406]

Gudridur was born at Laugarbrekka in Iceland. She later sailed to Greenland with her parents and foster parents, who settled in the colony established there by the famous Erik the Red. Here she married one of his sons: Thorsteinn. Another son, Leif the Lucky, had already ventured across the sea to America. Gudridur joined her husband on one of the early Viking voyages to Vinland, whose precise location on the eastern coast of North America is not known. After surviving a harrowing voyage home, plagued by storms, Thorsteinn and many of his malnourished crew died the following winter.

Following the death of her husband Gudridur fell in love with a wealthy Icelandic trader named Thorfinn Karlsefni, who had sailed to Greenland on a trading voyage. The two wed and decided to make a trip to Vinland, leading the first attempt to establish a settlement in the New World. With a carefully selected crew of sixty men and five women, they set sail with three ships; a variety of livestock were aboard. At their destination the expedition members moved into houses built by Leif on his earlier journey. Gudridur and Thorfinn spent three winters in North America, in a location that author Pall Bergthorsson believed to be near the site of what is now Saint John, New Brunswick.[407] The expedition is believed to have occurred between 1003 and 1014.[408]

It was here that Gudridur's son, Snorri, was born. Because of conflicts with the Native people of the area the colonists returned to Greenland. Thorfinn and his family sailed on to Norway with a cargo of trade goods. They then headed back to Thorfinn's home in northern Iceland, where they bought a farm in Skagafjord.

The adventurous Gudridur decided to continue her travels after becoming widowed again. She went to Denmark, then by foot on a pilgrimage to Rome. Committing herself to her new religion, Gudridur became a nun. On returning to the farm at Glaumbaer she passed her remaining years in seclusion at the church her son, Snorri, had built for her. Her descendants included three bishops in early Iceland.

Gudridur is a remarkable heroine in Canadian history. A courageous Viking explorer, she was known as "the most attractive of women and one to be reckoned with in all of her dealings."[409] She was probably one of the most travelled women in the world and presumably the first European female to visit what is now Canada.

Inspired by the fascinating life of this legendary explorer, Icelandic author Brynja Benediktsdóttir wrote the play *Saga of Gudridur*. First performed in 1998, it has played in several countries — including Canada. In the year 2000 special events were held throughout Canada to celebrate the first arrival in North America of European seafarers — the

Icelanders. On April 6, Iceland Prime Minister David Oddsson presented Canadian Prime Minister Jean Chrétien with a bronze statue of Gudridur and her baby, Snorri.

Quote:

"I have neither magical powers nor the gift of prophecy, but in Iceland my foster-mother, Halldis, taught me chants she called ward songs ... These are the sort of actions in which I intend to take no part, because I am a Christian woman."[410]

Gudridur speaking of her knowledge of the chants used in magical rites.

Mary Travers.

Songs of Quebec
Mary Travers
1894–1941

She mixed traditional music with her own words and innovative singing style, giving birth to an original sound.

When young Mary Travers was cooking and playing the accordion in a lumber camp she had no dreams of becoming a professional singer. But poverty pushed her to the stage and extraordinary talent made her a legend.

Mary Travers was born and raised in Newport, Quebec — an isolated fishing and lumbering town in the Gaspé Peninsula. She grew up in a large family with her French-Canadian mother and Irish father, from whom she learned to play the accordion, fiddle, harmonica, spoons, and Jew's harp. Music brought joy to the harsh realities of their existence. The musically gifted Mary could easily play traditional tunes and dances from memory. Poorly educated, she never received any formal music education and could not read music.

Mary left home at age thirteen for the promise of a better life in Montreal, where she worked as a maid and then in a factory. She married Édouard Bolduc at age twenty and in the following years gave birth to thirteen children — of whom just four survived to adulthood. The family lived in poverty even after Édouard became a plumber. Thanks to friends who performed at the Monument-National with a troupe organized by Conrad Gauthier (the noted folklorist and singer), the dynamic housewife replaced an absent violinist there, and in 1927 Gauthier asked her to sing. The audience loved Madame Bolduc and she was pleased to discover an unexpected means of supporting her family.

With Gauthier's encouragement she began composing songs: humorous, honest, folksy songs about the challenges faced by the common folks. Singing with a unique style, which included comical nonsense syllables — called "mouth music" or "turlutes" in French — the joyous woman quickly became known throughout the province as La Bolduc. She brought laughter and hope even in the dark days of the Depression, becoming an incredibly popular voice of her people. The singer had a great impact on French-Canadian women in particular.

In her relatively short eleven-year career La Bolduc performed in Quebec, Ontario, New Brunswick, and francophone areas of New England. She recorded about one hundred songs that she had composed, and a couple of her recordings sold an unprecedented twelve thousand copies. La Bolduc's work is now recognized as an important part of the culture of Quebec. She inspired future generations of Quebecois musicians and ushered in modern folk music to the province.[411] She is often called "The Queen of Canadian Folksingers."

Mary Travers' musical career ended abruptly after she was seriously injured in a car accident in 1937, at which time it was discovered she had cancer. The beloved singer and composer died in 1941 at the age of forty-six. The Historic Sites and Monuments Board of Canada commemorated her as a national historic person in 1992, and Canada Post honoured her with a stamp in 1994. There are many tributes to her throughout Quebec — from the portrait of her by Jean-Paul Riopelle, which is displayed in the Place des Arts in Montreal, to some mountains in the Gaspé and a street in Charlesbourg that bear her name.[412] When the Canadian Songwriters Hall of Fame was created in 2003, Madame Bolduc was selected as one of the first five popular song composers to be inducted.

Quote:

"The time will come, the time will come, but we can't lose hope."[413]

Mary Travers — La Bolduc.

Doctor Jenny

Jenny Gowanlock
Trout
1841–1921

A religious recluse with a mysterious nervous disorder, she became an unlikely heroine in the field of medicine.

Dr. Jenny Trout.

McDonald's Restaurants dubbed Jenny Trout as "Ms. M.D." in a promotional campaign that featured Canadian historical figures on placemats. In 1991 her portrait appeared on a Canada Post stamp that commemorated her accomplishments, and in 1999 a plaque commemorating the national historic significance of Dr. Jenny Trout was unveiled in Kingston, Ontario. But who was Jenny Trout — and why are we only recently rediscovering a Canadian heroine who seems to have been forgotten?

Jenny Trout holds the distinction of being the first Canadian woman licensed to practise medicine in Canada. Dr. Emily Stowe began her practice earlier but received her licence after Dr. Trout. The two women were once close friends who eventually became rivals. As suggested by historian Carlotta Hacker, the quiet and gentle Dr. Trout was probably overshadowed by the charismatic and outgoing Dr. Stowe — whose equally vivacious daughter, Dr. Augusta Stowe-Gullen, ensured that her mother featured prominently in the chronicles of early medical history in Canada.[414]

Jenny Gowanlock was a Scottish lass who came to Canada at age six when her parents settled on a farm near Stratford, Ontario. The Gowanlocks were descendants of a persecuted Swiss preacher and belonged to the Knox Presbyterian Church. The family had no problems financing the young girl's studies at Normal School in Toronto, where she received her teacher's certificate. Jenny taught school until marrying Edward Trout in 1865. Extremely ambitious, Edward became a prosperous businessman whose ventures included managing a commercial college in Toronto and publishing the *Monetary Times*.

For the first six years of her marriage Jenny was practically an invalid. She suffered from poor health much of her life, largely due to some sort of "nervous disorder."[415] After receiving mild electric shock treatments the young woman felt well enough to think about her future. Because of her own medical problems Jenny decided to become a medical doctor. It's hard to imagine today how tough it was to pursue this dream of entering a field that was not open to women. The obstacles were incredible.

When Jenny was healthy enough to begin her medical studies in the early 1870s her husband Edward was still establishing his career, so the Trouts were boarding with the Stowe family in their Toronto home. Jenny and Emily Stowe (who was already practising medicine but had not yet been able to obtain a licence) managed to get permission to attend the 1871–72 winter session of the Toronto School of Medicine. It was the first time that women were allowed to enter a recognized medical school in Canada — and the male students and professors were bent on ensuring they were the last. Though Jenny was a reserved woman who avoided confrontation whenever possible, she refused to accept the harassment without a fight. She finally threatened one of the professors with exposure to his wife if he did not stop telling lewd stories in class to upset the two female students.

After enduring the hostile treatment at the Toronto School of Medicine Jenny Trout decided she had no choice but to leave Canada. She completed her training at the Woman's Medical College of Pennsylvania in Philadelphia. Attracted by the Christian philosophy at this respected institution, she also had a special interest in its courses relating to electrotherapeutics. After three years of study Jenny Trout graduated with an M.D. degree in 1875. On passing licensing exams for Ontario, she became the first Canadian woman doctor licensed to practise as a physician there. Press comments on this impressive achievement included the remark: "That lady's scholastic experience must have been refreshing, particularly when we take into account the timidity, modesty, and general refinement of the sex."[416]

Dr. Trout established a Medical and Electro-Therapeutic Institute, which at one point accommodated up to sixty patients (primarily women) in six houses. Women stressed by family demands could stay and be treated for their "nervous diseases" with electricity and galvanic baths. Thanks to Edward Trout's business success, he was able to assist his wife in creating a stylish facility that included "splendidly furnished apartments" with delicious food. A genuinely caring and compassionate person, the religious Dr. Trout was remembered by patrons as kind and gentle. She was known to be sweet-natured and always willing to help needy people.

Due to popularity of the electrotherapy clinic Jenny opened branches of the Institute in Brantford and Hamilton. In her efforts to assist others Dr. Trout operated a short-lived dispensary for the poor, where she saw about fourteen patients per day. She gave medical lectures to pay the costs of the dispensary, but had to close the operation after six months because of insufficient funds and perhaps her growing fatigue. She had also become involved with a number of organizations, serving for a short while as Vice-President of the Association for the Advancement of Women and President of the Woman's Temperance Union.

Dr. Trout encouraged other women to pursue medical careers, going so far as to house some and pay for their college expenses. She was no doubt an inspiring role model. Convinced that Canadian women needed their own medical college, Dr. Trout initially worked with Emily Stowe on plans to set up such an institution in Toronto. Jenny offered to give $10,000 for the venture, but pulled out when the academics refused to accept her condition that women must sit on the governing board and be hired as staff. In 1883 she provided financial support for creation of another facility: the Women's Medical College in Kingston, Ontario.

When two medical colleges for women opened in October 1883 — the Toronto facility supported by Dr. Stowe and the Kingston one by Dr. Trout — Canadian women could more easily join the medical profession. Jenny Trout was appointed to the Board of Trustees of the Kingston Medical College for Women but was never able to attend any meetings. She was exhausted. Still plagued by her nervous disorder, Dr. Trout was by now bedridden much of the time. By 1882 she had closed her Institute, and she retired from medical practice at the age of forty-one. Anxious to lead a peaceful life, she retreated into Bible studies and pursued her interest in foreign missions. The Trouts also adopted and raised two children: a grand-niece and nephew.

As her brother-in-law noted, Jenny "never had any interest in society … [she] was always disposed to retirement and seclusion."[417] The pioneering doctor quietly faded into obscurity for the remainder of her life, away from the public attention that she had never enjoyed. Dr. Jenny Trout and her husband moved to California in 1908, where she died in 1921 at the age of eighty. A model of courage and determination, she helped pave the way for future generations of women pursuing careers in medicine. Dr. Trout has been recognized by the Historic Sites and Monuments Board of Canada as a national historic person, and a 1991 stamp from Canada Post honours her accomplishments.

Quote:

"I bethought me this evening that the moments were few ere 1880 became for all time a part of history not the least interesting part to me being the fact that our Queen's college opened its doors to Women. I regret very much that so few appear to avail themselves of the grand opportunity."[418]

Dr. Trout writing to a friend on New Year's Eve, 1880.

Harriet Tubman.

Wanted: Dead or Alive

Harriet Ross Tubman
ca. 1820–1913

Pistol in hand, she threatened a hesitant fugitive slave: "Move or die." He continued on to safety.[419]

Harriet Tubman couldn't read or write, and she suffered from seizures after a brutal slave overseer struck her on the head with a heavy weight. Such handicaps did not stop her from becoming the most successful conductor on the Underground Railroad. She never lost a passenger and freed more people than any other guide. Harriet led about three hundred slaves to freedom in the northern states and Canada, risking her own life to save them. Angry slave owners posted a $40,000 reward for her capture — dead or alive.[420]

Born to slaves on a Maryland plantation, Harriet Ross grew up in a family of eleven children. By the age of five she was labouring in the fields with other slaves. She married a free Black man called John Tubman but fled to Philadelphia without him in 1849 — fearful that she was going to be sold to a new master in the Deep South after her owner died. Harriet began cooking in hotels and clubs to earn money, which she used to finance her journeys to free states in the north with other Blacks escaping slavery.

Harriet was a tough conductor — lives depended on her leadership. She was a master of disguise, cunning, and ingenuity. A fearless commander who tolerated no laggards. Renowned for her physical stamina, she was a brilliant planner and strategist. Dedicated and deceptive, skilled in flattery and intimidation, she led her freedom seekers by night, using the North Star to guide the way along the network of secret contacts and safe shelters. Wading through swamps and bushwhacking through forests, the groups would bed down in barns or homes, dugouts, chimneys, etc.

Harriet at first took her charges to places like New York, Delaware, and Philadelphia. After the 1850 enactment of the Fugitive Slave Act compelled authorities in the north to return slaves to their owners, she began taking the escapees into Upper Canada at Niagara Falls. In 1851 Harriet Tubman moved to St. Catharines, Ontario. The settlement served as her home until 1857, during which time some of the freedom seekers stayed in the boarding house she'd rented there. A member of the Refugee Slaves' Friends Society, Harriet played an essential role in the Underground Railroad.

St. Catharines became Harriet's base of operation for anti-slavery activities for many years. She guided people to freedom there, then helped them adjust to their new home with the notable assistance of abolitionist Reverend Hiram Wilson. By 1855 there were 123 Black families living in the community. In late 1857 Harriet rescued her elderly parents from Maryland, bringing them up to St. Catharines in a daring escape after learning her father was to be tried for helping slaves. Another visitor was the famous abolitionist John Brown, who stayed with her to discuss some of his plans for liberating Blacks from slavery. Impressed by Harriet's legendary exploits, he always addressed her as General Tubman.[421]

Harriet Tubman eventually moved her base of operations to Auburn, New York, but continued to be involved in activities in St. Catharines. She served on the executive of the Fugitive Aid Society in 1861 and received funding from Canada for her work. The famous conductor led her last group of escaping slaves from Maryland in December 1860.

After the outbreak of the Civil War, Harriet headed south to help the Union Army. She served as a nurse, spy, and raider during the war, then returned to Auburn. Despite poor health and poverty, Harriet continued to help other people in any way she could — caring for her parents, supporting two schools for freed men, giving speeches along with suffragists such as Elizabeth Cady Stanton and Susan B. Anthony, helping build a church, and raising funds for good causes. When she finally received a government pension for her war service Tubman used the money to help create a home for the aged and needy, which was later called the Harriet Tubman Home. She died there at the age of ninety-three.

One of Harriet's contemporaries, Rev. Higginson of Massachusetts, described her as follows in a letter to his mother:

> We have had the greatest heroine of the age here, Harriet
> Tubman, a black woman and a fugitive slave ... Her tales
> of adventure are beyond anything in fiction & her gener-
> alship is extraordinary.[422]

During her years in Canada, Harriet and the refugees she conducted to St. Catharines often attended services at the British Methodist Episcopal Church; the house where she sheltered them was just behind it. The Historic Sites and Monuments Board of Canada recognized the church building as a national historic site because of its association with Harriet Tubman and the abolitionist activities. Tubman's heroism as a courageous conductor on the Underground Railroad has been recognized by the Ontario Heritage Foundation, which erected a plaque at the church to commemorate her important contribution in leading slaves to freedom in Canada.

Quote:

"I had seen their tears and sighs, and I had heard their groans, and I would give every drop of blood in my veins to free them."[423]

Harriet Tubman explaining her zeal for leading slaves to freedom.

Harriet Tubman woodcut, from an 1863 photograph.

Holding the Fort

Madeleine de Verchères
1687–1747

She was a teenage warrior who became one of the most famous heroines in Canadian history. A woman whose statue was deemed as important as New York's Statue of Liberty.

An imaginary historical portrait of Madeleine de Verchères by Gerald S. Hayward.

At the age of fourteen, Madeleine courageously took command of Fort de Verchères and successfully defended it against attacking Iroquois. She had only the help of two little brothers, an elderly servant, and two soldiers.

Madeleine was born in Verchères, Quebec, and grew up in a large family on her father's seigneury along the St. Lawrence River. Her father, François Jarret, had come from France with the Carignan Regiment in 1665. With a girl of twelve and a half as his bride, Jarret settled in Canada on land granted by Intendant Talon. The seigneury was called Verchères, and it was here that the family built a fort for protection from Iroquois raids. The manor house was surrounded by a rectangular stockade with walls about four metres high, and corner bastions.

Madeleine was minding the fort in 1692 when it was attacked by Iroquois who captured twenty people working in the surrounding fields. Both her parents were in Montreal, so the young girl quickly took charge of defending her home and family. There are different versions of what actually happened. Some indicate that after fleeing some Iroquois that were chasing her Madeleine scrambled up a bastion, donned a soldier's hat, and began to fire her gun.

Both fort and family survived the attack. Madeleine wrote about her defense of the fort in 1699 (seven years after the event) in petitioning the king's minister for a small pension or the position of ensign for her brother. With the death of François Jarret in 1700, the Verchères faced the challenge of looking after the seigneury without his guidance and salary as a half-pay lieutenant. After Intendant Jean Bochart de Champigny confirmed Madeleine's story, the minister agreed that her father's pension from the Carignan Regiment would be paid to her in recognition of her heroic behaviour in 1692. The young woman apparently delayed marriage to help look after her family, wedding Pierre-Thomas Tarieu de La Pérade at age twenty-eight.

Later accounts of the attack on the fort, another presumably penned by Madeleine and others written by historians La Potherie and Charlevoix, are coloured by more exciting details that embellished the performance of the young heroine. Madeleine was now reported to have escaped from as many as fifty Iroquois who were firing at her as they surrounded the fort. She was also further from the fort when the attack began. The basic story remained the same but seems to have been largely forgotten until the Canadian public learned about Madeleine's exploits after her letters were found in France in the 1860s.[424]

Madeleine de Verchères became a legendary heroine of New France — one of the most widely recognized figures in Canadian history. Governor General Lord Grey praised the high ideals of citizenship she had demonstrated and won support from Prime Minister Sir Wilfrid Laurier for the installation of a massive statue of the heroine along the St. Lawrence River at Verchères. Grey believed the monument would have the symbolic importance of the Statue of Liberty in New York City.[425] When the statue was unveiled in 1913 one speaker even compared young Madeleine to Joan of Arc. In 1923 the Historic Sites and Monuments Board of Canada designated Madeleine de Verchères as a national historic person and she remains a prominent heroine.

Quote:

"Although my sex does not permit me to have inclinations other than those it demands of me, allow me nevertheless, Madame, to tell you that, like many men, I have feelings which incline me to glory."[426]

A letter from Madeleine de Verchères to the Comtesse de Maurepas.

Can a Girl Learn to Fly?

Eileen Vollick
1908–1968

Eileen Vollick, 1928.

> She went where no Canadian woman had gone before: flying — as the first pilot to get her licence in this country.

"Can a girl learn to fly?" she asked. "I was fearful of being turned down or laughed at because women had not then entered this man's game in Canada." Eileen Vollick became Canada's first female licensed pilot in 1928 when she received private pilot's licence number 77.[427]

When Eileen arrived at the Jack V. Elliot flying school in Hamilton, Ontario, the instructors were skeptical about her ability to fly a plane: she was just five foot one, weighed eighty-nine pounds — and she was a woman. Elliot sent her application to the Department of National Defence for approval, a process that took three months. Officials finally accepted the request but stipulated that the female candidate must be nineteen to receive her licence — though males could obtain one at the age of seventeen. The discrimination continued when the school reluctantly agreed to teach the young woman, but fortunately most of her instructors were helpful.

Eileen was a natural flyer. All she needed for extra support were a couple more cushions on her seat to prop her up. She took her training in the winter months flying a Jenny: a World War I biplane with an open cockpit. Since the frozen Hamilton Harbour served as the landing strip, the aspiring pilot learned how to fly aircraft equipped with skis. After sixteen hours of training she passed her flying exams on March 13, 1928.

Jack Elliott quickly realized the publicity value of having the first accredited female pilot graduating from his flying school. He called some newspapers and Eileen's accomplishment was soon publicized, bringing her many invitations to give speeches. She continued her work as a textile analyst, but also began aerobatic flying and skydiving, becoming the first woman in Canada to parachute into water in the summer of 1928.

Eileen married James Hopkin and they raised a family in New York State, where she died in 1968. Though she was only an active flyer for a few years, Eileen Vollick demonstrated that women could be competent pilots. Many other daring women soon joined her on the list of Canada's licensed pilots. Eileen's important contribution to aviation was recognized when she was posthumously awarded the Amelia Earhart Medallion in 1975. In the following year the 99s, an International Organization of Women Pilots, and the Ontario Heritage Foundation organized a ceremony to unveil a historical plaque in honour of Eileen Vollick at Hamilton Airport.

Quote:

"Although it was against the rules to stunt with a passenger, on my first lesson he did spins, loops and zooms thinking he could either frighten me or find out how much courage I possessed! I loved it and showed up for my next lesson."[428]

Eileen Vollick's memories of the male instructor
for her first flying lesson.

Singing in Her Dreams

Portia White
1911–1968

Yousuf Karsh/National Archives of Canada/PA-192783

In her short but impressive career she became an internationally acclaimed singer.

Portia White.

The crowd loved her. So did the critics, when Portia White first sang on a major concert stage at Toronto's Eaton Auditorium. Portia White's debut on November 7, 1941, elicited glowing reviews from Hector Charlesworth writing for *Saturday Night* and the *Globe and Mail*: "...to only a few in her audience did the name of Portia White signify anything until they had heard her sing. Then they realized that they were listening to one of the most promising vocalists Canada has produced ... endowed by nature with a glorious voice..."[429]

But Portia White was already thirty years old. Her relatively short success on the stage was no doubt due to the fact that the extremely gifted contralto got the professional training she needed too late in her life.

Portia White was born in Truro, Nova Scotia, on June 24, 1911, the third of thirteen children in the family of William Andrew White and his wife, Izie Dora. William White was a descendant of slaves from Virginia, while Izie was from Mill Village and had some Mi'kmaq ancestors. Portia grew up in a loving family who were highly respected in the community. The Whites were prominent but didn't have a lot of money. William White was a well-educated Baptist minister and her talented mother was heavily involved in the musical life of his churches — playing piano, performing solos with her beautiful soprano voice, and directing the choirs.

The White household was full of music and Portia began singing in the church choir at age six. When she was eight her father was posted to the Cornwallis Street Baptist Church in Halifax, and Portia performed solos there and at a Halifax music festival. While attending school as a youngster, Portia's only musical instruction came from her mother. She was an average student who excelled at languages.

Portia took a teacher training course at Dalhousie University and taught in a number of all-Black primary schools in the Halifax area. Despite having no particular interest in teaching, there were apparently few career options for a young Black woman with limited funds. From her $30–35 monthly salary, Portia paid $3.50 per week for singing lessons at the Halifax Conservatory. They young singer continued to do solos at her father's church, sing on some of his radio shows, and perform at the Nova Scotia Music Festival — where she won the Helen Campbell Kennedy Cup four times. This success earned her the attention of the Halifax Ladies' Musical Club, who kindly offered financial assistance so Portia could continue music lessons.

Thanks to this help, Portia began studying with Dr. Ernesto Vinci at the Halifax Conservatory in 1939. Portia got a big break when Edith Read, a well-connected school principal who was visiting from Toronto, heard her sing. Within a couple weeks Edith Read had arranged for the debut of Portia White at Toronto's Eaton Auditorium. The day after the concert, Oxford University Press offered to manage her career. The hopeful singer quit her teaching job in Africville, Nova Scotia. She began giving concerts on tours across the country while continuing her musical studies and gave a command performance at Rideau Hall.

In March 1944 Portia White performed at New York's Town Hall, in a concert that the *New York Times* reported was "in many ways ... remarkable." One critic noted, "There is no question but that given time and further experience, Miss White's will be a talent to be reckoned with."[430]

Portia was swept up in a tide of success. The City of Halifax and the Province of Nova Scotia created a trust fund to help with her travel and living costs and provided a white fox cape for her to wear at performances. She performed at a United Nations Rally for Victory at Maple Leaf Gardens, then the Fifth Annual American Negro Music Festival in Detroit, Chicago, and St. Louis. Portia sang again at the Town Hall in October 1944, and after signing with Columbia Concerts Inc. was presented at concerts across North America. In early 1946 she began a three-month concert tour of Central and South America.

After Portia White performed at Massey Hall in April 1946, a critic for the *Globe and Mail* noted "a slight rasp" in her voice. Portia began to lose her singing voice, perhaps in part because of pleurisy. Concerts were cancelled and few opportunities were presented to her. She began worrying about supporting herself. In 1950 Portia White retired from the concert stage and began teaching music in Toronto. Her pupils included performers such as Robert Goulet, Lorne Greene, and Dinah Christie.

In the following years Portia performed a few more times on the stage with limited success; her early supporter, Edith Read, maintained that Portia should have been put on the stage earlier in her life. During the 1960s she gave public concerts just four times, one for a command performance attended by Queen Elizabeth II and the Duke of Edinburgh in 1964.

Portia White died of cancer in February 1968. The Nova Scotia school teacher with an extraordinary voice had a remarkable career as a concert singer, though it was unfortunately relatively short. She was one of the most celebrated singers in Canadian history and the first African Canadian to achieve success on the North American stage.[431]

The Historic Sites and Monuments Board of Canada recognized Portia White as a national historic person in 1995. In 1998 the Nova Scotia Arts Council created the Portia White Prize, which is awarded annually to recognize cultural and artistic excellence of an artist in the province. Portia White is also commemorated on a Canadian stamp, issued by Canada Post in 1999 as part of The Millennium Collection. The story of the internationally acclaimed singer has also been depicted in a moving documentary by Sylvia D. Hamilton.[432]

Quote:

"I had this dream — I was always bowing in my dreams, and singing before people and parading across the stage."[433]

Portia White recalling a childhood vision.

A Geologist — At Last!

Alice Wilson
1881–1964

Alice Wilson.

Canada's first female geologist blazed a path into a world where women weren't welcome.

She was a gangly girl who loved rocks. Alice Wilson made geology her hobby, her career, and her life. Even after retiring from the Geological Survey of Canada she continued to go to work in her office every working day until she was eighty-two.

It was only due to her iron will that Alice Wilson became the first woman to have a professional position at the Geological Survey of Canada — the first female permitted to do field work. She was the first Canadian woman Fellow of the Geological Society of America, the first woman Fellow in the Royal Society of Canada, and an honorary member of the Geological Association of Canada.[434]

Born in Cobourg, Ontario, Alice Evelyn Wilson grew up in a close family that thrived on learning and the outdoors. Her mother taught her Greek and Latin before she started grade one, but science became her passion. Alice entered Victoria University expecting to be a teacher, but snuck into science lectures since they were her primary interest. She dropped out of university and got a job as a clerk with the Geological Survey of Canada, where she worked for an invertebrate paleontologist named Percy Raymond. With his encouragement she returned to university to get a degree and came back with a Bachelor of Arts.

In 1911, at the age of thirty, Alice returned to the Geological Survey and became a Museum Assistant. After the war she became Assistant

Paleontologist, and in 1921 the results of some of her reports on field work in the Ottawa Valley were published. A change in management at the Geological Survey brought new roadblocks in her efforts to work as a geologist. For example, the men were issued cars to undertake their field work. Telling Alice that women shouldn't be driving cars, the powers that be gave her a bicycle. They were, however, impressed at how much ground she covered — not knowing that she bought herself a Model T Ford.

Aware that she wouldn't be able to advance without a degree in geology, Alice had been asking for ten years for educational leave. In 1926 she finally got permission to apply for a $1,000 scholarship from the Canadian Federation of University Women. She won, but the Survey presented many reasons why she could not accept: she was too ill (got a doctor's certificate); she was needed (got a woman geologist from the U.S. to work for her). A desperate Alice appealed to the CFUW and its members began lobbying for her. The Geological Survey gave in.

At the age of forty-five Alice Wilson began her studies at the University of Chicago. On December 17, 1929, she became a Doctor of Philosophy. She returned to the Survey, where she was unable to advance for seven years and management refused to publish a report on her dissertation.

Alice was becoming a bit of a legend: a high achiever with an adventurous spirit — a woman who had travelled alone down the Mackenzie River. In 1935 the federal government selected her as a notable woman in the civil service and she became a Member of the Order of the British Empire. Other honours followed.

In 1940, when Alice Wilson was fifty-nine years old, the Geological Survey of Canada appointed her as Associate Geologist. She became a full Geologist after World War II but had to accept retirement at age sixty-five. Alice Wilson continued to conduct field work, published academic reports, and wrote a book for young people called *The Earth Beneath Our Feet*. She travelled up the Amazon, flew over the Andes, and kept busy teaching others about geology.

An amazing Canadian pioneer in the field of geological science, Alice Wilson died in 1964. To honour the memory of this prominent geologist and world-renowned paleontologist, The Royal Society of Canada offers a scholarship each year in her name: The Alice Wilson Award, for the first woman elected to the Society.

Quote:

"The earth touches every life. Everyone should receive some understanding of it."[435]

Grey Nuns of the Sacred Heart

Marguerite d'Youville.

Marguerite's Mission
Marie-Marguerite d'Youville
1701–1771

She was a true saint — a woman that *Time* magazine called the Mother Theresa of her time.[436]

She continued to pay for the sins of her husband even after he was dead. Widowed at twenty-eight, Marie-Marguerite d'Youville discovered only after marriage that François d'Youville was a gambler, bootlegger, and womanizer. When he died in 1730 she was pregnant with their sixth child — and soon discovered she'd inherited his considerable debts and bad reputation. She opened a small shop to support the only two of her children that survived infancy; both sons became priests.

Born in Varennes, Quebec, in 1701, Marie-Marguerite Dufrost de Lajemmerais was the eldest child of one of the most respected families in New France.[437] When Marie-Marguerite was seven her father died, bringing financial insecurity to the family. Thanks to the generosity of relatives the young girl was able to study for several years with the Ursulines in Quebec City, before returning home. At the age of twenty she married François-Madeleine d'Youville in a ceremony that included the most prominent members of the colony.

Following the death of her husband Marguerite devoted herself to religion, raising her sons and helping the poor — giving them alms despite her own poverty, mending clothing, and begging for money to bury criminals. In 1737 she welcomed a blind woman into her home, and on December 31 of that year she joined with three other friends to create a lay association that would serve the poor and needy. This date marks the founding of the order that would become the Sisters of Charity, more commonly known as the Grey Nuns. The women moved into a large house in Montreal where they could help those in need.

Still tarnished by her husband's brandy trafficking, Marguerite and the other sisters were shunned in the streets and accused of continuing his illegal liquor sales. Some people even pelted the women with rocks and taunted them as "les soeurs grises," meaning tipsy women or grey sisters; Marguerite would later adopt the name of Grey Nuns for the order as an act of humility. They wore grey habits. For ten years Marguerite and the sisters faced hardship and harassment, including the denial of communion on one occasion, as they built their community and conducted good works. In 1747 Mme d'Youville was appointed director of a dilapidated, debt-ridden hospital: the Hôpital Général.

Using her impressive administrative talents, Marguerite transformed the facility into an efficient hospital funded by her creative methods of making money — from curing tobacco, selling produce from the sisters' farms, renting land, making sails and tents, to providing lodging for respectable ladies. The sisters cared for the poor, epileptics, the insane, lepers, the aged, "fallen women," British as well as French soldiers, and abandoned children. After a fire destroyed the hospital in 1765 Marguerite found the support to rebuild it and added a bakery, water mill, farm, and an orchard to help finance the many good works of the order. By the time of her death in 1771, Mother d'Youville had built a respected religious order that was well-known for charitable work. The Grey Nuns have established schools, hospitals, and orphanages in Canada, the United States, South America, and Africa.

Known as "Mother of the Poor," Marguerite was a courageous social activist who turned her own suffering into a mission to help others in need. Despite public ridicule and criticism from her own family, she founded a flourishing community of religious women that served outcasts from society. Marguerite d'Youville became the first Canadian-born saint when she was canonized by Pope John Paul II in 1990. The Historic Sites and Monuments Board of Canada has recognized her as a national historic person, and Canada Post has issued a commemorative stamp. St. Marguerite D'Youville is remembered in a multitude of murals, place names, and awards, as well as the living legacy of the Grey Nuns.

Quote:

"My dear Father, pray that God will give me the strength to bear all these crosses and to make saintly use of them. So much at one time: to lose one's king, one's country, one's possessions."[438]

Marguerite D'Youville writing following the conquest of New France
and the destruction of the Hôpital Général by fire in 1765.

Selected Bibliography

Books and Reports

Albini, Emma. *Forty Years of Song.* New York: Arno Press, 1977.

Ainley, Marianne Gosztonyi, ed. *Despite the Odds: Essays on Canadian Women and Science.* Montreal: Véhicule Press, 1990.

Atwood, Fred N., ed. *The Alaska Yukon Gold Book: A Roster.* Seattle: Sourdough Stampede Association, 1930.

Bannerman, Jean Mackay. *Leading Ladies Canada.* Belleville: Mika Publishing Company, 1977.

Bataille, Gretchen M., ed. *Native American Women: A Biographical Dictionary.* New York: Garland Publishing, 1993.

Black, Martha Louise. *My Ninety Years.* Anchorage: Alaska Northwest Publishing Company, 1976.

Brand, Johanna. *The Life and Death of Anna Mae Aquash.* Toronto: James Lorimer, 1978.

Bridge, Kathryn. *Phyllis Munday.* Montreal: XYZ Publishing, 2002.

Cameron, Agnes Deans. *The New North.* New York: D. Appleton and Co., 1910.

Carr, Emily. *Growing Pains: The Autobiography of Emily Carr.* Toronto: Oxford University Press, 1946.

Casgrain, Thérèse F. *A Woman in a Man's World.* Toronto: McClelland and Stewart Limited, 1972.

Chan, Arlene. *Spirit of the Dragon: The Story of Jean Lumb.* Toronto: Umbrella Press, 1997.

Chaput, Don. *Nellie Cashman and the North American Mining Frontier.* Tucson: Westernlore Press, 1995.

Chinese Canadian National Council, Women's Book Committee. *Jin Guo: Voices of Chinese Canadian Women.* Toronto: Toronto Women's Press, 1992.

The Clio Collective, Micheline Dumont et al. *Quebec Women: A History.* Toronto: The Women's Press, 1987.

Coates, Colin M. and Cecilia Morgan. *Heroines & History: Representations of Madeleine de Verchères and Laura Secord.* Toronto: University of Toronto Press, 2002.

Conrad, Earl. *Harriet Tubman: Negro Soldier and Abolitionist.* New York: International Publishers, 1942.

Cormack, Barbara Villy. *Perennials and Politics: The Life Story of the Hon. Irene Parlby.* Sherwood Park, AB: Professional Printing, 1968.

Cruikshank, Julie. *Life Lived Like a Story.* Lincoln, Neb.: University of Nebraska Press, 1990.

Davis, Angela E. and Sarah M. McKinnon. *No Man's Land: The Battlefield Paintings of Mary Riter Hamilton.* Winnipeg: University of Winnipeg, 1992.

De la Roche, Mazo. *Ringing the Changes.* Toronto: MacMillan, 1957.

Dictionary of Canadian Biography. Toronto: University of Toronto Press, 1987.

Dow, Leslie S. *Anna Leonowens: A Life Beyond the King and I.* Nova Scotia: Pottersfield Press, 1995.

Dressler, Marie. *My Own Story.* Boston: Little, Brown and Company, 1934.

Duvall, Paul. *Canadian Impressionism.* Toronto: McClelland & Stewart Inc., 1990.

Eber, Dorothy, ed. *Pitseolak: Pictures out of my life.* Toronto: Design Collaborative Books and Oxford University Press, 1971.

Epstein, Daniel Mark. *Sister Aimee: The Life of Aimee Semple McPherson.* New York: Harcourt Brace, 1993.

Eyman, Scott. *Mary Pickford, From Here to Hollywood.* Toronto: Harper Collins, 1990.

Feder, Alison. *Margaret Duley: Newfoundland Novelist.* St. John's: Harry Cuff Publications Ltd., 1983.

Ferguson, Ted. *Kit Coleman: Queen of Hearts.* Toronto: Doubleday Canada, 1978.

Fraser, Sylvia, ed. *A Woman's Place.* Toronto: Key Porter Books, 1997.

Freeman, Barbara M. *Kit's Kingdom: The Journalism of Kathleen Blake Coleman.* Ottawa: Carleton University Press, 1989.

French, Doris. *Ishbel and the Empire: A Biography of Lady Aberdeen.* Toronto: Dundurn Press, 1988.

Gaudreault, Laure. *Les Souvenirs de Laure Gaudreault.* Quebec: CEQ, 1997.

Gibbon, John Murray and Mary St. Mathewson. *Three Centuries of Canadian Nursing.* Toronto: MacMillan, 1947.

Gillett, Margaret. *We Walked Very Warily.* Montreal: Eden Press Women's Publications, c. 1981.

Givner, Joan. *Mazo de la Roche: The Hidden Life.* Toronto: Oxford University Press, 1989.

Gosztonyi Ainley, Marianne, ed. *Despite the Odds: Essays on Canadian Women and Science.* Montreal: Véhicule Press, 1990.

Grace, Sherrill E. *Canada and the idea of north.* Montreal: McGill-Queen's University Press, 2001.

Grant, Francis W. *Courage Below, White Wings Above.* Hantsport, Nova Scotia: Lancelot Press, 1979.

Gray, Charlotte. *Flint & Feather: The Life and Times of E. Pauline Johnson, Takahionwake.* Toronto: HarperFlamingoCanada, 2002.

Green, Stanley. *The Great Clowns of Broadway.* New York: Oxford University Press, 1984.

Grosskurth, Phyllis. *Canadian Writers & Their Works: Gabrielle Roy.* Toronto: Forum House, 1972.

Hacker, Carlotta. *The Indomitable Lady Doctors.* Toronto: Clarke, Irwin & Company Ltd., 1974.

Hall, Charles Francis. *Arctic researches and life among the Esquimaux: being the narrative of an expedition in search of Sir John Franklin, in the years 1860, 1861 and 1862.* New York: Harper, 1865.

Hill, Andria. *Mona Parsons.* Halifax: Nimbus Publishing, 2000.

Holmes, Rachel. *Scanty Particulars: The Life of Dr. James Barry.* London: Penguin Books, 2003.

Howley, J.P. *The Beothuks or Red Indians.* Cambridge: Cambridge University Press, 1915.

Huang, Evelyn. *Chinese Canadians: Voices From a Community.* Vancouver: Douglas & McIntyre, 1992.

Hubbard, Mina. *A Woman's Way Through Unknown Labrador.* New York: The McClure Company, 1908.

Huey, Lois M. and Bonnie Pullis. *Molly Brant: A Legacy of Her Own.* Youngstown, NY: Old Fort Niagara Publications, 1998.

Inglis, Bishop John. "Bishop John Inglis' Interview with Shanawdithit," in "Appendix: Letter from the Lord bishop of Nova Scotia," S.P.G. Annual Report 1827, London: S.P.G. and C. & J. Rivington, 1828.

Innis, Mary Quayle, ed. *The Clear Spirit: Twenty Canadian Women and Their Times.* Toronto: University of Toronto Press, 1967.

James, Donna. *Emily Murphy.* Markham: Fitzhenry & Whiteside, 2001.

James, Mel. "Margaret Newton 1887–1971: Defeating wheat rust disease." In *Wayfarers: Canadian Achievers* (Canadian Heirloom Series; volume V), 42–43, Mississauga: Heirloom Publishing, 1996.

Johnson, James Albert. *Carmack of the Klondike.* Seattle: Epicenter Press/Horsdal & Schubart, 1990.

Johnston, Sheila M.F. *Buckskin & Broadcloth.* Toronto: Natural Heritage /Natural History Inc., 1997.

Laffey, Bruce. *Beatrice Lillie: The Funniest Woman in the World.* New York: Wynwood Press, 1989.

Lai, David Chuenyan. *Chinatowns: Towns Within Cities in Canada.* Vancouver: University of British Columbia Press, 1989.

Lai, David Chuenyan. *The Forbidden City Within Victoria.* Victoria: Orca, 1991.

Lee, Betty. *The Unlikeliest Star.* Kentucky: The University Press of Kentucky, 1997.

Leonowens, Anna. *The English Governess at the Siamese Court.* New York: Oxford University Press, 1999.

Li, Peter S. *The Chinese in Canada.* Toronto: Oxford University Press, 1998.

Lillie, Beatrice. *Every Other Inch a Lady.* New York: Dell Publishing Co., 1973.

Livingstone, Donna. *Cowboy Spirit: Guy Weadick and the Calgary Stampede.* Vancouver: Greystone Books, 1996.

Luckyj, Natalie. *Helen McNicoll: a Canadian Impressionist.* Toronto: Art Gallery of Ontario, 1999.

MacDonald, Cheryl. *Emma Albani Victorian Diva.* Toronto: Dundurn Press Limited, 1984.

MacDonald, Colin S. "Mary Riter Hamilton." In Colin S. MacDonald. *A Dictionary of Canadian Artists.* Ottawa: Canadian Paperbacks, 1967.

MacEwan, Grant. *Mighty Women: Stories of Western Canadian Pioneers.* Vancouver: Greystone Books, 1995.

MacGill, Elsie Gregory. *My Mother the Judge: A Biography of Helen Gregory MacGill.* Toronto: PMA Books, 1981.

MacMillan, Viola. *From the Ground Up: An Autobiography.* Toronto: ECW Press, 2001.

Magnusson, Magnus and Hermann Palsson. *The Vinland Sagas.* Great Britain: Penguin Books, 1965.

Marshall, Ingeborg. *A History and Ethnography of the Beothuk.* Montreal: McGill-Queen's University Press, 1996.

McDonald, David. *For the Record: Canada's Greatest Women Athletes.* Rexdale: John Wiley & Sons Canada, 1981.

McKenzie, Ruth. *Laura Secord: The Legend and the Lady.* Toronto: McClelland and Stewart, 1971.

McKillop, A.B. *The Spinster & The Prophet.* Toronto: Macfarlane Walter & Ross, 2001.

McLaren, John. "Emily Ferguson Murphy." In *Women in Law*, 190–201, Westport, Connecticut: Greenwood Press, 1996.

McLean, Leonore. "Mrs. Weadick and I." In Thelma Poirier, ed. *Cowgirls: 100 Years of Writing the Range.* Red Deer: Red Deer College Press, 1997.

Montgomery, L.M. *The Alpine Path, The Story of My Career.* Don Mills: Fitzhenry & Whiteside, 1975.

Moritsugu, Frank and The Ghost-Town Teachers Historical Society. *Teaching in Canadian Exile.* Toronto: The Ghost-Town Teachers Historical Society, 2001.

Munday, Don. *The Unknown Mountain.* Seattle: The Mountaineers, 1975.

Murphy, Claire Rudolf and Jane G. Haigh. *Gold Rush Women.* Anchorage: Alaska Northwest Books, 1997.

Negodaeff-Tomsik, Margaret. *Honour Due: The Story of Dr. Leonora Howard King.* Ottawa: Canadian Medical Association, 1999.

Nickerson, Sheila. *Midnight to the North: The Untold Story of the Inuit Woman Who Saved the Polaris Expedition.* New York: Putnam, 2002.

Oleson, T.J. *The Norsemen in America.* Ottawa: Canadian Historical Association Booklets, No. 14, 1963.

Omatsu, Maryka. *Bittersweet Passage: Redress and the Japanese Canadian Experience.* Toronto: Between the Lines, 1992.

Pazdro, Roberta J. "Agnes Deans Cameron: Against the Current." In Barbara K. Latham and Cathy Kess, eds. *In Her Own Right: Selected Essays on Women's History in B.C.* Victoria: Camosun College, 1980.

Peyton, Amy Louise. *Nightingale of the North: Georgina Stirling.* St. John's: Jesperson Press, 1983.

Rayner-Canham, Marelene F. and Geoffrey W. Rayner-Canham. *Harriet Brooks: Pioneer Nuclear Scientist.* Montreal: McGill-Queen's University Press, 1992.

Rayner-Canham, Marelene F. and Geoffrey W. Rayner-Canham. *Women in Chemistry: their changing roles from alchemical times to the mid-twentieth century.* Washington, DC: American Chemical Society/Chemical Heritage Foundation, 1998.

Render, Shirley. *No Place for a Lady: The Story of Canadian Women Pilots 1928–1992.* Winnipeg: Portage & Main Press, 2000.

Rex, Kay. *No Daughter of Mine: The Women and History of the Canadian Women's Press Club, 1904–1971.* Toronto: University of Toronto Press, 1995.

Ricard, François. Translated by Patricia Claxton. *Gabrielle Roy: A Life.* Toronto: McClelland & Stewart, 1999.

Rijnhart, Susie Carson. *With the Tibetans in Tent & Temple*. Boston: Elibron Classics, 2001.

Roberts, Charles G.D. and Arthur L. Tunnell, eds. *A Standard Dictionary of Canadian Biography*, Vol. II. Toronto: Trans-Canada Press, 1938.

Roy, Gabrielle. Translated by Patricia Claxton. *Enchantment and Sorrow: The Autobiography of Gabrielle Roy*. Toronto: Lester & Orpen Dennys, 1987.

Roy, Patricia E. et al. *Mutual Hostages: Canadians and Japanese during the Second World War*. Toronto: University of Toronto Press, 1990.

Rubio, Mary and Elizabeth Waterston, eds. *Writing a Life: L.M. Montgomery*. Toronto: ECW Press, 1995.

Russell, Delbert W. *Anne Hébert*. Boston: Twayne Publishers, 1983.

Salverson, Laura Goodman. *Confessions of an Immigrant's Daughter*. Toronto: University of Toronto Press, 1981.

Savage, Candace. *Cowgirls*. Vancouver: Greystone Books, 1996.

Savage, Candace. *Our Nell: A Scrapbook Biography of Nellie L. McClung*. Halifax: Goodread Biographies, 1979.

Shadbolt, Doris. *Emily Carr*. Vancouver: Douglas & McIntyre, 1990.

Simpson, Patricia. *Marguerite Bourgeoys and Montreal, 1640–1665*. Montreal: McGill-Queen's University Press, 1997.

Smallwood, Joseph R., ed. *The Book of Newfoundland*. St. John's: Newfoundland Book Publishers, 1967.

Smiley, Jane. Preface. *The Sagas of Icelanders: A Selection*. New York: Viking, 2000.

Spring, Joyce. *Daring Lady Flyers: Canadian Women in the Early Years of Aviation*. Lawrencetown Beach: Pottersfield Press, 1994.

Steckley, John. *Beyond Their Years: Five Native Women's Stories*. Toronto: Canadian Scholars' Press Inc., 1999.

Toye, William, ed. *The Oxford Companion to Canadian Literature*. Toronto: Oxford University Press, 1983.

Trudel, Marcel. *Dictionnaire des esclaves et de leurs propriétaires au Canada Français*. Ville La Salle: Éditions Hurtubise, 1980.

Trudel, Marcel. *L'esclavage au Canada français* (Edition abrégée). Québec: Les Presses de l'Université Laval, 1960.

Tunnell, Roberts, ed. *The Canadian Who's Who 1938–1939*. Trans-Canada Press, 1939.

Van Kirk, Sylvia. *Many Tender Ties: Women in Fur-Trade Society, 1670–1870*. Winnipeg: Watson & Dwyer, 1980.

Weissman Wilks, Claire. *The Magic Box: The Eccentric Genius of Hannah Maynard*. Toronto: Exile Editions Ltd., 1980.

White, Donny. *Geraldine Moodie: An Inventory*. Regina: Canadian Plains Research Center, University of Regina, 1999.

White, Donny. *In Search of Geraldine Moodie*. Regina: Canadian Plains Research Center, University of Regina, 1998.

Winks, Robin W. *The Blacks in Canada: A History* (2nd Edition). Montreal: McGill-Queen's University Press, 1997.

Periodicals

Achard, Betty. "Laure Gaudreault, pionnière du syndicalisme enseignant au Québec." *Madame*, sept. 2003.

Anonymous Author. "Retrospect of the History of the Mission of the Brethren's Church in Labrador for the Past Hundred Years (1771-1871)." Translated by Dr. Hans Rollman. *Periodical Accounts*, 28 (1871), 1-19, 53-72.

Anonymous Author. "Shaa-naan-dithit, part II of Sketches of Savage Life." *Fraser's Magazine for Town and Country*, Vol. XIII, 1836.

Armstrong, Isabel C. "For She Was a Militant Rose!" *The Montreal Listening Post*, May 1924.

Bénesty-Sroka, Ghila. "Entrevue avec Léa Roback: une femme engagée." *Canadian Woman Studies*, Vol. 16, no. 128, Autumn 1996, 81-85.

Bolus, Malvina. "The son of I. Gunn." *The Beaver*, Winter 1971, 23-26.

Brown, Stephen R. "Cormack's Quest." *The Beaver*, April/May 2000, Vol. 80:2, 34-39.

Clum, John P. "Nellie Cashman, the Angel of Tombstone." *Arizona Historical Review*, January 1931, 9-34.

Coates, Colin M. "The legend of Madeleine de Verchères." *The Beaver*, April/May 2002, Vol. 82:2.

Craig, Terrence L. "The Confessional Revisited: Laura Salverson's Canadian Work." *Studies in Canadian Literature*, Volume 10.1 & 2, 1985.

Fischman, Sheila. "A literary gem cutter." *Maclean's*, Feb.7, 2000, Vol. 113, Iss. 6, 57.

Haven, Br. Jens. "Memoire of the Life of Br. Jens Haven." Translated by Dr. Hans Rollmann. *Periodical Accounts*, Vol. 2, 99-115.

Holt, Dit. "Viola MacMillan: remembering the Queen Bee." *The Northern Miner*, May 7/13, 2001, Vol. 87, Iss.11, 4

Johnson, A.M. "Edward and Frances Hopkins of Montreal." *The Beaver*, Autumn 1971: 4-19.

Page, Jake. "Arctic Arsenic." *Smithsonian*, Feb. 2001.

Parent, Madeleine. "Léa Roback 1903–2000." *Relations*, novembre 2000 (664): 5-6.

Powell, Barbara. "Laura Goodman Salverson." *Canadian Literature* No. 133, Summer, 1992: 78-89

Ricketts, Shannon. "Canadian Terminals on the Underground Railroad." *Heritage*, Spring 2000: 21-23.

Shiell, Mary. "Rediscovering Kate Carmack: True Queen of the Klondike." *Up-Here*, July/August 1996: 60-62.

Skloot, Rebecca. "Some Called Her Miss Menten." *PittMed*, October 2000: 18-21.

Smith, Helen. "Believing in Anne." *Canadian Heritage*, Summer 1988: 22-24.

Taylor, J. Garth. "The Two Worlds of Mikak: Part I." *The Beaver*, Winter 1983, 4-13.

Taylor, J. Garth. "The Two Worlds of Mikak: Part II." *The Beaver*, Spring 1984, 18-25.

Tremblay, Odile. "Anne Hébert." *Quille & Quire*, Mar. 2000, Vol. 66, Iss. 3, 8.

Van Kirk, Sylvia. "Thanadelthur." *The Beaver*, Spring 1974, 40-45.

Watson, Petra Rigby. "Hannah Maynard's Multiple Exposures." *History of Photography*, Summer 1996.

Wilson-Smith, Anthony. "Died: Léa Roback." Macelan's, Sept. 11, 2000, 9.

Newspapers

Major newspapers in Canada

Unpublished Sources

Anick, Norman. "Mrs. George Black." Historic Sites and Monuments Board of Canada Agenda Paper 1987-03.

Anonymous. "Ebierbing and Tookoolito." Historic Sites and Monuments Board of Canada Agenda Paper 1981-44.

Archives National du Quebec
Registre criminel, IV: 24-26; Procédures judiciaires, Matières criminelles, IV: 237.

Bazely, Susan M. "Who Was Molly Brant?" Presentation from Cataraqui Archaeological Research Foundation to Kingston Historical Society, April 17, 1996.

Board of School Trustees of School District No. 38 (Richmond). "In Memoriam — Mrs. Hide Shimizu." Minutes of Regular Meeting, Sept. 7, 1999.

Centre for Newfoundland Studies Archives, Memorial University of Newfoundland.

Mina Hubbard Papers COLL — 241, Description by Paul Hebbard.

Côté, Nathalie. "Marie Lacoste-Gérin-Lajoie." Commission des lieux et monuments historiques du Canada Rapport 1997-25.

Coutts, Robert. "Thanadelthur." Historic Sites and Monuments Board of Canada Agenda Paper 1999-50.

De Jonge, James. "The Site of Lucy Maud Montgomery's Cavendish Home." Historic Sites and Monuments Board of Canada Submission Report — Place, 1999-05.

Department of English, Memorial University of Newfoundland. "Margaret Iris Duley." Historic Sites and Monuments Board of Canada Agenda Paper 1976-24.

Dodd, Diane. "Helen MacMurchy." Historic Sites and Monuments Board of Canada Agenda Paper 1997-27.

Dodd, Diane. "Mary Meager Southcott." Historic Sites and Monuments Board of Canada Agenda Paper 1998-13.

Gisiason, David. "A Millennium to Celebrate." Report for The Millennium 125 Commission.

Guildford, Janet. "Edith Jessie Archibald." Historic Sites and Monuments Board of Canada Agenda Paper 1997-68.

Gutting, Patricia Bishop. Private Collection. Correspondence from Georgina Stirling to Janet Stirling.

Hay Snyder, Marsha. "Margaret Newton." Historic Sites and Monuments Board of Canada Agenda Paper 1996-15.

Johnson, Wendy. "Idola Saint-Jean." Historic Sites and Monuments Board of Canada Agenda Paper 1997-69.

Kelcey, Barbara Ellen. "Lost in the Rush: The Forgotten Women of the Klondike Stampede." M.A. Thesis, University of Victoria, 1989.

Lee, David. "Molly Brant." Historic Sites and Monuments Board of Canada Agenda Paper 1994-39.

Lee, David. "Pauline Johnson." Historic Sites and Monuments Board of Canada Agenda Paper 1983-02.

Léa Roback Foundation. http://www.foundationlearoback.org.

Maitland, Leslie. "Adelaide Hunter Hoodless Homestead: St. George, Ontario." Historic Sites and Monuments Board of Canada Agenda Paper 1995-47.

Mak, Eileen. "Helen Gregory MacGill, 1864–1947." Historic Sites and Monuments Board of Canada Agenda Paper 1998-17.

McCord Museum of Canadian History, Montreal.
McCord Family Papers, File 5031.
Artists: Hopkins, Frances Ann (3 items).

McDonnell, David. "Dr. Maude E. Abbott." Historic Sites and Monuments Board of Canada Agenda Paper 1993-14.

McKenna, Katherine M.J. "The Life of E. Cora Hind." Historic Sites and Monuments Board of Canada Agenda Paper 1997-24.

Noel, Julie. "L'euvre de Jeanne Mance." Commission des lieux et monuments historiques du Canada 1998-16.

Parent, Jean-Claude. "Turlutes et chansons canadiennes-françaises: Mary Travers dite La Bolduc." Commission des lieux et monuments historiques du Canada 1992-40.

Russell, Hilary. "Portia White." Historic Sites and Monuments Board of Canada Agenda Paper 1995-4.

Russell, W. "Agnes Campbell Macphail." Historic Sites and Monuments Board of Canada Agenda Paper 1985-18.

Secord, R.Y. "Henrietta Muir Edwards." Historic Sites and Monuments Board of Canada Agenda Paper 1962-81.

Sedgwick Stearns, Rhonda. "Flores Ladue." National Cowgirl Museum and Hall of Fame Biography 2001.

Smyth, David. "Demasduit and Shanawdithit." Historic Sites and Monuments Board of Canada Submission Report - Person, 2000-15.

Smyth, David. "Major Margaret C. Macdonald." Historic Sites and Monuments Board of Canada Agenda Paper 1982-33.

Smyth, David. "Matron Georgina Fane Pope." Historic Sites and Monuments Board of Canada Agenda Paper 1983-09.

Snyder, Marsha Hay. "Dr. Emily Stowe, Dr. Jenny Trout, and the Entry of Women Into the Profession of Medicine." Historic Sites and Monuments Board of Canada Agenda Paper 1995-23.

Taylor, C.J. "Lady Aberdeen." Historic Sites and Monuments Board of Canada Agenda Paper 1979-47.

Taylor, Georgina M. "Violet Clara McNaughton." Historic Sites and Monuments Board of Canada Agenda Paper 1997-70.

University of Victoria Archives
Margaret Newton Fonds: AR271
1.2 Aurora submission "Trip to Russia" 1933

University of Waterloo Library
Doris Lewis Rare Book Room
Collection: WA 10 Elizabeth Shortt File 442-443
Jennie Trout Correspondence

Wylie, William. "Mary Ann Shadd (Cary)." Historic Sites and Monuments Board of Canada Agenda Paper 1994-41.

Notes

Introduction

1. Dominion Institute and The Council for Canadian Unity, *Celebrating and Understanding Our Heroes: Canada's Top Heroes as chosen by Canadians* (1999) and Jack Aubry, "Secord is Canada's best-known hero: poll," *Ottawa Citizen*, 17 March 2002.
2. Colin M. Coates and Cecilia Morgan, *Heroines and History: Representations of Madeleine de Verchères and Laura Secord* (Toronto: University of Toronto Press, 2002), 95-97.
3. *The Other Side of the Picture*, National Film Board, 1999.

Maude Abbott

4. Certificate of Baptism, Anglican Church Records, St-André d'Argenteuil.
5. Jessie Boyd Scriver, "Maude Abbott," in *The Clear Spirit: Twenty Canadian Women and Their Times*, edited by Mary Q. Innis (Toronto: University of Toronto Press, 1966), 147.
6. Marie Gillett, "The Heart of the Matter," in *Despite the Odds: Essays on Canadian Women and Science*, edited by Marianne Gosztonyi Ainley, (Montreal: Véhicule Press, 1990), 184.
7. Gillett, 186.
8. Gillett, 190.
9. Dr. C.F. Martin, "Maude Abbott — An Appreciation," *McGill Medical Journal* no. 10 (1940) in Gillett, 194.
10. Maude Elizabeth Seymour Abbott, "Diary," McGill University Archives, MG 1070, in Gillett, 180.

Lady Aberdeen

11. Ishbel Gordon, Marchioness of Aberdeen and Temair, *The Canadian Journal of Lady Aberdeen, 1893-1898*, edited with an introduction by John T. Saywell (Toronto: Champlain Society, 1960), xxxii, in C.J. Taylor, "Lady Aberdeen," Historic Sites and Monuments Board of Canada 1979-47, 252.

12. John Campbell Gordon, first Marquess of Aberdeen and Temair, *We Twa', Reminiscences of Lord and Lady Aberdeen* (London: W. Collins, Son & Co., 1926), Vol. II, 297, in Taylor, 247.

13. Doris French, *Ishbel and the Empire: A Biography of Lady Aberdeen* (Toronto: Dundurn Press, 1988), 260.

14. French, 320.

Emma Albani

15. Paul Gissell, "Rejuvenating faded voice of Albani," *The Ottawa Citizen*, 23 January 1994, 5.

16. Emma Albini, *Forty Years of Song* (New York: Arno Press, 1977), 213.

Marie-Joseph Angélique

17. Marcel Trudel, *L'esclavage au Canada Français*, Edition abrégée (Québec: Les Presses de l'Université Laval, 1960), 25-54.

18. Marcel Trudel, *Dictionnaire des esclaves et de leurs propriétaires au Canada Français* (Ville La Salle: Éditions Hurtubise, 1980), 113-114, 400.

19. Trudel, *L'esclavage au Canada Français*, 92-97 and Archives de la province de Québec, Registre criminel, IV: 24-26; Procédures judiciaires, Matières criminelles, IV: 237.

20. Trudel, *L'esclavage au Canada Français*, 92-97.

21. Dalhousie University News Release, "First Holder of the James Robinson Johnston Chair in Black Canadian Studies Receives Second Honorary Degree," 6 August 1997.

22. Testimony at trial. 1036-5, Archives de la province de Québec.

Anna Mae Aquash

23. Johanna Brand, *The Life and Death of Anna Mae Aquash* (Toronto: James Lorimer, 1978).

24. Carson Walker, "Canadian native indicted in 1976 U.S. slaying," *Ottawa Citizen*, 4 April 2003.

25. Brand, 122.

Edith Jessie Archibald

26. Janet Guildford, "Edith Jessie Archibald," Historic Sites and Monuments Board of Canada Agenda Paper 1997-68, 2050.

27. Guildford, 2057.

28. Guildford, 2050.

Pitseolak Ashoona

29. Dorothy Eber, ed. *Pitseolak: Pictures out of my life* (Toronto: Design Collaborative Books and Oxford University Press, 1971).

30. Eber.

James Miranda Barry

31. Carlotta Hacker, *The Indomitable Lady Doctors* (Toronto: Clarke, Irwin & Co. Ltd., 1974), 3.

32. Rachel Holmes, *Scanty Particulars: The Life of Dr. James Barry* (London: Penguin Books, 2003).

33. Holmes, 249.

34. Holmes, 5, 49.

35. Holmes, photo section after 162.

Martha Black

36. Martha Louise Black, *My Ninety Years* (Anchorage: Alaska Northwest Publishing Company, 1976), 25.

37. Black, 45.

38. Norman Anick, "Mrs. George Black," Historic Sites and Monuments Board of Canada Agenda Paper 1987-03, 83.

39. Black, 59.

Marguerite Bourgeoys

40. Patricia Simpson, *Marguerite Bourgeoys and Montreal, 1640–1665* (Montreal: McGill-Queen's University Press, 1997), 15.

41. Hélène Bernier, "Marguerite Bourgeoys," DCB, I, 326.

42. Marie Morin, *Histoire simple et véritable, les annales de L'Hôtel Dieu de Montréal*, 1659-1725, critical edition by Ghislaine Legendre (Montreal: Presses de l'Université de Montréal, 1979), 64, in "The Clio Collective," *Quebec Women: A History* by Micheline Dumont et al., (Toronto: The Women's Press, 1987), 36.

43. *Marguerite Bourgeoys* texts in "Classiques canadiens," no. 3 selected by H. Bernier, (Montreal, Fides, 1958), 66, in "The Clio Collective," 38.

Molly Brant

44. David Lee, "Molly Brant," Historic Sites and Monuments Board of Canada Agenda Paper 1994-39, 401-413.

45. Susan M. Bazely, "Who was Molly Brant?," Presentation to Kingston Historical Society, April 17, 1996.

46. Lois M. Huey and Bonnie Pulis, *Molly Brant: A Legacy of Her Own* (Youngstown, New York: Fort Niagara Association, Inc., 1997), 10.

47. Barbara Graymont, "Gonwatsijayenni, Mary Brant," in *Dictionary of Canadian Biography*, 1771 to 1880, 417.

48. Leopold Lamontagne, "Petticoats and Coifs in Old Kingston," *Historic Kingston*, Vol. 8 (Kingston), 23, in Bazely, 9.

49. Ian Wilson, "Molly Brant: A Tribute," *Historic Kingston*, Vol. 2 (Kingston), 57, in Bazely, 11.

50. Mary Brant to Col. Daniel Claus, Oct. 5, 1779, Claus Papers, MG19, F1, 2:135-36, in *Molly Brant: A Legacy of Her Own* by Huey and Pulis, 63.

Harriet Brooks

51. Marlene F. Rayner-Canham and Geoffrey W. Rayner-Canham, *Harriet Brooks: Pioneer Nuclear Scientist* (Montreal: McGill-Queen's University Press, 1992), 46-51.

52. E. Rutherford to A. Schuster, 25 March 1907, The Royal Society, London, in *Despite the Odds* by Marianne Gosztonyi Ainley, 201.

53. H. Brooks to L. Gill, 18 July 1906, Barnard College Archives in Rayner-Canham, *Harriet Brooks: Pioneer Nuclear Scientist*, 46-47.

Agnes Deans Cameron

54. Agnes Deans Cameron, *The New North* (New York: D. Appleton and Co., 1910).

55. *The Daily Colonist*, 27 February 1919, 6, in *In Her Own Right: Selected Essays on Women's History in B.C.*, edited by Barbara K. Latham and Cathy Kess (Victoria: Camosun College, 1980).

56. Agnes Deans Cameron, "The Idea of True Citizenship — How Shall We Develop It?," *Educational Journal of Western Canada*, Vol. 1, no.8 (December 1899), 233, in Latham and Kess.

57. Agnes Deans Cameron, "In the Mother-Land," *Educational Journal of Western Canada*, Vol. 3, no. 9 (January 1902), 261, in Latham and Kess.

58. Pazdro, "Agnes Deans Cameron: Against the Current," in Latham and Kess. See also Linda L. Hale, "Agnes Deans Cameron", DCB, XIV, 169.

59. Agnes Deans Cameron, *The New North*, 393.

60. *The Daily Colonist*, 14 May 1912, 1, in Latham and Kess.

61. Hale, 169.

62. Hale, 169.

Emily Carr

63. Emily Carr, *Growing Pains: The Autobiography of Emily Carr* (Toronto: Oxford, 1946), 294-295.

64. Doris Shadbolt, *Emily Carr* (Vancouver: Douglas & McIntyre, 1990), 41-47.

65. Flora Hamilton Burns, "Emily Carr," in *The Clear Spirit: Twenty Canadian Women and Their Times*, edited by Mary Q. Innis (Toronto: University of Toronto Press, 1966), 236.

66. Carr, 372.

67. Emily Carr, *Hundreds and Thousands: The Journals of Emily Carr* (Toronto: Clarke, Irwin, 1966), 101.

Thérèse Casgrain

68. A term used by Thérèse Casgrain in her autobiography, *A Woman in a Man's World* (Toronto: McClelland and Steward, 1972), 115.

69. Clio Collective, *Quebec Women: A History* (Toronto: The Women's Press, 1987), 285.

70. Casgrain, 106-107.

71. Casgrain, 115.

72. Casgrain, 190.

Nellie Cashman

73. *Alaska Weekly*, 19 February 1932 in *Nellie Cashman* by Don Chaput, (Tucson, Arizona: Westernlore Press, 1995), 20.

74. Interview with Mike Cunningham, *Bisbee Daily Review*, 1 April, 1948, in Chaput, 84.

75. John P. Clum, "Nellie Cashman, the Angel of Tombstone," *Arizona Historical Review*, 1931.

76. Sister Mary Theodore, "The sisters of St. Ann on North Pacific Shores," typescript, Part 2, 420-21; Archives, Sisters of St. Ann, Victoria, in Chaput, 111.

77. Chaput, 150.

78. *Victoria Daily Colonist*, 11 January 1925, in Chaput, 156.

Kit Coleman

79. Barbara M. Freeman, *Kit's Kingdom* (Ottawa: Carleton University Press, 1989), 11.

80. *Daily Mail*, Saturday Supplement, 25 June 1892, 1, in Freeman, 83.

81. Ted Ferguson, *Kit Coleman: Queen of Hearts* (Toronto: Doubleday, 1978), 10.

82. Ferguson, 172.

Laure Conan

83. Micheline Dumont, "Laure Conan," in Innis, 94.

84. Laure Conan, *Angéline de Montbrun*. (Quebec: Brousseau, 1884).

Florence Deeks

85. A.B. McKillop, *The Spinster & The Prophet* (Toronto: Macfarlane Walter & Ross, 2001).

86. McKillop, 102.

87. McKillop, 351.

Mazo de la Roche

88. Joan Givner, *Mazo de la Roche: The Hidden Life* (Toronto: Oxford University Press, 1989), 1-10.

89. Mazo de la Roche, *Ringing the Changes: An Autobiography by Mazo de la Roche* (Toronto: Little, Brown and Company, 1957).

90. Givner, 239.

91. Givner, 224.

92. de la Roche, 217.

Carrie Derick

93. For complete list see "Carrie Matilda Derick" in *The Canadian Who's Who 1938-39* (Trans-Canada Press, 1939).

94. Margaret Gillett, "Carrie Derick (1862-1941) and the Chair of Botany at McGill" in *Despite the Odds: Essays on Canadian Women and Science*, edited by Marianne Gosztonyi Ainley, (Montreal: Véhicule Press, 1990), 81.

95. Gillett, 85.

96. Carrie M. Derick, "Professions and Careers Open to Women," in *Women of Canada — Their Life and Work* (Minister of Agriculture, 1900).

97. Derrick.

Marie Dressler

98. Betty Lee, *The Unlikeliest Star* (Kentucky: The University Press of Kentucky, 1997), 2.

99. Marie Dressler, *My Own Story* (Boston: Little, Brown, and Company, 1934), 13.

100. Dressler, 7.

Margaret Duley

101. Margaret Duley, *Highway to Valour* (Toronto: Macmillan, 1941), dedication page.

102. William Arthur Deacon, "Sea, Love and Death," *Globe and Mail,* 4 October 1941.

103. For background see Alison Feder, *Margaret Duley: Newfoundland Novelist* (St. John's, Nfld.: Harry Cuff Publications Limited, 1983).

104. Department of English, "Margaret Iris Duley," Historic Sites and

Monuments Board of Canada Agenda Paper 1976-24, 421.

105. Marian Frances White, *The Finest Kind: Voices of Newfoundland and Labrador Women* (St. John's, Newfoundland: Creative Publishers, 1992), 52.

106. Department of English, 411.

107. Feder, 147.

108. Margaret Duley, *The Caribou Hut* (Toronto: Ryerson Press, 1949).

Henrietta Muir Edwards

109. R.Y. Secord, "Henrietta Muir Edwards," Historic Sites and Monuments Board of Canada Agenda Paper 1962-81 and Grant MacEwan, *Mighty Women* (Vancouver: Douglas & McIntyre, 1975), 27.

110. Eleanor Harman, "Five Persons from Alberta," in Innis, 172-173.

111. Heritage Community Foundation/Famous 5 Foundation, "Henrietta Muir Edwards — Legislation Championed," http://collections.ic.gc.ca/famous 5.

Rose Fortune

112. "The Lewises of Annapolis Royal," Public Archives of Nova Scotia, MG 100, vol.143, no. 11.

113. *Rhythm Stick to Freedom*, Great North Productions, Inc., 1988.

114. Isabel C. Armstrong, "For She Was a Militant Rose," *The Montreal Listening Post*, May 1924.

Laure Gaudreault

115. Betty Archard, "Laure Gaudreault, pionnière du syndicalisme enseignant au Québec," *Madame*, sept. 2003.

116. Louis Cornellier, "Défense de l'école québécoise et de ses profs," *Le Devoir*, 6 sept. 2003.

117. Archard.

Marie Lacoste Gérin-Lajoie

118. Nathalie Côté, "Marie Lacoste-Gérin-Lajoie," Commission des lieux et monuments historiques du Canada Rapport 1997-25, 689.

119. Côté, 688.

120. Côté, 691.

Helen Grant

121. Francis W. Grant, *Courage Below, White Wings Above* (Hantsport, Nova Scotia: Lancelot Press, 1979), 57-65.

122. Grant, 61.

Isobel Gunn

123. *Through Her Eyes: The Orkney Lad*, Wheelwright Ink Ltd, 2001.

124. Sylvia Van Kirk, "Isabel Gunn," DCB, V, 394.

125. Elliot Coues, ed., *New Light on the Early History of the Greater Northwest* (Minneapolis, Minn., 1965), 427n, in *"Many Tender Ties,"* by Sylvia Van Kirk (Winnipeg: Watson & Dwyer Publishing Ltd.), 177.

126. Malvina Bolus, "The Son of I. Gunn," *The Beaver*, Winter 1971, 24.

Marie Guyart (Marie de l'Incarnation)

127. Marie-Emmanuel Chabot, O.S.U., "Marie Guyart," DCB, I, 352.

128. Ursulines Archives, Letter LXXXVI from Quebec to her son September 15, 1644.

Mary Riter Hamilton

129. Mary Riter Hamilton interview with Frederick G. Falla, *The McClure Newspaper Syndicate*, 10 September 1922.

130. Robert Amos, *Mary Riter Hamilton 1873-1954*. (Victoria: Art Gallery of Greater Victoria, 1978), 16-17, in *No Man's Land* edited by Angela E. Davis (Winnipeg: University of Winnipeg, 1992), 30.

131. Amos, see the exhibition catalogue for more info.

132. Letter from Mary Riter Hamilton to Dr. Arthur Doughty, Dominion Archivist, 27 July 1926.

Helen Harrison

133. Shirley Render, *No Place for a Lady* (Winnipeg: Portage & Main Press, 2000), 135.

134. For more info on background and career see Render and Joyce Spring, *Daring Lady Flyers* (Porters Lake, Nova Scotia: Pottersfield Press, 1994), 139-156.

135. Render, 64.

136. Render, 90.

137. Render, 136.

138. Render, 137.

139. Render, 137.

140. Render, 86-87.

Ann Harvey

141. "The Loss of the Brig Dispatch," *The Strabane Morning Post*, Londonderry, No. 958 Tuesday, 2 September 1828.

142. "Ann Harvey — 'The Grace Darling of Newfoundland,'" in *The Book of Newfoundland*, Vol. 3, edited by Joseph R. Smallwood (Saint John's:

Newfoundland Book Publishers, 1967), 454-455.

143. Info from The Harvey Trail, South West Coast Development Association, Newfoundland.

Anne Hébert

144. Delbert W. Russell, *Anne Hébert* (Boston: Twayne Publishers, 1983), 3.

145. Pierre H. Lemieux, "Anne Hébert," in *The Oxford Companion to Canadian Literature* (Toronto: Oxford University Press, 1983), 342.

146. Jacques Godbout, *Anne Hébert 1916-2000* (National Film Board of Canada, 2000).

147. Sheila Fischman, "A literary gem cutter," *Maclean's*, 7 Feb. 2000, Vol. 113, Iss. 6, 57. See also Odile Tremblay, "Anne Hébert: a singular voice of wisdom and rigour," *Quill & Quire*, Mar 2000, Vol.66, Iss.3, 8.

148. Tremblay, 8.

E. Cora Hind

149. John W. Dafoe, "Foreword" in *Seeing For Myself: Agricultural Conditions Around the World* by Cora Hind (Toronto: Macmillan, 1937), v.

150. Manitoba Free Press, November 29, 1916, in "The Life of E. Cora Hind," by Katherine M.J. McKenna, Historic Sites and Monuments Board of Canada Agenda Paper 1997-24, 675.

151. Kenneth M. Haig, *Brave Harvest: The Life Story of E. Cora Hind, LL.D.* (Toronto: Thomas Allen, Limited, 1945), 69-70, in McKenna.

152. Kenneth Haig, "E. Cora Hind," in Innis, 140.

153. Speech to the University Women's Club, "Progress of Women in the Last Fifty Years," 1935, E. Cora Hind Papers, Mss Sc 7, University of Manitoba Dafoe Library Archives, Winnipeg, Manitoba, 4-5, in McKenna, 670.

Adelaide Hunter Hoodless

154. Ruth Howes, "Adelaide Hoodless," in Innis, 106.

155. *Empire*, Toronto, 28 Oct. 1893.

156. Terry Crowley, "Adelaide Sophia Hunter," DCB, Vol. 13.

157. Leslie Maitland, "Adelaide Hunter Hoodless Homestead," Historic Site and Monuments Board of Canada Agenda Paper 1995-47, 267.

158. Cheryl MacDonald, *Adelaide Hoodless; Domestic Crusader* (Toronto: Dundurn, 1986), 46, in Maitland, 266.

Frances Anne Hopkins

159. Philip Shackleton, "Frances Anne Beechey," DCB, Vol. 14, 49.

160. Alice M. Johnson, "Edward and Frances Hopkins of Montreal," *The Beaver*, Autumn 1971, 13.

161. Letter from Frances Anne Hopkins to Mr. McCord July 12,1910, McCord Museum, McCord Family Papers, file 5031.

Mina Hubbard

162. Biographical information from Mina Hubbard Papers COLL — 241, Centre for Newfoundland Studies Archives, Memorial University of Newfoundland.

163. Mina Hubbard, *A Woman's Way Through Unknown Labrador* (New York: The McClure Company, 1908).

164. Bert Riggs, "Lured to the Labrador Wild," *Telegram*, St. John's, 28 Sept.1999.

165. Gerard Kenney, "Against all odds," *The Citizen's Weekly*, 5 Dec.1999, D8.

166. Hubbard, 82.

Françoise-Marie Jacquelin (Marie de la Tour)

167. For discussion of her background see George MacBeath, "Françoise-Marie Jacquelin," DCB, Vol. I, 383 and Ethel Bennett, "Madame de La Tour," in Innis, 3-24.

E. Pauline Johnson

168. For discussion of the engagement see Sheila M.F. Johnston, *Buckskin & Broadcloth* (Toronto: Natural Heritage Books, 1997), 150-151 and Charlotte Gray, *Flint & Feather* (Toronto: HarperFlamingo Canada, 2002), 240-43, 246-48, 255.

169. For discussion of her writing see Elizabeth Loosely, "Pauline Johnson," in Innis 74-90 and David Lee, "Pauline Johnson," Historic Sites and Monuments Board of Canada Agenda Paper 1983-02,18-25.

170. Paul Gessell, "Rediscovering Pauline," *The Ottawa Citizen*, 29 July 2000, I1and I2.

171. Introduction to *E. Pauline Johnson: The Shagganappi* (Toronto, 1913), 8, in David Lee, "Pauline Johnson," 22.

Leonora Howard King

172. Margaret Negodaeff-Tomsik, *Honour Due* (Ottawa: Canadian Medical Association, 1999), xiv.

173. "FMWC nominee to be in Canadian Medical Hall of Fame," *The Federation of Medical Women of Canada*, Winter, vol. 12, No. 1, 1.

174. Negodaeff-Tomsik, xv.

175. Negodaeff-Tomsik, 219-220.

176. Negodaeff-Tomsik, 101.

Flores La Due

177. For background info see Donna Livingstone, *Cowboy Spirit* (Vancouver: Greystone Books, 1996), 24-33 and Rhonda Sedgwick Stearns, "Flores Ladue," National Cowgirl Museum and Hall of Fame Biography 2001.

178. Juliet Briskin, "Hall of Fame cowgirls bring a historical past," *Country World*, Texas, 15 November 2001 and Sedgwick Stearns.

179. Livingstone, 64.

180. Sedgwick Stearns.

181. Candace Savage, *Cowgirls* (Vancouver: Greystone Books, 1996), 62.

Mrs. Kwong Lee

182. Chinese Canadian National Council, *Jin Guo: Voices of Chinese Canadian Women* (Toronto: Toronto Women's Press, 1992), 18 and *The British Colonist*, Victoria, "Arrival of Chinaman"(sic), 1 March 1860.

183. David Chuenyan Lai, *Chinatowns* (Vancouver, University of British Columbia Press, 1988), 190-191.

184. Chuenyan Lai, 187-191.

185. David Chuenyan Lai, *The Forbidden City Within Victoria* (Victoria: Orca Book Publishers, 1991).

186. *The British Colonist*, 3 Apr.1908, in Chuenyan Lai, *Chinatowns*, 190.

187. Chinese Canadian National Council, *Jin Guo*, 18.

188. Chuenyan Lai, *Chinatowns*, 186.

Anna Leonowens

189. W.S. Bristowe, *Louis and the King of Siam* (London: Chatto & Windus, 1976), 26-31.

190. Lois K. Yorke, "Anna Harriette Edwards," DCB, XIV, 332.

191. Yorke, 332.

192. Leslie Smith Dow, *Anna Leonowens* (Lawrencetown Beach, N.S.: Pottersfield Press, 1991), 108.

193. Smith Dow, 111.

Beatrice Lillie

194. Beatrice Lillie, *Every Other Inch a Lady* (New York: Dell, 1972), 207.

195. Lillie, 14.

196. Lillie, 53.

197. Lillie, 42.

198. Lillie, 44.

199. Lillie, 136.

200. Lillie, 296.

201. Lillie, 171, 326.

202. Stanley Green, *The Great Clowns of Broadway* (New York: Oxford University Press, 1984), 153.

203. Lillie, 72.

204. Bruce Laffey, *Beatrice Lillie: The Funniest Woman in the World* (New York: Wynwood Press, 1989), 229.

Jean Lumb

205. Arlene Chan, *Spirit of the Dragon* (Toronto: Umbrella Press, 1997), 18.

206. Chan, 23.

207. Evelyn Huang, *Chinese Canadians: Voices from a Community* (Vancouver: Douglas & McIntryre, 1992), 34.

Major Margaret C. Macdonald

208. G.W.L. Nicholson, *Canadian Nursing Sisters* (Toronto: A.M. Hakkert Ltd., 1975), 49-55, in "Major Margaret C. Macdonald," by David Smyth, Historic Sites and Monuments Board of Canada Agenda Paper 1982-33.

209. For more information see Smyth, op. cit. and John Murray Gibbon and Mary S. Mathewson, *Three Centuries of Canadian Nursing* (Toronto: Macmillan Co., 1947), 289-310.

210. Smyth, 307.

Elizabeth Gregory MacGill

211. Elsie Gregory MacGill, *My Mother The Judge* (Toronto: Ryerson Press, 1955), 133.

212. Library and Archives Canada, "Living Memory – Elsie MacGill," http://www.collectionscanada.ca.

Helen Gregory MacGill

213. Linda Kealey, *A Not Unreasonable Claim: Women and Reform in Canada, 1880s-1920s* (Toronto: Women's Educational Press, 1979), 7, in "Helen Gregory MacGill," by Eileen Mak, Historic Sites and Monuments Board of Canada Agenda Paper 1998-17, 451.

214. MacGill, *My Mother The Judge*, 225.

215. MacGill, 226.

216. MacGill, 219.

Viola MacMillan

217. Viola MacMillan, *From the Ground Up* (Toronto: ECW Press, 2001).

218. JL Granatstein, "They all had a vision and the drive to pursue it," *Macleans*, Toronto, 1 July 1998, 56 and Diane Francis, "Miners back on solid ground," *National Post*, 13 March 2003, FP3.

219. Dit Holt, "Voila MacMillan: remembering the Queen Bee," *The Northern Miner*, Toronto, 7 May 2001, 4.

220. Holt, 4.

221. MacMillan, 28.

Helen MacMurchy

222. *Globe and Mail*, 30 March 1921, 16.

223. Dianne Dodd, "Helen MacMurchy," Historic Sites and Monuments Board of Canada Agenda Paper 1997-27, 763-871.

224. Dodd, 780.

225. "Dr. Helen MacMurchy, C.B.E. Honored by Her Profession, Portrait Presented for Hall", *Globe and Mail*, 10 January 1940.

226. "Dr. Helen MacMurchy Addressed Women's Institutes," *Globe and Mail*, 16 Nov. 1911, 9.

Agnes Macphail

227. M. Stewart and D. French, *A Biography of Agnes Macphail — Ask No Quarter* (Toronto: Longmans, Green & Company, 1959), 74, in "Agnes Campbell Macphail," by W. Russell, Historic Sites and Monuments Board of Canada Agenda Paper 1985-18, 422-3.

228. Doris French, "Agnes Macphail," in Innis,186.

229. French, 192.

230. French, 195.

231. French, 195.

232. French, 184.

Jeanne Mance

233. For background see Marie-Claire Daveluy, "Jeanne Mance," DCB, Vol.I, 483-487 and Julie Noel, "L'oeuvre de Janne Mance," Commission des lieux et monuments historiques du Canada 1998-16.

234. Archives des religieuses hospitalières de Saint-Joseph, in Noel, 440.

Hannah Maynard

235. Claire Weissman Wilks, *The Magic Box: The Eccentric Genius of Hannah Maynard* (Toronto: Exile Editions Ltd., 1980), 5.

236. Weissman Wilks,5 & 7.

237. *Saint Louis and Canadian Photographer*, September 1879.

238. For analysis of her work see Petra Rigby Watson, "Hannah Maynard's Multiple Exposures," *History of Photography*, Summer 1996 and Wilks.

239. *The New West* (Winnipeg), 1888.

240. Wilks, 7.

Nellie McClung

241. Natalie Symmes, "Nellie McClung of the West," *Canada Monthly*, February 1916, 217, in *Our Nell: A Scrapbook Biography of Nellie L. McClung*, by Candace Savage (Halifax: Goodread Biographies, 1979), 1.

242. Dominion Institute and The Council for Canadian Unity, *Celebrating and Understanding Our Heroes: Canada's Top 20 Heroes as chosen by Canadians* (1999). An Internet survey with 28,000 respondents showed for women heroes Laura Secord ranked no. 1 and Nellie McClung placed second.

243. Gwen Matheson & V.E. Lang, "No 'Nice Nellie' Was Nellie," *Chatelaine*, November 1974: repr. in *A Woman's Place*, edited by Sylvia Fraser (Toronto: Key Porter Books, 1997), 248.

244. Nellie McClung, *Nellie McClung: The Complete Autobiography. Clearing in the West and The Stream Runs Fast* (Peterborough: Broadview Press), 235.

245. Savage, *Our Nell*, illustrations after 138.

246. Archives and Library Canada, "Living Memory – Nellie McClung," http://www.collectionscanada.ca.

Louise McKinney

247. Charles G.D. Roberts, ed., "Louise Crummy," in *Canadian Who Was Who 1875-1936* (Toronto: Trans-Canada Press, 1938), 84.

248. Louise C. McKinney, "Where are Canadian Women Going — Back to Their Homes or Continue in Business Life?," *Canadian Home Journal*, Aug. 1991.

Violet McNaughton

249. Georgina M. Taylor, "Violet Clara McNaughton," Historic Sites and Monuments Board of Canada Agenda Paper 1997-70, 2090.

250. Taylor, 2085.

251. Saskatchewan Archives Board (SAB), McNaughton Papers A1 D58(2), McNaughton, 2 September 1938, in Taylor, 2088.

252. Taylor, 2091.

253. SAB, pamphlet G35.1, in Taylor, 2093.

254. Taylor, 2092.

Helen McNicoll

255. Natalie Luckyj, *Helen McNicoll: A Canadian Impressionist* (Toronto: Art Gallery of Ontario, 1999).

256. "A Loss to Canadian Art," *Saturday Night*, 3, in Luckyj, 70.

257. Natalie Luckyj, "Helen Galloway McNicoll," DCB, Vol. XIV, 731.

Aimee Semple McPherson

258. Daniel Mark Epstein, *Sister Aimee* (San Diego/New York/London: Harcourt Brace & Company, 1993), 82.

259. Louise Weicke, *San Francisco Chronicle*, 1921, in Epstein, 230.

260. Epstein, 247.

261. Epstein, 255.

262. Epstein, 378.

263. Epstein, back cover.

264. Aimee Semple McPherson, "This Is My Task: A sermon by Aimee Semple McPherson," Given at Angelus Temple, Los Angeles, California, 12 March, 1939.

Maud Menten

265. Marelene F. Rayner-Canham, *Women in Chemistry* (Washington: America Chemical Society/Chemical Heritage Foundation, 1998), 157.

266. Rebecca Skloot, "Some Called Her Miss Menten," in *PittMed*, Oct. 2000, 20.

267. Skloot, 21.

268. Skloot, 21.

Mikak

269. J. Garth Taylor, "The Two Worlds of Mikak: Part I," The Beaver, Winter 1983, 6.

270. Br. Jens Haven, "Memoir of the Life of Br. Jens Haven," (translation by Dr. Hans Rollmann), *Periodical Accounts*, Vol. 2, 99-115.

271. William H. Whiteley, "Mikak," in *Dictionary of Canadian Biography, online.*

272. Taylor, 8.

Lucy Maud Montgomery

273. See L.M. Montgomery, *The Alpine Path: The Story of my Career* (Markam: Fitzhenry & Whiteside Limited, 2001;reprint of 1917) and Mario Rubio and Elizabeth Waterston, *Writing a Life: L.M. Montgomery* (Toronto: ECW Press, 1995).

274. For info on home see James De Jonge, "The Site of Lucy Maud Montgomery's Cavendish Home," Historic Sites and Monuments Board of Canada Submission Report - Place, 1999-05.

275. Innis, 203.

276. Montgomery, *The Alpine Path*, 64.

Geraldine Moodie

277. Donny White, *Geraldine Moodie: An Inventory* (Regina: Great Plains Research Center, University of Regina, 1999) and *In Search of Geraldine*

Moodie (Regina: Great Plains Research Center, University of Regina, 1998).

278. RCMP, RG 18, Vol. 3459, file 0-66, Comptroller White to Commissioner Perry, 22 September 1910 in White, 152.

279. National Archives of Canada, Traill Family Collection, MG29D81 V.1, Geraldine Moodie to Catharine Parr Traill, 8 May 1895, in White, *In Search of Geraldine Moodie*, 10.

Phyllis Munday

280. Kathryn Bridge, *Phyllis Munday* (Montreal: XYZ Publishing, 2002), 135.

281. For details see Don Munday, *The Unknown Mountain* (Seattle: The Mountaineers, 1975 reprint of 1948 edition).

282. Munday, xiv.

283. Bridge, 136.

Asayo Murakami

284. *Obaachan's Garden*, National Film Board, 2001.

285. *Obaachan's Garden.*

Emily Murphy

286. Letter dated October 25, 1917, Judge Murphy to E. Jackson. ECA, Emily Murphy Papers, MG2, Box 1, in "Emily Murphy," by John McLaren, in *Women in Law* (Westport: Greenwood Press, 1996), 192.

287. Heritage Community Foundation/Famous 5 Foundation, "The Famous 5: Their Legacy", http://collections.ic.gc.ca/famous 5.

Nahnebahwequay

288. Donald Smith, "Nahnebahwequay," DCB, Vol. IX, 591.

289. John Steckley, *Beyond Their Years: Five Native Women's Stories* (Toronto: Canadian Scholars' Press Inc., 1999), 169.

290. *The Colonial Intelligencer*, 1866, 155, in Steckley, 174.

291. Steckley, 140.

292. *Friends' Intelligencer* 1861, in Steckley, 155.

Margaret Newton

293. Ralph H. Estey, "Margaret Newton 1887-1971," in *Despite the Odds: Essays on Canadian Women and Science*, edited by Marianne Gosztonyi Ainley, (Montreal: Véhicule Press, 1990), 184.

294. Marsha Hay Snyder, "Margaret Newton," Historic Sites and Monuments Board of Canada Agenda Paper 1996-15, 455-459.

295. Aurora submission, "Trip to Russia" 1933, Margaret Newton Fonds AR271, University of Victoria Archives.

Mary Irene Parlby

296. See Barbara Villy Cormack, *Perennials and Politics* (Sherwood Park: Professional Printing Ltd.) and *The Reluctant Politician: The Story of Irene Parlby*. White Pine Pictures, A Scattering of Seeds — The Creation of Canada.

297. Cormack, 98.

298. Cormack, 98.

299. Cormack, 137.

300. Cormack, 159.

Mona Parsons

301. Andria Hill, *Mona Parsons* (Halifax: Nimbus Publishing Ltd., 2000).

302. Hill, 111.

Mary Pickford

303. Scott Eyman, *Mary Pickford* (Toronto: Harper Collins, 1990), cover, 2, 85.

304. Robert Windeler, *Sweetheart: The Story of Mary Pickford* (New York/Washington: Praeger Publishers, 1974), 94.

305. Windeler, 165.

306. Eyman, 304.

307. Eyman, 247.

Georgina Pope

308. Canada, Parliament, 1901 Sessional Paper No. 35a. Report by Georgina Fane Pope, 17 January 1901, 63, in "Matron Georgina Fane Pope," by David Smyth, Historic Sites and Monuments Board of Canada Agenda Paper 1983-09,130.

309. Smyth, 130.

310. PAC Personnel Files, Macdonald to Major-General J.T. Fotheringham, 11 December 1918, in Smyth, 132. See also John Murray Gibbon and Mary S. Mathewson, *Three Centuries of Canadian Nursing* (Toronto: Macmillan, 1947), 292.

311. Gibbon and Mathewson, 291.

Isabella Preston

312. See Edwinna Von Baeyer, "Isabella Preston," in *Despite the Odds: Essays on Canadian Women and Science*, edited by Marianne Gosztonyi Ainley, (Montreal: Véhicule Press, 1990), 220-235 and *Rhetoric and Roses: A History of Canadian Gardening 1900-1930* (Markham: Fitzhenry & Whiteside, 1984), 164-170.

313. Royal Botanical Gardens Library, Preston Coll., Percy Wright to I.

Preston, 17 March 1950, in "Isabella Preston," by Von Baeyer, 229.

314. Royal Botanical Gardens Library, typewritten draft of autobiography, 2., in Von Baeyer, 224.

Susanna Carson Rijnhart

315. C.T. Paul, "Dr. Susie C. Rijnhart," in *Churches of Christ* (Louisville, KY: John P. Morton, 1904), 462-463.

316. For details see Susie Carson Rijnhart, *With the Tibetans in Tent & Temple* (Boston: Elibron Classics).

317. Rijnhart, 193.

318. Alvyn J. Austin, "Susanna Carson," in DCB, online.

319. Rijnhart, 250.

Léa Roback

320. Helena Katz, "Knitting isn't my passion — social causes are," *The Gazette*, Montreal, 2 Dec., 1993, 5.

321. Michael Livingstone, "Lives lived: Léa Roback," *Globe & Mail,* 11 Sept., 2000.

322. Examples include Susan Schwartz, "Life on the frontline," *The Gazette*, 2 Nov.1998, where author Irène Demzcuk is quoted: "...it is the dauntless faith in emancipating women and men that makes Léa Roback not only a model, but a heroine..."; see Susan Schwartz, "Activists gather to honor their inspiration," *The Gazette*, 4 Nov. 1993, where lawyer Juanita Westmoreland is quoted: "A woman 10 times bigger than her size, Leah is the universal woman."

323. *A vision of darkness*, Productions Contre-Jour, Montreal, 1992 (Producer Sophie Bissonette).

Fanny Rosenfeld

324. David McDonald, *For the record: Canada's Greatest Women Athletes* (Toronto: Mesa Associates, 1981), 13.

325. McDonald, 10.

326. Jewish Women's Archives, Brookline, MA, Bobbie Rosenfeld.

327. McDonald, 13.

328. Jewish Women's Archives.

Gabrielle Roy

329. Publisher Jack McClelland said "She was the only Canadian novelist ever to fully bridge our bilingual nation both in the critical and popular sense." Doug Whiteway, "Roy Valued Prairie Roots," *Winnipeg Free Press*, 15 July 1983.

330. Gabrielle Roy, translated by Patricia Claxton, *Enchantment and Sorrow* (Toronto: Lester & Orpen Dennys, 1987), 58.

331. Roy, 193.

332. François Ricard, translated by Patricia Claxton, *Gabrielle Roy A Life* (Toronto, McClelland & Stewart Inc., 1999), 418.

333. Phyllis Grosskurth, *Canadian Writers & their Works: Gabrielle Roy* (Toronto: Forum House, 1972), 7.

334. Doug Whiteway, "Roy Valued Prairie Roots," *Winnipeg Free Press*, 15 July 1983.

335. Gabrielle Roy, *The Fragile Lights of Earth* (Toronto: McClelland, 1982), 150.

Idola Saint-Jean

336. Montreal *Standard*, 23 March 1940, in "Idola Saint-Jean," by Wendy Johnston, Historic Sites and Monuments Board of Canada Agenda Paper 1997-69, 2069.

337. Thérèse Casgrain, *Une femme chez les hommes*, 108, in Johnston, 2068.

338. "Are Women Chattels?," *The Montreal Herald*, 1929, in Johnston, 2070.

339. Johnston, 2069-70.

Laura Goodman Salverson

340. Laura Goodman Salverson, *Confessions of an Immigrant's Daughter* (Toronto: University of Toronto Press, 1981), 395.

341. Salverson, 405.

342. Terrence L. Craig, "The Confessional Revisited: Laura Salverson's Canadian Work," Studies in Canadian Literature, Volume 1 & 2, 1985 (online version), 2 and 4.

343. Craig, 7 and Athabasca University: Canadian Writers - Laura Goodman Salverson (www.athabascau.ca/writers/goodman.html).

344. Salverson, 357.

Margaret Marshall Saunders

345. Lorraine McMullen, "Margaret Marshall Saunders," in *The Canadian Encyclopedia* (Historica Foundation of Canada: 2003).

346. "Margaret Marshall Saunders," in *Contemporary Authors Online* (The Gale Group: 2001) and "Beautiful Joe" Plaque, Ontario Heritage Foundation.

347. Barry M. Moody, "Edward Manning Saunders," in DCB, online.

348. Elizabeth Waterston, "Marshall Saunders," in *The Oxford Companion to Canadian Literature* (Toronto: Oxford University Press, 1983), 728-729 and Carole Gerson, *Dictionary of Literary Biography*, Volume 92: *Canadian Writers*, 1890-1920 (Detroit: Gale, 1990), in *Contemporary Authors Online* (The Gale Group: 2001).

349. Anonymous, "'Dumb Folks' Friend is Gifted Creator of 'Beautiful Joe,'" *The Register*, 5 September 1923.

350. Margaret Marshall Saunders, "The Story of My Life," *Ontario Library*

Review, 1927, in *Contemporary Authors Online* (The Gale Group: 2001).

Laura Secord
351. Ruth McKenzie, *Laura Secord: the legend and the lady* (Toronto: McClelland and Stewart, 1971), 90-93 for accounts by Laura Secord and Fitzgibbon.
352. See "Secord is Canada's best-known hero: poll," Ottawa Citizen, 17 March, 2002 re Ipsos-Reid poll and *Celebrating and Understanding Our Heroes: Canada's Top 20 Heroes as chosen by Canadians* (The Dominion Institute and Council for Canadian Unity). An Internet survey (1999) conducted for the report showed the top women heroes were Laura Secord, Nellie McClung, L.M. Montgomery, Emily Murphy, Margaret Laurence, Agnes Macphail, E. Pauline Johnson, Emily Carr, Barbara Frum and Susanna Moodie.
353. McKenzie, 98-99.

Shaaw Tlaa (Kate Carmack)
354. Charlene Porsild, "Shaaw Tlaa," DCB, XIV, 923.
355. Armstrong, Major Nevill, *Yukon Yesterdays: Thirty Years of Adventure in the Klondike* (London: John Long Ltd., 1936), 27, in "Lost in the Rush: The Forgotten Women of the Klondike Stampede," by Barbara Ellen Kelcey (MA Thesis, University of Victoria, 1989), 154.
356. Fred N. Atwood, ed., *The Alaska-Yukon Gold Book* (Seattle: Sourdough Stampede Association, Inc., 1930), 30.
357. James Albert Johnson, *Carmack of the Klondike* (Seattle: Epicenter Press and Horsdal & Schubart, 1990), 112-124.
358. Mary Shiell, "Rediscovering Kate Carmack: True Queen of the Klondike," *Up-here*, July/August 1996.
359. Sherrill E. Grace, *Canada and The Idea of North* (Montreal/Kingston: McGill-Queen's University Press, 2001), 92-103.
360. Johnson, 156.
361. Wheelock, Angela, "Daughter of the Wolf," Unpublished typescript, 12, in Grace, 98.

Mary Ann Shadd
362. William Wylie, "Mary Ann Shadd," Historic Sites and Monuments Board of Canada Agenda Paper 1994-41, 461.
363. Wylie, 464.

Shanawdithit
364. J.P. Howley, *The Beothuks or Red Indians* (Toronto: Coles Publishing Col

Ltd, 1974) and Ralph T. Pastore and G.M. Story, "Shawnadithit," DCB, online version.

365. Proclamation by His Excellency John Holloway, Commander-in-Chief of the Island of Newfoundland, July 30, 1807, in Howley, 64.

366. Letter from E.S. (probably Mr. E. Slade) to Editor of *Liverpool Mercy*, in Howley, 100.

367. John McGregor, "Shaa-naan-dithit, or The Last of the Beothics," in part II of "Sketches of Savage Life" by an Anonymous Author, *Fraser's Magazine for Town and Country*, Vol. XIII, No. LXXV (March 1836): 316-323 (Rpt. Canadiana House, Toronto, 1969).

368. David Smith, "Demasduit and Shanawdithit," Historic Sites and Monuments Board of Canada Submission Report - Person, 2000-15.

369. "Bishop John Inglis' Interview with Shanawdithit," in Appendix: Letter from the Lord bishop of Nova Scotia," S.P. G. Annual Report 1827 (London: S.P.G. and C.&J. Rivington, 1828), 85-88.

Hide Hyodo Shimizu

370. Randy Boswell, "WWII internment became lifetime cause," *National Post*, 28 Aug. 1999, A14.

371. Centennial Japanese United Church, "We remember Hide Hyodo Shimizu...," *CJUC Newsletter*, Fall 1999.

372. Maryka Omatsu, *Bittersweet Passage* (Toronto: Between the Lines, 1992), 64-65.

373. For details see Patricia E. Roy et al., *Mutual Hostages* (Toronto: University of Toronto Press, 1990), 131-133.

374. "In Memoriam – Mrs. Hide Shimizu," Minutes of Board of School Trustees, School District No. 38 (Richmond), 7 September, 1999.

375. Boswell, A14.

Mary Meager Southcott

376. Dianne Dodd, "Mary Meager Southcott," Historic Sites and Monuments Board of Canada Agenda Paper 1998-13, 369.

377. *Remarkable Women of Newfoundland and Labrador* (St. John's: St. John's Local Council of women, n.d.) 23, in Dodd, 374.

378. Dodd, 373.

Georgina Ann Stirling

379. See Amy Louise Peyton, *Nightingale of the North* (St. John's, Jesperson Press, 1983).

380. Peyton, 77.

381. Peyton, 104.

382. Peyton, 141.

383. Georgina Stirling to sister Janet, from Paris, n.d. Private Collection of Patricia Bishop Gutting.

Emily Stowe

384. Marsha Hay Snyder, "Dr. Emily Stowe, Dr. Jenny Trout, and the Entry of Women Into the Profession of Medicine," Historic Sites and Monuments Board of Canada Agenda Paper 1995-23, 759.

385. Carlotta Hacker, *The Indomitable Lady Doctors* (Toronto: Clarke, Irwin & Co. Ltd.), 21.

386. Gina Feldberg, "Emily Howard Jennings," DCB, 509 and Synder, 768.

387. Newspaper cutting in Scrapbook No. 3, Stowe Collection, Wilfrid Laurier University Archives, in Hacker, 21.

Taqulittuq (Tookoolito)

388. Anonymous, "Ebierbing and Tookoolito," Historic Sites and Monuments Board of Canada Agenda Paper 1981-44, 224.

389. Charles Francis Hall, *Arctic researches and life among the Esquimaux: being the narrative of an expedition in search of Sir John Franklin, in the years 1860, 1861 and 1862* (New York: Harper, 1865), 158.

390. Hall, 158.

391. Jake Page, "Arctic Arsenic," *Smithsonian*, Feb. 2001.

392. Sheila Nickerson, *Midnight to the North* (New York: Tarcher/Putnam, 2002).

393. Anonymous, "Ebierbing and Tookoolito," 234-5.

394. Hall, 158.

Kateri Tekakwitha

395. Henri Béchard, "Tekakwitha," DCB, I, 635.

396. Béchard, 636.

397. John Steckley, *Beyond Their Years* (Toronto: Canadian Scholars' Press Inc., 1999), 13, 59.

398. William Ingraham Kip, *The Early Jesuit Missions in North America* (Albany: Joel Munsell, 1873), 103-4, in Ibid., 33.

Thanadelthur

399. See Robert Coutts, "Thanadelthur," Historic Sites and Monuments Board of Canada Agenda Paper 1999-50 and John Steckley, 68-95

400. Sylvia Van Kirk, "*Many Tender Ties*," (Winnipeg: Watson & Dwyer Publishing Ltd., 1980), 69.

401. Van Kirk, 70.

402. Coutts, 359.

403. Van Kirk, 77.

404. Edward S. Curtis, *The North American Indian*, 8-9, in Coutts, 363.

Gudridur Thorbjarnardottir

405. Jane Smiley, preface, *The Sagas of Icelanders* (New York: Viking, 2000), xxxiii.

406. Smiley, 644, 665 and Magnus Magnusson and Hermann Palsson, *The Vinland Sagas* (Great Britain: Penguin Books, 1965), 78.

407. Pall Bergthorsson, *Vinlands Gatan* (the Vineland riddle) and *The Wineland Millennium: Saga and Evidence* (2000).

408. T.J. Oleson, *The Norsemen in America* (Ottawa: The Canadian Historical Association, 1963), 4.

409. Smiley, 655.

410. Smiley, 659.

Mary Travers

411. See Réal Benoît, *La Bolduc* (Montréal: Éditions de l'Homme, 1959), 111-119 and Jean-Claude Parent, "Turlutes et chansons canadiennes-français-es: Mary Travers dite La Bolduc," Commission des lieux et monuments historiques du Canada 1992-40, 413-414.

412. For more info see Jean-Claude Parent, 414.

413. Mary Travers, Translation from the song " Ça va venir, découragez-vous pas," (1930).

Jenny Trout

414. Carlotta Hacker, *The Indomitable Lady Doctors*, 38-52.

415. Hacker, 41-42 and Synder, "Dr. Emily Stowe, Dr. Jenny Trout, and the Entry of Women Into the Profession of Medicine," 770.

416. *Advocate*, May, 7 1875, in Darrell Buchanan, "'In His Name' – The Life and Times of Jenny Kidd Trout," *Leaven: A Publication for Ministry in the Churches of Christ*, 3/3 1995.

417. W.H. Trout, *Trout Family History* (Milwaukee, Meyer-Rotier Printing Co., 1916), 280, in Hacker, 39.

418. Jennie Trout to My Dear Friend, 31 Dec. 1880. University of Waterloo Library, WA10 Eliz. Shortt File 442-443.

Harriet Tubman

419. Earl Conrad, *Harriet Tubman* (New York: International Publishers, 1942), 14. The more common version of the quote is used in Library and Archives Canada, "Canadian Confederation Towards Confederation: Influence of the American Civil War – Harriet Tubman," http://www.collectionscanada.ca.

420. Owen Thomas, "Harriet Ross," DCB, XIV, 896.

421. Conrad, 25.

422. Conrad, 26.

423. Conrad, 8.

Madeleine de Verchères

424. Colin M. Coates, "Warrior Woman," *The Beaver*, April/May 2002, 11.

425. Coates, 12.

426. André Vachon, "Marie-Madeleine Jarret de Verchères," DCB, III, 310.

Eileen Vollick

427. Shirley Render, *No Place for a Lady*, 11.

428. Render, 13.

Portia White

429. Hector Charlesworth, "Portia White's Rare Promise," *Saturday Night*, 15 Sept. 1941, in "Portia White," by Hilary Russell, Historic Sites and Monuments Board of Canada Agenda Paper, 1995-4, 81-82.

430. *New York Times*, 14 March 1944, in Russell, 83.

431. Russell, 91.

432. *Portia White: Think on Me.* Sylvia Hamilton, 2000.

433. Russell, 77.

Alice Wilson

434. See Anne Montagnes, "Alice Wilson," in Innis, 260-278 and Barbara Meadowcroft, "Alice Wilson, 1881-1964," in *Despite the Odds: Essays on Canadian Women and Science*, edited by Marianne Gosztonyi Ainley, (Montreal: Véhicule Press, 1990), 204-219.

435. Montagnes, 260.

Marie-Marguerite d'Youville

436. Jeffery C. Rubin, "Admirers call Marie Marguerite d'Youville the Mother Teresa of her time," *Time International*, 24 Dec. 1990.

437. See Claudette Lacelle, "Marie-Marguerite Dufrost de Lajemmerais," DCB, IV, 234-238.

438. Lacelle, 238.

Acknowledgments

I'd like to express my appreciation to the Ontario Arts Council.

Thanks to the encouragement of my husband, Glen, and my young sons, Gavin (nine) and Lawren (seven), I took the big plunge and decided to temporarily leave my job as a federal civil servant in order to research and write this book. They have probably heard more about women in Canadian history than they ever wanted to know — and I expect the boys are the only ones in their school that recognize illustrations of Marie de la Tour and Pitseolak Ashoona, and know the story of "Beautiful Joe." Glen served as my resident computer expert and photographer, doing everything from touching up photos to burning CDs of the book illustrations. Thanks guys for being my sounding board and cheering squad!

A special thanks goes to my mother, Joyce, for believing I could write a great book, and for being interested in every story I uncovered.

I also owe a big thanks to Luce Vermette (Ph.D., Ethnology; former Parks Canada historian) for her support, encouragement, and careful review of my manuscript. Luce was an enthusiastic believer in the worthiness of my project and a major source of good advice and information. And merci to her husband René Chartrand for identifying some great historical images for the book. It was an added bonus that Luce and René provided their advice at cozy lunches with fine wine!

To Roberta Russell (Ph.D., Education: former Director, Research & Stats Division, Department of Justice) I want to extend a special thanks for taking time out of her retirement to read the manuscript and provide very helpful comments.

Many historians, librarians, archivists, family of the heroines in the book, friends, etc. from across Canada and the United States contributed to the development of this book. Some provided helpful resource materials and others helped me discover some wonderful illustrations that I hoped existed and wasn't sure where to find.

I'd like to extend special thanks to Michele Barusta for finding time to send emails of support as she travelled in Europe for a year; Michel Audy and Margaret Peck at the Historic Sites and Monuments Board of Canada for research assistance; Ted Shimizu for spending hours collecting information and photos and sharing stories of his step-mother Hide; the staff of the Ottawa Public Library, in particular those at the Emerald Plaza Branch; Arlene Chan for allowing me to copy a treasured family photo; Penny Wheelwright for providing photos from her movie about Isobel Gunn; Linda Ohama for sharing images of her grandmother; teacher Vickie MacDougall and her students in Port Aux Basques for providing photos of their hike on the Harvey Trail; Mickey King at the Archives of the Sisters of Saint Ann for having a great sense of humour and being extremely helpful; the Heritage Department of the International Church of the Foursquare Gospel for reviewing the text on Sister Aimee and providing great photos; Professor David Lai, University of Victoria for reviewing the text on Mrs. Kwong Lee; Jeffrey C. Golden of Minnesota for providing me with a copy of a fascinating letter belonging to his relative Georgina Stirling; Joellen ElBashir, Moorland-Spingarn Research Center, Howard University for being especially helpful; Margaret Negodaeff for providing an image of Dr. King; Sister Marlene Butler, Grey Nuns of the Sacred Heart, Yardley, PA and Sister Thérèse Pelletier, SGM, Montreal for personal notes of encouragement and images of St. Marguerite d'Youville; Denise and Deborah Pictou Maloney for providing a photo of their mother; author Andria Hill for sharing her photo of Mona Parsons; David Dewar, Wallace and Area Museum, N.S. for finding an image of Helen Grant when I'd almost given up hope; Dr. Clarence Bayne, Black Studies Centre, Montreal for doing everything in his power to help me; and author Valerie Knowles for sharing her experience with a novice. Thanks for the co-operation and contribution of the Hudson's Bay Company in providing an image of Thanadelthur, and to the very helpful staff at the Library and Archives Canada.

Last but not least, I want to thank Tony Hawke at The Dundurn Group for believing that this project was "a good thing."

Illustrations

Every reasonable effort has been made to identify and acknowledge the copyright owners of images reproduced in this book, and this information has been included with the illustrations. For most images in this volume the copyright has expired and they are in the public domain. Should any errors or omissions have been made, please advise the author and the publishers.

Some historical illustrations have been modified slightly to enhance the quality by removal of spotting and other indications of age.

Front Cover Illustrations

Top left to right: Flores La Due (Glenbow Archives NA-3164-371), Harriet Tubman (Moorland-Spingarn Research Center, Howard University), Marie de La Tour (New Brunswick Museum) and Mary Pickford (National Archives of Canada C-016958). Bottom left to right: Mikak (John Russell portrait), Hide Shimizu (Courtesy Ted Shimizu) and Thérèse Casgrain (Yousuf Karsh/National Archives of Canada/PA-178177).

The registration card that Hide Shimizu was required to carry During WWII.
(See Hide Shimizu, p. 237.)

About the Author

Merna Forster developed public education programs for national parks and national historic sites across Canada for twenty years while employed by Parks Canada. She also worked in the field of Canadian Studies. An arts and sciences graduate from the University of Alberta, the author received her M.A. in History at Laval University as a Richard J. Schmeelk Canada Fellow. A recipient of the Canada 125 Commemorative Medal from the Governor General, the native of Alberta has been discovering historical heroines from coast to coast during her travels in Canada. Merna now lives in Ottawa with her husband and two sons. She can be contacted through her website at **www.heroines.ca**.